200 Ways of Using IMAGERY in the Classroom

Michael T. Bagley
Karin Hess

Trillium Press
New York

ACKNOWLEDGMENTS

We wish to extend a sincere thanks to Drs. M. Jerry Weiss, Leo Buscaglia, and Dorothy Sisk.
A special thanks to Carol Canariato.
Other individuals who contributed to the development of this project and to whom we wish to express a deep appreciation are: Dr. Akhter Ahsen, Dr. Robert Rotella and Hale Rowland.
A **big** thanks to all the students who contributed to our growth and understanding of imagery and its application to learning.

Trillium Press
Box 921
Madison Square Station
New York NY 10159

ISBN: 0-89824-084-0
Printed in the United States of America

Edited by Frederick Kaufman
Cover Design by Lori Schlendorf

TABLE OF CONTENTS

CHAPTER   **PAGE**

6. IMAGERY IN SOCIAL STUDIES

7. IMAGERY IN ART

8. IMAGERY IN MUSIC

9. IMAGERY IN GUIDED FANTASY

1. Introduction

Imagery has become an exciting phenomenon that is beginning to capture the attention of those individuals in the field of education devoted to the enhancement of creativity. Never before has there been such a desperate need for incorporating creativity and imagination into the basic curriculum. Our society is becoming more and more complex, and our problems are becoming more diversified; life in general requires a great degree of problem solving. As educators, it is our responsibility to nurture and cultivate the creative potential in our young, so that they will have the mind power to challenge the future. We must enable them to dictate and not be dictated by the future.

Our objective in this text is simple. We ask that you open your minds to the possibility of using imagery as a means of exposing your students to the creative process. We have introduced imagery to many students at all grade levels over the last few years, and have found the approach to be remarkably successful and rewarding. Students enjoy imagery as they do most creative experiences. They welcome it and see it as relief from drill work and test preparation. More important, imagery provides both a focus and a more open-minded attitude toward the concepts and subjects that are being covered in the basic curriculum.

We believe that this text has the potential for increasing the instructional capabilities of teachers. For students, imagery is new, exciting and highly motivating. It results in the achievement of new levels of personal, social and academic growth. As a result of incorporating imagery experiences in your basic teaching methodology, you will be a richer, more open, sensitive human being and a beautiful model for the children who will shape tomorrow's future.

The purpose of this first chapter is to provide the reader with the following: (a) some basic terminology related to imagery, (b) a frame of reference for categorizing and classifying various types of imagery, (c) a list and description of major conditions that are necessary for enhancing the skill of imagery and (d) a brief overview of the use of imagery in today's world.

The content of this first chapter is especially relevant and important in terms of becoming aware of and understanding the dynamics of imagery.

The second chapter deals with the basic steps and procedures for introducing imagery to students. There are a number of instructional imagery exercises designed to help students learn about the process of imagery. You will also find guidelines on how to use subject-related, academic imagery exercises in the basic curriculum.

Chapters 3 through 8 have been developed with the intention of providing a diversified range of imagery activities which can be incorporated into any curriculum, in any school, for any level of student. They are easy to follow, sophisticated enough to challenge the imagination, filled with the facts and information necessary for growth and development in the cognitive domain. The activities are designed to encourage both teachers and students to develop new and expanded imagery experiences.

As educators, we have often heard distinguished philosophers and psychologists remark that human beings are functioning only at ten percent of their true capacity. It is our contention that a significant part of the other ninety percent lies within the visual, imaginative and creative side of the brain. Not to tap this rich natural resource is truly a waste of human potential.

We appeal to all educators: recognize the importance of individual creative potential; and nurture and develop it to its highest possible level. A direct and positive tool for meeting this challenge is imagery.

DEFINITION OF IMAGERY

Imagery is a process whereby a person can visualize an object, event or situation in his mind. These visual pictures represent photographic records of objects, interactions and impressions of the external environment. They are often vivid, highly detailed representations of real-life experiences. While images may draw upon previous memories, specific experiences are not prerequisite to the process. The mind is capable of combining previous experiences in a way that produces "new thoughts" which form the content of the images. These visualizations are most vivid when the mind is least distracted by interfering thoughts. As one focuses on a particular image, the mind automatically begins to slow down and limit the number of distractions and thought messages. The creative process (Imagination) becomes more active. This "stilling of the mind" increases the vividness and clarity of an image. The longer the mind remains in this restful, visual state, the longer the image will be projected in the mind's eye. The more a person uses his power to visualize, the greater control he will have over the skill. When you image, you become a projectionist capable of speeding up, slowing down or stilling a particular picture. The slowing down of the picture provides a detailed means to examine the elements in such a way that the individual gains new thoughts and emotional perspectives. The process of imagery will be discussed in greater detail in the following section.

Psychologists have had difficulty establishing criteria to distinguish types of images. In a book entitled *Mental Imagery* (1969), Dr. Alan Richardson attempted a formal definition:

> *Mental imagery refers to (1) all those quasi-perceptual experiences of which (2) we are self consciously aware, and which (3) exist for us in the absence of those stimulus conditions that are known to produce their genuine sensory or perceptual counterparts, and which (4) may be expected to have different consequences from their sensory or perceptual counterparts.*

In an article published in the "Journal of Mental Imagery" (1972), Dr. Akhter Ahsen presents a comprehensive discussion of the definition of the phenomenon as well as criteria for distinguishing various types of images. The lack of agreement among psychologists in terms of a general definition of imagery is clearly presented in Ahsen's article.

Despite the confusion and obvious difficulties concerning the definition of the term, most researchers will agree to the existence of certain types of images. The four types of images discussed most often in the literature are: Memory Image, Imagination Image, Dream Image and Eidetic Image.

From work with both students and teachers, we have found that we enhance the comprehension of the meaning of imagery when we discuss visual experiences in terms of memory, imagination or dream. We can distinguish criteria for each type of image. Although a strong interrelatedness exists among the types of imagery, the delineation of specific characteristics helps explain the intricacies of this mental phenomenon.

BASIC IMAGERY TYPES

Since the 1880's, psychologists have studied man's ability to use imagery both as an inner source for new thoughts and feelings, and as a vehicle for reconstructing the past or projecting future experiences. The most popular theme for study has been the MEMORY IMAGE. The memory image may be experienced in a spontaneous manner as a person actively calls upon a previous experience in an attempt to remember certain facts or details. Memory images are useful for recollecting facts. Memory images are usually evoked by a sensory stimulus, either a picture, taste, smell or verbal utterance. According to Richardson (1969), memory images are previously experienced events or situations that have a high degree of personal reference.

The EIDETIC IMAGE, according to both Richardson (1969) and Ahsen (1977), is a vision, a new thought, a feeling which can be scanned by a person as he would scan a real current event in his environment. It is a material picture, a potent, highly significant stimulus which arises from within the mind and throws the mind itself into a series of self-revealing imagery effects. Most researchers believe that the eidetic image is an image of unusual vividness, seen only by a minority of people (Hebb, 1972, Jaensch, 1930, Haber R. N. and Haber, R. B., 1964). However, Ahsen (1977) believes that many more people are capable of experiencing this especially vivid and detailed image than was previously thought. Ahsen claims that, "the memory image is always open to arbitrary change but the eidetic image is closed to arbitrary change or revision but subject to further progression in a definite direction, i.e., it is corrective in nature."

Different from both memory and eidetic, the IMAGINATION IMAGE has no fixed reference point; that is, it does not necessarily relate to a specific event or situation. Imagination images are spontaneous, free, unstructured creative experiences which integrate the past and the present in newly organized patterns. Creative imagery often provides the artist or poet with the central idea for a picture or poem (Richardson 1969).

Finally we come to the DREAM IMAGE, considered by some to be the most important type (Samuels and Samuels, 1975). Dream images are perhaps the most real in terms of their vividness. Dream content varies significantly among people; however, the frequency of dreams per night remains fairly constant. Most people have between three and five dreams per night. Unlike the previous image types, most people have little or no control over images in their dreams.

"All of the imagery types briefly discussed above share a common link -- visual images -- and can be looked upon as a continuum, rather than as entirely separate experiences" (Samuels and Samuels, 1975).

The interrelatedness of imagery types will become evident later, as the reader begins to experiment with the imagery exercises. Having the imagery process broken down into categories may assist the imager in gaining greater awareness of the inner function of the mind. It may equally demonstrate the source and fuel for creating and controlling images. The imagery type most often used in education is Imagination Imagery. Memory, Dream and Eidetic Imagery are important aspects of psychotherapy.

It is our experience that once the students are comfortable with your explanations of imagery and have used imagery successfully, the need for delineation of imagery types or characteristics is greatly reduced. The need for drawing their attention to different imagery types or classifications really becomes a low priority. It is best not to confuse the matter any more than is necessary. More important than criteria for definition are the many conditions necessary for enhancing the skill of imaging.

The next section deals specifically with the critical variables associated with successful imagery.

IMAGERY: CHARACTERISTICS AND CONDITIONS

The purpose of this section is to provide the reader with a basic overview of the imagery process. We will present the characteristics and the important conditions which enhance the imagery process. Each of the following elements can be critical factors in achieving success in imagery. It is important for the reader to become very familiar with these concepts, ready to apply the ideas to various situations.

VISUAL IMAGE

The image is perceived as a picture, a visual element. The vividness and clarity of the image will vary among people. It should be noted that through practice one can achieve greater profoundness of the visual picture. The visual image can be seen in real-life colors with multiple shades and contrasts. First and foremost in the process of imagery is the visual image. Without the visual image, feeling and meaning would be difficult to generate. Visual identification with a concrete stimulus (object, event, etc.) is the first step in the imagery process.

SOMATIC RESPONSE

The imagery process involves the whole psychological system and allows various senses and physiological sectors to participate in a spontaneous manner. Different senses should be stimulated simultaneously, e.g., auditory, kinesthetic, olfactory, gustatory. The image should be capable of evoking a somatic (feeling) response. This emotional response may be characterized as a joyful, happy experience. Imagination imagery can create a very positive emotional feeling. Somatic response allows the perceiver to gain meaning from the image. However, not all images will provoke an emotional response.

MEANING

A complete image experience should involve all three dimensions: visual, somatic and meaning. Meaning is achieved as the imager becomes engaged in an *interactive relationship* with some aspect or feature of the image. When the visual picture is clearly in focus and is generating some type of emotional response, the end result is meaning. Sparked by the image, meaning is a message that flows into your consciousness. The meaning provides the imager with a new understanding and a new perspective about the content (e.g., an event, a situation or a skill).

CLARITY AND COMPLETENESS OF IMAGE

Images are generally less clear and stable during early practice experiences. They improve in clarity and depth as one progresses through the various imagery stages and begins to trust his visual abilities. An image may exist in every stage of completeness, from the most fleeting fragment to the most literal reinstatement of reality. Nature images usually provoke the highest degree of clarity, especially for beginning imagers.

CONTROLLABILITY

Controllability involves the actual manipulation, movement or reconstruction of an image by the imager. The ability to control the image will enable the person to increase the length or duration of the image and, at the same time, allow the image to expand in terms of its features, depth, variations, etc. The ability to control an image may be more important than the ability to conjure clear mental pictures. Controllability is a skill that can be developed through imagery practice.

SCANNING

This feature is most critical to imaging as it provides the mechanism for capturing specific *detail* within the image. It allows the imager to study, analyze and draw meaning from a particular aspect of the image. Scanning becomes important when you encourage a student to continue her exploration of the content of an image for the purpose of tapping creative responses or acquiring a new skill, e.g., learning about the digestive system.

PRINCIPLE OF REPETITION

A vivid image usually can be repeated over and over with little difficulty. The repetition factor increases the capacity to observe an image from different perspectives at different times. Each time the image is projected, the potential for new emotional feelings and thought is dramatically increased. Learning can be reinforced through the repetition of images. This is very important when dealing with subject-related material.

ACCEPTANCE

A non-judgmental attitude is critical to the success of imagery. Negatives will serve to diminish the potency of the image experience. A positive, accepting attitude must prevail at all times. The accepting attitude must be present in the students' and teacher's discussion of the imagery experiences. Imagery can only be sustained in a supportive environment. Since imagery taps the creative, intuitive side of our brain, an infinite number of outrageous, wild, inventive and futuristic images are very probable. Therefore, you must be prepared for those creative experiences which are out of the ordinary. Don't fight an image or thought; just allow it to pass if it is unpleasant or disturbing and wait for the next image to flow into your consciousness.

BODY POSITION

Any position that keeps the right and left sides of your body in equal balance and that can be maintained comfortably without moving for the length of your imaging is the right position for you. (Sitting, standing, crossed-leg sitting, lying down -- all are acceptable positions if they allow the imager to be comfortable and relaxed.) Body position is a highly individual matter; therefore, you must allow students the freedom to choose what is best for them. Most students enjoy lying down, especially after they have had some experience with imagery or when they are doing guided fantasy.

SHOULD YOUR EYES BE KEPT CLOSED?

Most individuals prefer to keep their eyes closed. This enables them to concentrate more deeply on the image. When our eyes are open there's a tendency to allow environmental stimuli to break our concentration and interfere with the image. Although eyes closed is preferred, you will find individuals who are more comfortable having their eyes open. You must encourage them to do what is comfortable and safe for them. You must let these individuals know that it is okay to have their eyes open.

IS THERE A BEST TIME OF THE DAY TO IMAGE?

Basically any time of the day is appropriate for imaging, especially with children. More important than time of day is freedom from interruption or distraction by something or someone. Some psychologists suggest that the period right before sleep (hypnagogic) is a good time, because the mind is beginning to slow down naturally and effortlessly. During this period your mind and body become more relaxed and capable of deep concentration. In school, we suggest that imagery exercises follow cognitive experiences (spelling, math, science, etc.). This provides a nice shift, allowing students to go from the verbal to the visual. Some teachers prefer to use imagery after gym or recess. Imagery has the potential to act as a relaxant, thereby having a calming effect that can help the student regain focus or concentration necessary and vital for task commitment. Therefore, any time of the day can be used for imagery. A teacher must explore the different periods of the day in order to find which period yields the best results. We encourage teachers to try different times of the day and observe the reactions of their students. Also, allow the students to suggest times when the class might engage in imagery.

FREQUENCY OF IMAGERY EXERCISES

Imagery, like other skills, needs sharpening. The more students are exposed to visualization experiences, the more competent they become and the more high quality images they will produce. On the other hand, if students rarely use imagery, their potential for using visualization as a learning tool will never be fully realized. Most educators will agree that the basic school curriculum is heavily weighted toward verbalization, cognition, and evaluation, all of which could be classified as non-creative experiences. The proponents of creative education feel strongly about the integration of more visual, imaginative and holistic experiences into the regular curriculum. Imagery can be the means of creating more balance between verbalization and visualization.

As proponents of the creative education movement, we urge teachers to incorporate visualization experience into their basic teaching menu. It would be difficult to offer a specific percentage of a day or week, since there are so many situations that must be considered: grade level, subject area, school philosophy, training, class size, grouping, etc. However, here are a few suggestions which might help you decide when and how to incorporate imagery into the basic school curriculum.

1. Expose students to the introductory exercises (Chapter 2) and the guided fantasy exercises first. Then introduce subject area imagery exercises.

2. Examine the range of activities suggested for teaching a specific subject area. Categorize the activities in terms of whether you could present all or part of the content through imagery-type experiences. Rate the curriculum activities according to the following: 1 -- High Imagery Potential, 2 -- Moderate Imagery Potential and 3 -- Low Imagery Potential. Obviously, activities rated as (1) would be most appropriate for incorporating visualization experiences. We suggest that after you read the first few chapters which deal with the imagery process, you examine the various activities we have developed under the heading of Language Arts, Social Studies, Science, etc., which are found in Chapters 3 through 8.

3. Begin using some of the imagery experiences for the purpose of relaxing the students. This could be done at the beginning of a lesson, after lunch, etc. Do it for 5 or 10 minutes at first. Let the students' reactions and discussions dictate your planning and scheduling.

4. During the first few weeks you might conduct two imagery exercises per week, e.g., Monday AM and Wednesday PM, or any other alternating day arrangement. This is a nice way to introduce the students to a whole new way of learning.

5. Allow the students an opportunity to suggest different ways in which to use
   imagery in learning basic school content.

Encourage students to develop their own guided fantasies. They could then present
them to the class.

HOW LONG SHOULD IMAGERY EXERCISES BE?

At first, your exercises should only be 5 to 10 minutes long. After that, students will respond well to exercises that last 15 to 30 minutes. This may seem like a rather lengthy period; however, due to the relaxing nature of imagery and to the fact that a person's mind has shifted from a temporal (aware of time) to a non-temporal awareness, a 30 minute experience will feel like a 15 minute experience.

A teacher must plan according to certain schedules. The teacher must also rotate the nature of different learning experiences, e.g., lecture, hands-on, discussion, independent study, etc., to keep learning active, reflective, concrete, abstract and experimental. It is the teacher's responsibility to meet the individual learning styles of students.

We suggest that teachers explore different periods of time, starting with imagery exercises of short duration and increasing to a longer duration. Let the students be the guide. Observe their reactions, observe their follow-up activities, observe their ability to shift to a verbal activity; observe whether they are imaging on their own, and observe any changes in their attitudes toward certain content or subject areas.

CAN ALL STUDENTS IMAGE?

Research has shown that more than 95% of adults can see visual images. This percentage figure drops as we look at other sense modalities. Auditory - 93%, Olfactory - 76%, Kinesthetic - 62%. Most psychologists will agree that children can image more easily than adults. It appears that the ability to see images is an inherited trait, given to all human beings at birth. If we do not use this ability, it will fade away, and we lose one of our most precious gifts.

The phenomenon is experienced by children naturally and spontaneously in the form of dreams, daydreams and fantasies. Richardson reports that as young people enter the third year of high school, there is a noticeable decline in the ability to image. This decline maintains throughout one's adult life. The literature suggests that children are better imagers than adults.

In a recent study, Bagley, M. T. & Barrett, M. (1982) found that fourth and fifth grade students with learning styles categorized as *Active Experimenters* (doing, risktakers, experimenters, intuitive, present-oriented) rated their ability to image significantly higher than students with learning styles categorized as *Abstract Conceptualizers* (logical, rational, evaluative, abstracting and judgmental). These results suggest that students that are more *right brain* dominant tend to have an easier time at imaging than students who are more *left brain* dominant. Since imaging is a visual, creative process located in the right hemisphere of the brain, it would appear that these findings have some validity. However, we are only suggesting that certain students have a greater potential or tendency toward imaging than other students. Some students have thinking and learning characteristics that interfere with the evocation and control of images. Teachers need to be aware of the effects of these personality traits so that they can be identified and discussed with students. Students need to know that differences exist in one's ability to see and control vivid images. Despite these discrepancies, most, if not all students are capable of evoking high quality images.

THREE DIMENSIONAL IMAGERY MODEL

Three major components of imagery comprise the model presented in Figure 1. We present the model in order to reinforce the understanding of the nature of imagery. The model highlights the key elements and necessary conditions for effective imagery. The first component (A) deals with the basic parts found within the imagery process. These are: (1) visual image (picture), (2) somatic response (feeling) and (3) meaning (understanding). The second component (B) deals with the different degrees in which people experience images. Again, there are three levels beginning with the lowest (Level 1), which is seeing images at a superficial level. The next level is covert (Level 2), which is a deeper degree of image experience. The final level (Level 3) is called the interactive association, the highest degree of imagery.

The final component of the three dimensional model consists of the major conditions that are necessary for high quality imagery. These conditions, in sequential order, are:

1. Identification
2. Relaxation
3. Acceptance
4. Concentration

We will briefly describe each of the components of the model in order to provide the reader with an additional frame of reference for understanding the imagery process.

Note: The basic concepts and ideas discussed in the Model presented in Figure 1 are derived from the work of the distinguished psychologist, author and lecturer, Dr. Akhter Ahsen. With his permission, Dr. Michael Bagley has developed the Three Dimensional Imagery Model.

FIGURE 1

Three Dimensional Imagery Model

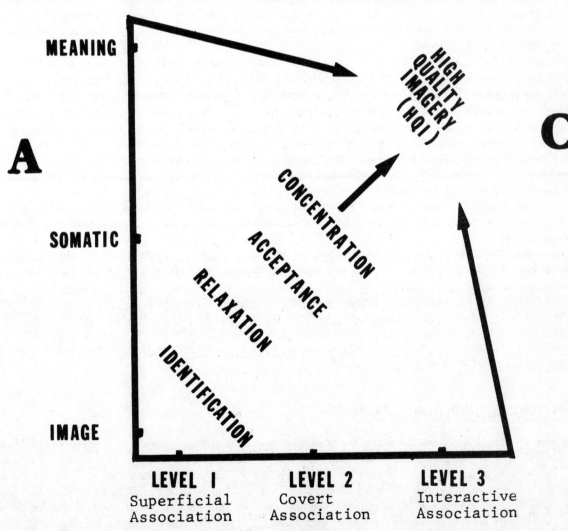

COMPONENT A: ELEMENTS OF AN IMAGE

The first element of an image is a pictorial one, the *visual* representation of an object, thing or event which has either appeared in a person's previous experience or is a newly created image centered in one's imagination. Once a person has identified with the visual image, it is possible to receive a *somatic* experience in the form of positive or negative feelings (joy, pleasure, love, excitement, fear, anxiety, happiness, etc.). The nature and degree of somatic experience is contingent on the vividness of the image, the content of the image, and the manner in which the imager associates with the image. The next element is *meaning*, which is the degree of understanding generated by the evoked image. Meaning is transmitted in the form of a message, an insightful thought or idea, a new perspective, a new emotional feeling.

For imagery to be successful and beneficial, each of these elements must be incorporated into the experience. If these elements are potent and interrelated, the quality of the imagery experience will be enhanced.

COMPONENT B: LEVELS OF ASSOCIATION

According to A. Ahsen (1977), there are three levels or degrees of association potentially present in the imager. These are: a) Superficial Level, b) Covert (deeper association) and c) Interactive Association.

As we discussed earlier, people see images in varying degrees of vividness. At Level 1, people may attempt to evoke an image but find only a vague, unclear picture projected on their screen. They can see neither detail nor an array of colors and shades. A faint outline might be seen, or absolutely nothing. There might also occur an intellectualization of what the people wish to see.

At the second level of association people are capable of seeing an image very clearly, in all of its detail -- a rather authentic approximation of reality. They are able to see themselves in the image even to the extent of facial detail. The only aspect that might be lacking at this level is a real state of interactive behavior, either with things or other individuals. Most people are capable of achieving the second level of imagery after some basic instruction. At the covert level, the imager is capable of evoking emotion, since the visual or pictorial image has a reality representation.

The final and deepest level of association is interactive. Here, the imager is capable of evoking a very powerful image which will include strong emotional responses and highly authentic meanings. The imager sees him/herself interacting within the environment with something or someone as if he/she were watching an actual movie. Images at this level are highly detailed and can almost always be repeated over and over again.

The interactive level of imaging has all the ingredients for a total learning experience. Level 3 associations are multi-sensory, and give the student the greatest possibility for achieving a high level of understanding and meaning. The imagery exercises included in this text are capable of evoking Level 3 imagery experiences for students, providing you have slowly introduced the instructional exercises and have created a positive, non-judgmental climate. If students have trust, feel relaxed and are open to explore with their imaginations, the results will be rewarding and educationally stimulating.

Not all students will be capable of achieving Level 3 associations at the beginning. Therefore, you need to discuss individual differences in imaging ability just as you would in other skill areas, e.g., reading, spelling, etc. However, as we have said earlier, most if not all the students in your class have the potential for achieving high quality images.

In addition to establishing a supportive imagery climate, teachers must continue to emphasize and reinforce those conditions which enhance the imagery process.

COMPONENT C: CONDITIONS FOR IMAGING

In Figure 1 you will notice that the four major conditions have been arranged sequentially, in order to highlight the progressive flow of the imagery process. The initial step for the imager is to IDENTIFY with some object, thing, or event, i.e., acquire a mental picture of what he/she will evoke onto his/her screen of the mind's eye. At this point, the student will draw upon various concepts and/or previous meanings in order to formulate an identification with the object, thing or event to be imaged. For instance, you might ask the students to image themselves walking through a forest. Immediately prior to beginning the image, each student will form or conceptualize a meaning of forest. This conceptualization process allows the student to form an identification with the construct, forest. The identification state could be conjured as an activator which generates the early motivation and power which will ignite the images that

8

will follow. Since our brains work at an amazing speed, identifying with something may require only a few seconds of rapid association.

The second condition, noted earlier as most important, is RELAXATION. Relaxation of the mind allows the student to experience deep concentration. An overly tense and anxious mind will interfere with the natural flow of images. When the mind is racing, filled with many thoughts, distraction is unavoidable. Although the imagery process can result in a state of relaxation, it is advisable to start the imagery exercise with a certain degree of relaxation already in operation. You may even wish to use a relaxation technique prior to administering some imagery exercises. This procedure will assure that your students are relaxed, ready to shift into the visualization mode. Again, discuss this feature (relaxation) of the imagery process with your students, and allow them to appreciate its value and special relationship to imagery.

The next condition in the model is ACCEPTANCE. Neither fight nor evaluate the image that appears on the screen. If you analyze or verbalize, your consciousness will change. Verbalization (labeling, categorizing, analyzing) automatically knocks the visualized picture right off the screen. Some individuals experience extreme difficulty as they try to remain in a visualization state. Highly conditioned to be verbal, logical and analytical, these individuals will need a lot of practice. Children will adapt more easily to a non-verbal state than adults because they have had less conditioning and formal education.

The other issue to discuss with your students relates to the nature of imagination. The origin of creative ideas is hard to explain, especially to children. Imagination is a beautiful thing, pure and provocative, exciting, explanation defying; and students must realize that the imagery process ignites imagination. We suggest that teachers take time to discuss the characteristics of imagination. A good discussion will make students more accepting of the unexplained images which float in and out of their consciousness with remarkable regularity. Do not analyze the images evoked by students. Discuss the image openly if the student wishes to, and deal on a descriptive, non-evaluative level. The analysis of a person's images or dreams is the work of the psychologist, not the educator.

The final condition necessary for insuring high fidelity imagery is CONCENTRATION. After the student has successfully identified with an object, thing or event, is relaxed, accepting the flow of images, the remaining goal is to achieve deep concentration. The stronger the concentration is, the greater the meaning. In other words, if the student progresses to a level of concentration where all extraneous noise, time factors, etc., are totally removed from conscious awareness, images will spontaneously develop. They will evoke both positive emotional responses and meanings which may appear in the form of new ideas, thoughts and actions. A student who images the growth of a plant may gain new emotional perspectives about plant life that quite possibly would never have occurred if he/she had not experienced that image in a highly concentrated manner.

As students become more involved in imagery experiences and grow in confidence, their level of concentration will automatically deepen. They will be capable of concentrating on the images suggested by the teacher, and on any image which they personally wish to evoke.

To heighten concentration, we suggest that teachers ask the students to focus on specific details in an image and scan the entire image for *colors, shapes* and *texture*. Another method to increase concentration involves asking the students to refocus on the same image two or three times. Each time the student repeats any image, he/she will usually see something new, something that was not previously realized. Recently, some sixth graders were asked to image their favorite flower three times. Each flower image lasted approximately 30 seconds. They were then asked to open their eyes for 10 seconds, then return to their flower image. All 12 students saw something different each time they returned to their flower. One student saw the flower in the ground among an assortment of beautiful flowers. In the second image she saw the flower wrapped in multi-colored paper and, finally, in her last image she saw the flower pinned on the lapel of her father's new suit.

If all of the prerequisite conditions are operating (identification, relaxation, acceptance), chances are that the concentration aspect will automatically activate and provide the imager with new thoughts, feelings and ideas.

If you turn again to Figure 1, note that the upper dimension of each component has a strong interrelationship. This formula illustrates the point:

INTERACTIVE ASSOCIATION (LEVEL 3) *plus* CONCENTRATION *plus* MEANING
equals
A HIGH QUALITY IMAGE (HQI)

The imagery exercises presented in this text and the methodologies discussed earlier aim at enhancing students' ability to achieve high quality images.

As you experience the variety of imagery exercises outlined in the remaining chapters of the text, you will achieve a greater understanding of the imagery process.

We suggest that after you have experienced imagery for a while, go back to this chapter and reread it. You will be surprised at your increased level of understanding.

THE IMPORTANCE OF RELAXATION AND CONCENTRATION

Educators generally agree that the ability to relax and concentrate are two very significant and important skills, highly related to academic growth, productivity and task commitment. As we shall see, both relaxation and concentration are of paramount importance in imagery exercises. We will first deal with the concept of relaxation, then the art of concentration.

Relaxation is one of the most important elements of successful imagery. When a person's mind and body are tense, anxious or filled with numerous thoughts (and the mind begins to race like an over-active piston), imaging becomes a difficult task. For example, we have had students in our graduate program who were not able to relax their minds for most of the course and, as a result, never saw images on any level other than the superficial. One day, class was held at a different time and location (a more relaxed environment) and, for the first time, one student evoked very vivid images. When we had a chance to discuss this experience, she explained that for the first time she had felt completely relaxed. It was obvious that the rigid classroom environment was not conducive for her relaxation and, consequently, she had not seen vivid images.

The effect of relaxation has also been demonstrated numerous times during introductory imagery training sessions. Asked to evoke an image and then discuss it in a group setting, many participants will be unable to image. As we continue the session, steadily moving forward with the instructional imagery exercises, suddenly those individuals who had been experiencing difficulty begin to see images with greater clarity. When asked, we are invariably told by these individuals that they were more relaxed than when they had started the imagery exercises.

We purposely begin imaging without having achieved any degree of relaxation in the group in order to highlight the progression of increased relaxation and its positive effect on imagery. Thus, participants learn about the relationship between a relaxed mind and body and imaging. Relaxation achieved, the mind begins to slow from its normal, highly active moving state and, as a result, becomes capable of deep levels of concentration. The mind can evoke a vivid image, scan its details and, to some degree, control the image while it is projected on the screen of the mind's eye. A relaxed mind has a very limited number of thoughts that penetrate consciousness. It is like a lake that is very still and quiet, motionless and peaceful.

Relaxed, you experience images more clearly and vividly than ever before. Our students have described these periods of deep relaxation as tingling, radiating and pulsing. They have expressed the feelings of heaviness, warmth, coolness, and even a floating sensation.

A pertinent dimension of the relaxation process is *trust*. When students begin to develop trust in you and the imagery process, relaxation increases. Trust cannot be fully established unless a non-judgmental climate has been created. Students need to know that there is no one right way to image, that people see images differently, and that evoked images shouldn't be evaluated or criticized. A climate of trust is crucial for establishing relaxation.

We recommend that you administer to your class some of the relaxation exercises presented in Chapter 2. Ask the students to describe what it felt like, i.e., "how did you feel during the exercise?" In addition to having a positive effect on imagery, learning the techniques of relaxation can be instrumental in reducing school related stress and anxiety. The only way to examine this contention is to observe your students' behavior over the course of a semester. You will note positive changes in attitude and performance, providing you follow the recommendations and suggestions outlined in this text.

SOME RELAXATION TECHNIQUES

During the 1920's, Dr. Edmund Jacobson conducted numerous research studies in muscle physiology. As a result, Dr. Jacobson developed a technique called PROGRESSIVE RELAXATION. Essentially, the technique required that a person go through a series of tensing and relaxing exercises which centered around relaxing different parts of the body. Dr. Jacobson suggested that a person concentrate on a designated area of the body, e.g., the feet: tense feet; then relax feet; again tense -- relax. This procedure would continue until all the most basic tensing areas of the body were done. According to Samuels and Samuels (1975), "most people find the muscles with the greatest residual tension to be the face and neck, especially those around the eyes and jaw."

Another method commonly used for achieving deep relaxation is AUTOSUGGESTION. The basic principle of autosuggestion is that most bodies respond to ideas, i.e., the thoughts a person has affect emotions, which in turn affect behavior. For example, ask the students in your class to close their eyes and inhale slowly and deeply several times; then suggest that they feel the different body zones become more relaxed, e.g., have them say, "my lower legs are becoming more and more relaxed. . ." Continue the process until all the designated body parts have been treated.

We have found that the 5 minutes taken to relax a class is worth the effort: it enables everyone to enjoy the subsequent experience as well as image clearly and productively. The more you experience the autosuggestion technique of relaxation, the easier it becomes and the more deeply relaxed you feel. Again, deep relaxation serves to clear the mind and reduce normal muscle tension which often interferes with the ability to concentrate.

Another relaxation method is the slow countdown. For example:

Twenty-one -- twenty -- nineteen: feel yourself going deeper.
Eighteen -- seventeen -- sixteen: go deeper within.
Fifteen -- fourteen -- thirteen: deeper and deeper.
Twelve -- eleven -- ten: feel yourself going inward.
Nine -- eight -- seven: go more inward.
Six -- five -- four: inner and inner.
Three -- two -- one: you are now completely relaxed and comfortable.

It is important to remember that these suggestions, whether in the form of relaxing a particular part of your body, counting methodically, or seeing a beautiful passive scene, must be administered *slowly* and *clearly*. One error that novice trainers make is that they go too fast. Suggestions for body relaxation should be verbalized in an *effortless, smooth* manner. It takes practice to perfect this skill of suggesting. Several relaxation exercises are presented in Chapter 2, Instructional Imagery.

Note: The relaxation techniques described above and the exercises in Chapter 2 are generally not necessary for imagery activities. The imagery exercise itself has a relaxing effect which works rather quickly. However, if the class is unusually anxious, or if you would like them to experience increased relaxation, you might administer one of the exercises. To reiterate, you do *not* have to use a relaxation exercise prior to a subject-related imagery exercise.

ART OF CONCENTRATION

Concentration is a mother robin perched on a nearby branch as little children discover her nest of newborns; concentration is walking a high wire connecting the two World Trade Towers; a pilot landing a jumbo jet in zero visibility; a surgeon performing micro-surgery; catching an arrow fired toward you in mid-air with your hand. Each of these situations describes a moment when the brain is highly stilled, engrossed, deeply centered on a single stimulus or event. All irrelevant thoughts are blocked at this heightened period when the mind is centered on a single object. "Concentration is the supreme art, because no art can be achieved without it, while with it anything can be achieved," W. Timothy Gallwey (1974).

The ability to concentrate is something you can develop and cultivate -- something you can learn. Many of us handicap ourselves by harboring the fallacy that we are simply unable to improve our level of concentration. We rationalize and tell ourselves that some people are just naturally gifted, as if they were endowed at birth with special powers of concentration. If you wish to be convinced that concentration is a talent or an asset which anyone can acquire, that there are specific techniques by which you can develop your powers of concentration, we recommend that you read *A Practical Guide to Better Concentration* by Robert Starrett and Melvin Powers.

In order to image effectively, people must be able to concentrate, to fix their mind on one thought or image, and to hold it there. The object on which a person concentrates should fill the entire consciousness. The only thoughts that should be registered by the brain are those related to the object. All interfering thoughts should not be allowed to penetrate the conscious mind.

We said that concentration can be maintained if we block or get rid of interfering thoughts. This is a lot easier to express than to do. However, there are two basic techniques we have developed in our training programs which enhance concentration.

First, develop a word which can be used as a trigger for activating a feeling or condition which blocks out or stops negative incoming thoughts. For instance, one student used the word "release" whenever he needed to deepen his concentration or block a negative incoming thought. As he continues to use it successfully and believes in its ability to perform effectively, his association of the word "release" and getting rid of unwanted thoughts will become a conditioned response that will help him increase his level of concentration. Second is a technique we call the "cloud response." When a person experiences an interfering thought or a negative thought, he/she will put that thought into a cloud and allow the thought to drift slowly out of his/her consciousness. We all understand the concept of a drifting cloud, so the image is fairly easy to create.

The ability to concentrate on images can be improved by following these simple rules:

1. Allow relaxation time prior to imaging (a few minutes is sufficient).

2. Maintain a non-threatening climate where students' images are not analyzed or criticized.

3. Develop and personalize a system in which the individual can get rid of interfering or negative thoughts, e.g., a trigger word, cloud response.

4. Reduce the number of distracting variables within the classroom, e.g., students leaving room opening and shutting the door, open windows with outside noise, etc. All of these variables will interfere with concentration and should be minimized.

5. Avoid asking questions during imagery.

6. Pace your suggestions, pausing frequently and expressing yourself in an effortless manner.

SOME CONCENTRATION TECHNIQUES

A popular technique for enhancing concentration is the ancient practice of breath meditation. Used primarily in Yoga, the activity requires the student to observe the rhythmic nature of breathing, count breathing cycles and establish breath control. A decrease in breaths per minute increases sensations and interactions with the environment and clears the mind.

A slow, steady rhythm automatically cancels conflicting thoughts, which in turn fosters better concentration. As you become better able to concentrate on your breathing, you will find yourself better able to concentrate on a single image. Samuels and Samuels (1975) have suggested that people who practice breathing exercises are better able to hold an image for longer periods of time and are less bothered by intruding thoughts.

Another technique is to look at one characteristic of an object after another. For instance, notice the color of a leaf, notice the texture, the lines, shades, the total shape, etc. By directing your focus on the various elements of the leaf, you can guide and strengthen your ability to concentrate on details, shift and reconcentrate.

Another way of looking at objects is to stare and experience it. Allow thoughts to arise freely as you fix your eyes on different aspects of an object. Do not react verbally or label what you see; just experience the images and the feelings that surround those images. If you do this for a long time (15 to 30 minutes) you will discover a great deal about the object, and go beyond its labeled aspects.

Another way for students to develop their ability to concentrate is to look at an object from different mental points of view. Look at an orange. First, look at it as something to be eaten; then become aware of the color of the orange, the texture. Imagine how it would be to paint the orange. See the orange in its growth stages, see it being picked, see it being sold at a market. Each time your point of view changes, there will be a new awareness of different aspects of the orange.

You will find that your students' ability to concentrate will be enhanced as a result of the exercises and activities in this text.

IMAGERY IN TODAY'S WORLD

Since the turn of the century, imagery has become more and more prevalent in all aspects of human life. Today we find imagery utilized in fields such as science, medicine, industry, education and, most recently, sports.

In psychology, therapists have their patients use images taken from the memory and imagination as a means to explore traumatic emotional experiences of the past. The process allows both the patient and the therapist to gain important insight into personality structures and psychological variables which contribute to mental health problems.

In addition to its wide use in psychotherapy, imagery is being used with patients in hospitals and clinics all over the world as a stress reducing mechanism. Dr. Herbert Benson of Harvard Medical School, author of the best-selling book, *Relaxation Response*, has demonstrated that patients who use relaxation and imagery techniques can reduce their oxygen consumption, respiratory rate, heart rate and muscle tension. Dr. Benson even recorded numerous cases of decreased blood pressure in patients who suffered from high blood pressure.

These results have provided the impetus for the growth of Biofeedback clinics. These are special clinics where patients are trained to concentrate on an apparatus that graphically and continuously monitors blood pressure. As the patient relaxes and heightens his/her degree of concentration, he/she can actually raise or lower his blood pressure rate as measured by an electronic gauge. In essence, people are learning how to alter physiological behavior through imagery-related techniques; they are gaining greater control over the relationship between mind and body.

Other patients train to apply imagery techniques to ease pain. Asked to concentrate on the specific area of pain (headache, strained muscle, etc.), the patient describes it completely inside the framework of the following four questions: How big is it in inches or in feet? What color is it? What does it look like? How does it feel? After doing this several times in a relaxed state of mind, the person will notice that the pain is becoming smaller, lighter, thinner. . . gone. Many burn centers throughout the United States use imagery techniques.

Even more dramatic is the number of doctors at major hospitals throughout the country who use imagery exercises with their patients. Dr. Carl Simnonton of Fort Worth, Texas, a radiologist specializing in the treatment of cancer, describes how his patients use imagery to reduce pain and fight the growth of diseased cancer cells. The patient learns how to relax and apply visualization techniques to become familiar with the diseased cells. The focus then shifts to an imagined army (or positive force) that the patient sees slowly and methodically destroying each individual diseased cancer cell. There have been numerous cases where patients have used imagery techniques two or three times a day for a period of six to eight weeks. The results: an amazing, inexplicable, complete remission of the cancer growth.

Other doctors use imagery to treat obesity problems. Patients with serious weight problems image themselves as both slender and attractive. The combination of different imagery approaches has been successful with a number of people.

In each of the cases described thus far, the process began with relaxation, continued with deeper and deeper levels of concentration and finally culminated in the controlled state of advanced imagery. These dramatic findings are not new to the scientific community; it is just that they are no longer being ignored.

Many of the practices (relaxation, concentration, imagery) can be traced back to the eastern cultures (India, China, Japan, etc.). The philosophers of Meditation and Yoga are beginning to have a greater influence on western psychologists, medical and educational practitioners.

Industry has become interested in imagery as a possible vehicle for creative problem solving. Managers and executives learn various relaxation and concentration exercises and, subsequently, a range of diversified imagery exercises. These imagery exercises provide executives with skills which can be applied toward improving business results. The imagery process acts as an energizer for each individual's creative imagination. Unlike forced creative thinking such as brainstorming, creative ideas generated as a result of imagery may be more imaginative and promising. This altered state of consciousness, the mind relaxed and open, in a slowed-up state of being, allows creativity to flourish.

For the past ten years, creativity training has continued to surge within the educational system. Educators are beginning to realize the value of nurturing creativity in students, and they have taken major steps to incorporate it into the basic school curriculum. An aspect of creativity which is becoming widely used by teachers is imagination imagery. Students are taught to relax their minds, and allow their consciousness to take them on a guided fantasy (some are related to the future, e.g., space travel or underwater exploration). In this shift of consciousness, we find combinations of experiences melded together in inexplicable ways, forming new and exciting ideas. A student might be asked to visualize a nature scene, scan its detail, allowing the mind to focus on whatever it desires. Then the student might be asked to write about the experience in a free, descriptive manner. Thus, imagery fueled the student's creative imagination. Imagery techniques are being used in schools for problem solving, creative writing, and to gain greater insight and understanding of literature and mythology. Students enjoy the imagery process and its visual component, especially in light of the fact that ninety percent of schooling is cognitive and verbal. We will continue to see imagery gain in popularity throughout the classrooms of America.

13

A final area in which imagery has appeared and developed is in the world of sports. There have been hundreds of articles and several books devoted to the subject of imagery in sports. Perhaps the most popular is a book written by a professional tennis coach, W. Timothy Gallwey, entitled, *The Inner Game of Tennis* (first published by Random House, 1974). Gallwey describes the techniques for using imagery as a basic means to improve a person's performance in tennis. Gallwey states that, "getting it together mentally in tennis involves the learning of several internal skills:

"1. Learning to program your computer [which he calls the subconscious mind] with images rather than instructing yourself with words;

"2. Learning to trust thyself (subconscious), and

"3. Learning to see non-judgmentally -- that is, to see what is happening rather than merely noticing how well or how badly it is happening."

Alex Morrison, a professional golfer, has written a book called *Better Golf Without Practice*. Morrison instructs players how to develop clear mental images of the correct swing. He has a player sit in a comfortable chair, go through a series of relaxation exercises, and then concentrate deeply (using imagery) in order to see him/herself swing correctly.

Having read this first chapter you should have a basic understanding of the imagery process and should be ready to experiment with the instructional exercises presented in the next chapter. We realize that much of the material in this chapter is new; therefore, we encourage you to read it slowly, perhaps *rereading* it prior to beginning any real work with students. *It is also advisable to practice imaging yourself before you try it with your students.* Learn the pacing and the poetic nature in which images should be presented to the students. Remember: go slowly, relax, be patient, allow plenty of discussion time, provide a safe, protective climate, and truly enjoy the remarkable gift of imagery.

IMAGERY AND THE CREATIVE PROCESS

The creative process has primarily been studied in relationship to techniques such as creative problem solving, brainstorming, forced relationships, etc. All of these techniques share their dependency on verbalization. The other strong similarity that exists among all of them is forced thinking. Unlike these typical creative problem-solving techniques, imagery is highly visual and it is not an exercise in forced thinking.

Figure 2 (Column 1), is a model developed by Dr. Sidney Parnes which describes three stages of the creative process. We will use this model to demonstrate how imagery relates to the creative process (Column 3) and how it differs from ordinary creative problem solving (Column 2).

For each of the three stages of the creative process, we have drawn some comparisons and listed some attributes for Category 1 (Standard Creative Problem Solving) and Category 2 (Imagery). Stop now and carefully read the characteristics listed under each column. After you have read them return and read the following conclusions:

1. CPS requires more preparation time than imagery.

2. More materials are needed for CPS than Imagery (e.g., newsprint, board space, markers, etc.).

3. CPS can be more distracting than Imagery. Participants shout and move about actively, resulting in frequent interruptions and loss of time.

4. CPS activates more analytical thinking in many of the participants than does Imagery. As concepts are verbalized, people analyze various words, terms or phrases; and the result is a loss of time spent on generating new ideas.

5. CPS is more limiting than Imagery in terms of seeing the problem from different perspectives. A good imager can control the image, scan it from many different perspectives, all in a matter of a few minutes.

Figure 2

STAGES OF THE CREATIVE PROCESS	CATEGORY 1 CREATIVE PROBLEM SOLVING (CPS)	CATEGORY 2 IMAGERY
Stage 1: SENSORY IMPRESSIONS (preparation stage)	Concrete material is presented: pictures, diagrams, objects, etc. Instructions and objectives are verbalized. Problem is defined.	Read problem or related data Identify with a certain visual image Select content for initial image
Stage 2: ASSOCIATIVE PROCESS (incubation stage)	Discussion of facts relating to problem Review concrete data Facts are verbalized and listed as data Read all data Ask questions and discuss data	Begin to project detail of image Scan image -- repeat image See image from different perspectives Control image and change content Begin to receive somatic response
Stage 3: INTERRELATIONSHIP PROCESS (illumination stage)	Approach problem through logical and illogical thought, resulting in ideas which are verbalized to group facilitator Ideas are listed and read Participants continue to generate new ideas Spontaneous responses from group Some members record ideas	Problem is seen vividly Ideas begin to float into conscious mind, effortlessly and naturally New Perspectives are received New feelings are received Problem is seen with magnification Mind is relaxed and open Ideas are clear and can be easily remembered

15

•

6. Imagery taps the subconscious mind faster, easier, and more consistently than does CPS, resulting in superior quality of ideas and heightened imagination.

7. Due to the high dependency and use of verbalization, CPS interferes with images relating to the problem. When we verbalize, we activate a logical thought system, a system that is not known for its creative ingenuity. On the other hand, when we visualize, we activate an intuitive, sensory and imaginative system.

Although we have built a case to demonstrate the superiority of imagery over common creative problem solving, we would not want the reader to lose sight of the importance and potential of the latter. Creative problem solving (brainstorming) has been used to ignite the imagination and creativity of students for years. It has a marvelous track record with tremendous supportive research data. Our claims about the superiority of imagery are solely based on observation. Therefore, our contentions must be considered as hypotheses which will wait for supportive evidence in the form of research data. On that note, we invite our readers to engage in imagery research.

Perhaps our point can best be illustrated by a quote from Harold Rugg (1963):

"We have had millions of hours devoted to training in solving problems by reasoning, but almost none devoted to cultivation of the imagination."

Dr. Sidney Parnes defined the creative process as "the fresh, meaningful association in elements from our knowledge and experience " (1972). Creativity is a means of examining old facts and experiences in new ways. Carl Rogers defines the creative process:

". . . as the emergence in action of a novel relational product growing out of the uniqueness of the individual on the one hand, and the materials, events, people, or circumstances of his/her life on the other."

There are hundreds of definitions of creativity found in the literature, and most of them underscore the process of seeing something in a new, original way. Consistent with that thought, we must view imagery as a potent tool for igniting an internal system which focuses on divergent ways of sensing and perceiving our environment. Through imagery, students will be able to increase their ability to associate facts, knowledge, and draw unique interrelationships beyond the content of their experiences. These interrelationships which result in the illumination of new ideas will foster a more positive, healthier attitude in the student.

Wonder, wonder
Wonder with me
Wonderment is
Fancy free!
And what we wonder
Is apt to be
Tomorrow's
Actuality.

Bert J. Decker

Imagery should be viewed as more than a component of the creative process. . . it *is* the creative process.

Perhaps the anecdote presented in Joe Khatena's new book, *Educational Psychology of the Gifted* (1982), best sums up the potential of imagery in terms of its relationship to creativity and imagination:

"I shut my eyes for a few minutes with my portable typewriter on my knee. I make my mind a blank and wait and then, as clearly as I would see real children, my characters stand before me in my mind's eye. . . . The story enacted almost as if I had a private cinema screen there. . . . I don't know what is going to happen. I am in the happy position of being able to write a story and read it for the first time at one and the same moment. . . . Sometimes a character makes a joke, a really funny one that makes me laugh as I type it on my paper and I think, 'Well, I couldn't have thought of that myself in a hundred years!' And then I think, 'Well who did think of it?'" (Stone, 1974)

Cinematographic imagery of Enid Blyton relative to the occurrence of her ideas for the *Noddy* stories.

2. Instructional Imagery

INTRODUCTION TO INSTRUCTIONAL IMAGERY

We are now ready to apply the concepts and conditions presented in Chapter 1. If you have taken sufficient time to learn the new terminology relating to the imagery process, you should have a base for the exercises in this Chapter. We suggest that as you experiment with the exercises, you go back and reread the section on characteristics and conditions. This will reinforce and strengthen your understanding of the process.

The basic purpose of this Chapter is to provide teachers with the following:

1. Important methodologies concerning the introduction of imagery.

2. Several instructional imagery exercises which are diverse, controlled and sequential.

3. Additional exercises for the purpose of enhancing mental and physical relaxation.

4. Guidelines for using the subject-related developmental imagery exercises in Chapters 3-8.

On the assumption that controlled imagery will represent a new experience for students, it is most important that their initial encounter with imagery be successful and pleasant. To achieve this goal, we recommend that you introduce the exercises to your students according to the sequence outlined in this chapter. We have introduced hundreds of students to imagery using our sequential approach and have met with good success. We do not recommend that you administer any of the subject-related exercises until you have gone through the instructional exercises. Students need to be comfortable with imagery and assured that a supportive, non-judgmental climate exists.

Subject-related imagery exercises relate to the academic curriculum and, as a result, create an expectation of evaluative learning. Therefore, if you expose students to academic imagery first, the "evaluation effect" will be present and perhaps stifle creative thinking and learning. Get rid of student fears, deal with their questions, demonstrate non-judgmental learning, give them time to adjust to visual learning. Let them build trust in you and the imagery process and then, finally, they will be ready for some very productive academic imagery experiences.

PROCESSING OUT

One of the important factors in instructional imagery is the time given to students for discussing their reactions to the various experiences. We call this time "processing out." At the completion of a particular exercise, class members are asked if they would like to share what they saw, what they didn't see, how they saw, how they felt. Students will provide you with important feedback on their progress, enabling you to identify any youngsters who might be experiencing initial difficulties. Processing out also provides an excellent opportunity for students to observe the amazing and pleasant creative imagination. Students will be most eager to share their exciting experiences. We have never gone through an instructional imagery session where there weren't some fantastically vivid and creative images seen by some members of the group. This shared creativity stimulates and ignites the imagination in other students. Any student who wishes to share an imagery experience should be given the opportunity and the time.

Another important dimension of processing out is the establishment of a supportive and trusting climate. Teachers can demonstrate non-judgmental behavior and alert students of the safeness of the classroom and their general acceptance of divergent thinking.

During processing out, students will learn that they do not necessarily have to share any or all of their experiences. If they wish to *pass*, allow it. The safer the climate, the more students will want to share.

Therefore, discussion time is an integral part of the instructional imagery training. It allows students to theorize or conjecture why and how they see or can't see images. These discussion periods help students confirm their previously held views about imaging. Through their own inquiry, they can draw conclusions about the imagery process.

POINTS TO REMEMBER ABOUT PROCESSING OUT

1. A person's thinking and learning styles can influence and affect the clarity and completeness of images.

2. A threatening or evaluative classroom climate prohibits students from relaxing their minds and allowing imagination to flow.

3. Not all students will achieve equal success with all types of imagery activities. Again, because of differences in thinking styles and previous experiences, some students will find that certain exercises are not stimulating or provoking and may even be threatening. Always allow an "OUT," i.e., give students the option of doing or not doing an imagery exercise. This rule should be maintained in a consistent manner for the duration of imagery learning.

4. Students need to be continually reminded that they should *never force images. . . let them happen!*

5. We all see images differently. There's not one right way of seeing images.

You will learn a great deal about the imagery process and about creative thinking during these discussion periods. Take the time that is needed and gain tremendous benefit for you and your students.

INSTRUCTIONAL IMAGERY EXERCISES

The following chart lists the ten basic instructional exercises and their respective features and characteristics. They are presented and sequenced according to their complexity and sophistication. Exercises seven through ten incorporate the characteristics of earlier exercises and are, therefore, not repeated in the listing.

TITLE	FEATURES/CHARACTERISTICS
1. Picture/Painting	Two-dimensional, black and white, short-term memory
2. Pencil/Pen	Three-dimensional, color, shape, design, texture
3. Childhood Room	Long term memory, objects, things, events, spatial relationships
4. Flower	Multi-sensory
5. Apple	Multi-sensory (additional)
6. Balloon	Transformational, controllability
7. Tranquil Scene	Relaxation effect, covert, deeper association
8. Guided Fantasy	Imagination, interactive association
9. Other Person	Facial and bodily features, detailed human characteristics
10. Yourself	Self-image, reality-based

TEN INSTRUCTIONAL EXERCISES

The introductory imagery exercise that we suggest uses a simple two-dimensional (IIE-1) black and white picture or painting that might be found in any typical classroom. The students are asked to look at the picture for a moment, then to close their eyes and see it with the mind's eye. Some students might wish to keep their eyes open, especially at the beginning. Always allow them to do so. This type of exercise draws on each student's short term memory or after-image. You may have the students repeat this a few times and suggest that they look at the detail of the picture first with eyes open, then with the mind's eye. Specific relaxation techniques are not usually introduced at this time. It is better to build toward a state of relaxation with a more sophisticated and detailed image.

Allow the students approximately 15 seconds to look at the picture; then have them image the picture for approximately 30 seconds (the amount of time allowed for imaging is somewhat flexible, so feel free to alter it). After 2 or 3 times, process out with the students saying, "Would anyone like to share?" Then relax and wait. Listen to the students and be non-judgmental. Don't allow other students to make judgmental statements about anyone's images.

The next imagery exercise (IIE-2), Pencil or Pen, introduces the three-dimensional concept, shape, design and color. Suggest that the students hold their pencil or pen approximately 2 feet in front of their eyes and scan its detail. After inspecting the pencil with eyes open, have the students close their eyes and see it with their mind's eye. Repeat 2 or 3 times. While they're looking at the pencil with eyes open, you might encourage them to notice details. As with all instructional imagery exercises, follow with the "processing out" period.

The third imagery exercise (IIE-3), a Childhood Room, requires the student to draw on long-term memory. Here, the student begins to experience controllability. As you give the suggestions, he/she controls the image and locates the item or thing suggested. From this point on you will usually find that students will be most eager to share, especially if a non-judgmental climate was established during exercises 1 and 2. On occasion some will experience a negative image. If that happens, just show empathy and tell them it's okay and tell them to feel free to stop. Thus, you would avoid any images that might provoke negative feelings.

The next exercise (IIE-4), a Flower, introduces a nature image which is multi-sensory in that it involves not only the visual but olfactory (smell) and kinesthetic (touch and feel) senses. The flower image is relatively easy and enjoyable for most students. Because of its nature and beauty component, the flower image has the potential to create a very relaxed feeling in the student.

At this time, you may wish to introduce some relaxation suggestions to accompany exercises 4 through 10. Do the flower image at least three times. You will notice that each time the students image their favorite flower they will see it differently, i.e., from a different perspective. Allow the students 1 or 2 minutes for the repetitions. Point out this important feature brought about through repetitive imaging. After the second flower image, you may suggest that they go inside the flower and see something they have never seen before. This suggestion usually evokes interesting and imaginative images with great descriptiveness.

The fifth exercise (IIE-5), is the Apple Image, which is multi-sensory and has a strong taste image component. It is not necessary that you repeat the apple image more than once. You may wish to change the food element and have them experience something different, e.g., peach, pear. Taste is the big element in this exercise, just as smell and touch were paramount in exercise 4. The students may also experience a vivid *auditory image* as they bite into the apple, taste and enjoy it.

The sixth exercise (IIE-6), the Balloon, introduces the concept of transformation. Students are asked to change a balloon into several colors and to have the balloon do various things, e.g., bounce along the ceiling, floor, have it slowly rise, etc. Each of the suggestions provides students an opportunity to control the projected image, a very important dimension of advanced imagery. Some psychologists feel controllability is more important than the degree of vividness. Usually there will be several students who are not completely able to transform the balloon into new colors. Just tell them to accept it and that we all experience and relate to colors in different ways.

If you have not introduced any relaxation exercises up to this point, we suggest that for (IIE-7) Tranquil Scene, you try one with your students. Experiencing a relaxed state prior to the tranquil scene will serve to heighten the quality of the image. Try one of the relaxation exercises listed in this chapter. The tranquil scene image is a very peaceful and relaxing experience which usually evokes very real and vivid images. It is very important that you administer the suggestions for IIE-7 slowly, smoothly and in an effortless manner. Teachers who first begin with imagery tend to rush the suggestions. Slowing down the suggestions is an important aspect in creating high quality images.

If you would like to try a few more instructional imagery exercises of the tranquil scene variety before moving into subject-related imagery, we suggest that you and/or your students write a few. Keep your statements simple and avoid asking questions. Use words such as *see, feel, notice, look,* etc., to start each suggestion. Imagination usually begins to flourish at this level of the imagery instruction. Pause a lot, allow plenty of time and offer the suggestions in a soft, poetic voice. Try exercise IIE-7 for at least 10 minutes. Again, the tranquil scene image has a strong relaxation and imagination effect.

The next exercise (IIE-8), Guided Fantasy, aims at evoking imagination. Unlike the previous exercise, the guided fantasy has an unrealness to it, and it is capable of arousing vivid fantasies. This is a good exercise to determine the level of trust established in the classroom. If students enjoy imaging and find it pleasurable, chances are they will allow their minds the freedom to explore in an uninhibiting manner. If, on the other hand, students have not had sufficient time or practice to discuss the process, they may be skeptical about the guided fantasy. The net result is a superficial involvement.

Some of the students might resist the guided fantasy suggestions on the basis of the non-reality of the circumstances. They will consciously reject all suggestions, and say to themselves, "this is ridiculous," or "this doesn't make sense." The verbal and logical side of their brains will shut down the visual side, and the students will lose the images. Adults tend to do this more than children, as the former have had more training in logical behavior. A child can imagine himself floating on a cloud fairly well; however, an adult who has had limited imagery experiences may find it impossible. Be patient with those who find it difficult to follow guided fantasies. All that is needed is some practice, a good trusting climate and encouragement.

The first eight imagery exercises have dealt with objects, places or things. Instructional imagery exercise nine (IIE-9), Other Person, relates to the ability of the imager to see the face and body of another person. This is generally a difficult image. The imager must pay close attention to specific facial detail (eye color, shape of nose, mouth and chin, etc.). This experience will be important for later images which will deal with specific interactions with people. The exercise helps to train the student to scan for detail and to be very observant.

The final exercise (IIE-10), Yourself, is by far the most difficult; yet it is a requisite skill, necessary for reaching the highest level of imagery: interactive association. At this level of imagery, the person actually and vividly sees him/herself engaged in some form of interactive behavior. Students can observe themselves engaged in social interactions, work-related interactions, family interactions and, as a result, can learn a lot about their behavior. Seeing yourself clearly in all of these situations helps you understand any problems you might be having. Once the students have imaged themselves in detail, they will be capable of using the image in many situations for many reasons. Throughout the subject-related imagery exercises, students will be asked to image themselves in many different ways. Exercise 10 provides the means to become more observant of how we look and act.

How long should it take to go through the instructional exercises? We suggest at least two weeks for introducing all the different facets relating to imagery. As we have said earlier, it is important that all or most of the elements and conditions of imagery be presented to the students during the instructional period. You also need time to establish a climate for non-judgmental learning. In addition, you want students to be successful with the introductory exercises so that they have a good foundation for advanced, subject-related imagery activities. While we have suggested that you follow the sequence outlined in this text, you may wish to alter or modify it somewhat. We encourage you to develop images to use for instructional purposes.

To conclude this section, here are some suggestions for presenting the instructional imagery exercises.

1. Present the suggestions (verbal commands) very slowly and naturally, pausing frequently.

2. Allow plenty of time for students to share their imagery experiences, both negative and positive.

3. Introduce relaxation techniques slowly.

4. Don't ask questions or make suggestions too complicated; keep them free and easy.

5. Discuss the characteristics found in the various exercises (color, shape, controllability, imagination) so that participants understand the process better.

6. Create a supportive climate that is non-judgmental, free of criticism.

7. Encourage the use of imagination; after all, the subconscious is the key to our creative potential.

8. Instruct participants to accept what they see, how they see it and where they see it, e.g., some people see images behind their eyelids, others behind their foreheads, etc. Remember, there are no right or wrong ways to see images.

9. Try to control the level of distracting variables by finding a quiet area. Avoid interruptions.

Sit comfortably
Relax
Look at this picture
Close your eyes
See the picture in your mind's eye
Open your eyes
Look at the picture again noticing its detail
Close your eyes again
Relax....take a deep breath
See the picture in your mind's eye
Notice the detail in the picture
Now open your eyes

Instructions:

1. Select a simple two-dimensional picture or painting found in the classroom.
2. Have students look at the picture for 10 sec.
3. Ask students to close their eyes and see it in their mind's eye for 10 sec.
4. Discussion.
5. Have students again look at the picture and concentrate on detail for 15 sec.
6. Ask students to close their eyes and see it in their mind's eye for 30 sec.
7. Discussion.

Sit comfortably
Relax
Hold a pencil horizontally in front of your eyes approximately two feet away
Allow your eyes to scan its detail
Now take a deep breath
Close your eyes
See the pencil
Notice its shape and design
See its point
See its color
Notice any writing or logos on it
When I count to three, open your eyes

Instructions:

1. Any pen or pencil will do.
2. Have students first look at the pencil for 15 sec., scanning its detail.
3. Ask students to close their eyes and see the pencil in their mind's eye for 30 sec.
4. Discussion
5. Repeat exercise.
6. Be sure to minimize the noise and distractions during all imagery exercises.

Sit comfortably
Relax
Take a slow deep breath
Close your eyes
See yourself standing in the middle of a childhood room
See the wall in front of you
Notice a window
See the view through the window
See the curtains hanging on the window
Locate an object that brought you great pleasure as a young child
See the rug on the floor
Look around and notice the whole room
When I count to five, open your eyes

Instructions:

1. Allow approximately 15 seconds for each suggestion.
2. Again, don't call on students, wait for them to volunteer during discussion period.

3. **With younger children you may wish to have them see their present bedroom and locate an object or toy that brings them great pleasure.**

Sit comfortably
Relax
Close your eyes
See a flower
Allow your eyes to roam over the whole flower stopping wherever you like
Notice its color
Smell the flower
Feel its texture
See it gently blowing in the wind
Look again at the whole flower
When I count to five, open your eyes

(Discuss flower image with students, then ask them to
  see their flower again for approximately three mins.)

Instructions:
    1. During the second flower image, you may want
       to suggest the following:
         a) Go inside the flower and see something
            you have never seen before.....
         b) See yourself doing something with the
            flower....
    2. Be non-judgmental as students describe their
       images (from here on in, imagination images
       will begin to flourish).

    3. Discuss which senses were easiest to experience.

Sit comfortably
Relax
Close your eyes
See a large red apple
Allow yourself to scan its detail
Notice any small imperfections
See the stem
Notice its size and shape, feel its weight
See yourself taking a big bite
Hear the crunch
Enjoy the taste
Smell the apple
Feel the skin and make it shiny
Look at the whole apple again
When I count to five, open your eyes

Instructions:

1. Any type of fruit could be used for this exercise

2. Allow 15 seconds for each suggestion.

3. Observe student differences in being able to use the senses while imaging an apple.

Sit comfortably
Relax
Close your eyes
Take a deep breath
You're in your bedroom
See yourself filling up a red balloon with helium
See yourself knotting it
Allow the red balloon to rise slowly to the ceiling, stopping it just before it reaches the ceiling
Have it bounce along the ceiling
Now bring it down in front of you
Change its color to blue
Have it bounce along the floor
Stop it and change its color to yellow
Have the yellow balloon slowly move up the wall
Put the yellow balloon on the table
Watch the helium slowly leave the balloon
When I count to five, open your eyes

Instructions:

    1. Other colors could be substituted.
    2. Allow 15 seconds for each suggestion.

    3. With younger children, a brief explanation of helium may be necessary before you begin.
    4. Some may not be able to change to all colors suggested. Explain that control will increase when they can "let go of" logic.

Sit comfortably and relax
You're standing on a sandy beach on a beautiful resort island
Feel the sand under your feet
Feel the sand between your toes
Feel the warm water gently running over your ankles
Smell the salt in the air
Hear the waves breaking in the distance
Feel the hot sun
Feel its warmth on your arms...legs...entire body
Look up and see a beautiful blue sky
See little white fluffy clouds drifting...drifting
See some birds flying by
Listen to them
Notice how clear everything is
Look far out into the ocean
See a ship in the distance
Now see yourself doing something you enjoy
Enjoy this calm and peaceful place
See yourself sipping your favorite drink
Taste it...enjoy
See yourself returning to the classroom
When I count to ten, open your eyes

Instructions:

1. Use appropriate pausing

2. Express yourself in a very pleasant, soft voice.

3. Use guided fantasy images as follow up.

4. Count to ten for this exercise, giving the
   students an opportunity to adjust to returning.

Sit comfortably and relax
Take some slow deep breaths
Close your eyes
See yourself getting onto a safe, magical balloon
Feel the balloon slowly beginning to go up into the sky
Direct the balloon to your favorite vacation place
Travel there now
Feel yourself floating through soft white clouds
See the green trees below
Notice how clear everything is
Feel how relaxed you are
You're now over your favorite place
Go down and visit for a while*
Take pictures of all that you see
Now see an unoccupied house...go inside and look around
Go into each room
Find something to take with you
Now see yourself leaving the house
Feel youself going back up into the sky
Look again at your favorite vacation place
See all the beautiful places and things
See yourself making the trip home
You're now returning to the classroom
When I count to ten, open your eyes

Instructions:
1. Have students relax for a moment prior to
   starting the exercise.
2. We suggest that you limit yourself to no more
   than one guided fantasy in any given day.
3. See Guided Fantasy section for more exercises
   of this nature.
4. Encourage students to develop guided fantasy
   exercises.
5. Remember to pause at least 15 seconds per line.

(* = 1 or 2 min. pause)

Sit comfortably and relax
Close your eyes
See someone you know well standing in front of you
Look at the face
Notice the eyes
See the nose
Notice the color of the hair
Notice the skin
See the whole body standing in front of you
Listen to the person talk
Hear the volume of speech
See the person doing something s/he frequently does
Look again at all of the features
When I count to ten, open your eyes

Instructions:

1. Let students know that person images may be more difficult than object images.

2. You may wish to do this exercise several times; the first time everyone could see you, the teacher, the next time as written, and finally with the line, "See the person doing something he or she would never do."

Sit comfortably and relax
Close your eyes
See yourself standing in a room
Notice your face
See the color of your eyes
See the features of your nose...cheeks...and jaw
See your whole body
Notice the clothes you are wearing
See yourself doing something familiar
Listen carefully to your voice as you speak
Look at yourself from different angles
When I count to ten, open your eyes

Instructions:
1. Be aware that this image may be difficult for some students to evoke.
2. Create person images using different content, i.e., different situations.

Lie down with your legs uncrossed and your arms at your side, palms up

Let your eyes gently close

Inhale through your nose and sense your chest expanding

Then release your breath

Repeat this same breathing sequence until it becomes natural and effortless*

As you continue, begin to place stronger and stronger emphasis on your exhalation

Now inhale to a silent count of four

Hold for a silent count of four before you exhale

Exhale to a silent count of eight

You are now becoming relaxed...continue the slow and even breathing

Inhale again to a silent count of four

Hold for a count of four

Exhale to a silent count of eight

Concentrate on the rhythmic cycle of your breathing

Increase the silent exhalation...count to 12 on your next breath

Continue at this rate*

Feel this rhythmic breathing beginning to clear your mind

You are now calm and comfortable

You are deeply relaxed

* = 1 or 2 min. pause

Let your legs spread slightly apart with toes and feet hanging loosely from your ankles

Let your hands fall to your sides, palms up

Close your eyes

Inhale slowly and deeply

Concentrate on your abdomen rising and falling

Do this several times

You now feel calm, comfortable and more relaxed

Now relax your feet...feel them becoming heavier

Relax your ankles

Say to yourself, my ankles are becoming more and more relaxed

Relax your lower legs

Relax your thighs

You are becoming more and more relaxed

Relax your pelvis, abdomen, muscles of your back

Feel your chest relaxing

Relax your fingers, hands, forearms, upperarms

Feel your body becoming totally relaxed

Now feel your neck relaxing

Relax your face, cheeks, eyes and tongue

Relax your forehead, top of your head

You now feel deeply relaxed and your mind is open

Lie comfortably on your back
Allow your hands and feet to loosely rest against the floor
Close your eyes and begin to inhale slowly and deeply
Listen to the music
Immerse yourself in the music
Listen so carefully and so completely that you lose all outside thoughts
Just listen*
Become one with the sound
Listen to the flow of the music
Just listen*
As you let the sound encompass you, enjoy this calm and comfortable feeling
Allow these beautiful sounds to continue, peacefully and freely
You are now deeply relaxed and your mind is open

Note: Select soft gentle music for this exercise.

* = 1 to 2 min. pause

Sit comfortably and relax
Let your hands fall loosely on your thighs with your palms up
Take a slow deep breath, expanding your chest and abdomen
Then exhale slowly, feeling your chest and abdomen relax
Breath in this way until you begin to feel quite relaxed*
As you become more relaxed, your breathing will become slow and even
Now feel soft, warm air gently coming through the holes in your shoes
Feel the warm air moving slowly through you ankles
Feel it move slowly upward through your lower legs
Feel the warm air rising gently up...up through your thighs
Feel its warmth in your pelvic area
Feel the warm air moving up through your stomach and into your chest
You are now becoming more and more relaxed
Feel the warmth gently running down your one arm
Feel it going through each finger
Now feel it coming up and moving down the other arm slowly and warmly
Feel the warm sensations moving through your neck
Feel its inner softness gently passing through your face
Feel its warmth against your eyes, nose, forehead
You are now deeply relaxed

* = 1 or 2 min. pause

Find a comfortable position with your eyes closed
Take some deep breaths
Breathe slowly and deeply and every time you breathe out, feel
yourself becoming more and more relaxed
Just let your body go and relax
Breathe in and out and relax
Now feel the muscles of your face contract...tense then let
go...relax
Contract your neck and let go
Allow your shoulders to tense and then relax
As you relax, your breathing will become slow and even
Contract your forearms and let go
Now relax your hands and fingers in the same manner*
Repeat the same suggestions for your stomach and pelvis
Feel your thighs contract and then let go
Feel your body becoming deeply relaxed
Enjoy this calm and comfortable feeling
Now feel your ankles tense and relax
Feel your feet tense and relax
Your body has let go and you are now in a deep state of mind,
free and open

Note: Have students tense body parts for at least 15
      seconds before letting go.

* = 1 to 2 min. pause

Find a comfortable position and relax
Sit erect and straighten your spine
Place both feet squarely on the floor, a comfortable distance apart
Allow both hands to fall loosely in your lap
Close your eyes and begin to inhale slowly and deeply
Continue to take slow deep breaths, expanding your chest and abdomen
Breathe in this way until you begin to feel quite relaxed*
As you continue to relax...getting ever more deeply into your inner level
See first the color Red...visualizing an apple
See yourself biting into it
See the color Orange...visualizing an orange
See Yellow...visualize yourself basking in the golden sunshine of your mind and growing calmer
See the soothing color Green and...visualize the forest and inner peace
See Blue...visualizing an azure sky and a feeling of love
See Purple and...visualize a mystical twilight
See Violet and...visualize a misty haze gradually merging into the endless sea
Enjoy the feeling of total body relaxation
You are now in a calm, relaxed state of being

* = 1 or 2 min. pause

Sit erect and straighten your spine

Place both feet squarely on the floor, a comfortable distance apart

Allow both hands to fall loosely in your lap

Tilt your head back a little so that your neck and spine form one continuous vertical line

Close your eyes gently and begin to inhale slowly and deeply

I shall now count from twenty-one down to one

On every descending number you will feel yourself going deeper and more inward

Twenty-one - Twenty - Nineteen...Feel yourself going deeper

Eighteen - Seventeen - Sixteen...Go deeper within

Fifteen - Fourteen - Thirteen...Deeper and deeper

Twelve - Eleven - Ten...Feel youself going inward

Nine - Eight - Seven...Go more inward

Six - Five - Four...Inner and inner

Three - Two - One

You are now calm, comfortable and deeply relaxed

GUIDELINES FOR USING THE SUBJECT-RELATED DEVELOPMENTAL IMAGERY EXERCISE

In the following chapters (3 - 8) you will find two hundred imagery exercises which relate to the major subject areas in the basic school curriculum: Language Arts, Science, Social Studies, Math, Music and Art. In addition, there are several guided fantasy imagery exercises listed at the end of the academic section. We have developed the exercises after a careful review of the curriculum scope and sequence at the primary and intermediate levels. We have tried to vary the activities as much as possible, so that teachers can appreciate the flexibility and potential of imagery related activities. The imagery exercises are presented in a clear, concise manner with a sufficient number of suggestions (verbal commands) to evoke vivid images from the students. They are general enough to be used at different grade levels. We suggest that if teachers wish to modify or change some of the suggestions in the imagery exercise in order to personalize them, they do so.

BASIC FORMAT OF THE DEVELOPMENTAL IMAGERY ACTIVITIES

The subject-related activities are presented in the following format:

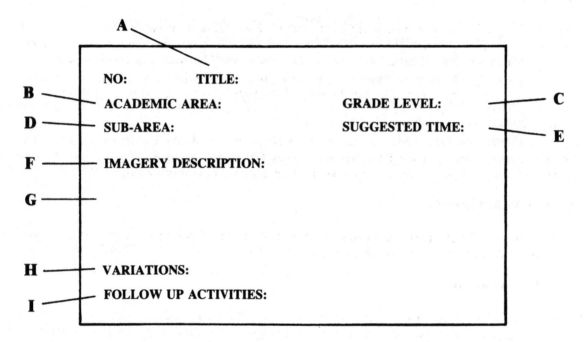

A. ACTIVITY TITLE

Each of the activity areas have been selected from curriculum guides developed by major publishing houses. They represent important content within a particular unit of study. There are approximately thirty different activity titles for each of the academic subject areas presented in the text.

The activities are diverse and demonstrate the feasibility of using visualization as a major tool for learning.

Our primary objective has been to offer a sufficient number of activities so that teachers would have some foundation for creating their own imagery experiences.

B. ACADEMIC AREA

At the top of each activity you will find the corresponding academic area in which the activity is classified: Language Arts, Science, Social Studies, Math, Music and Art.

C. GRADE LEVEL

We have designated two basic grade levels for the purpose of identifying the appropriateness of certain activities for different age groups: Primary (Grades 1, 2 and 3) and Intermediate (Grades 4 -8).

We found that the content for some activities is appropriate for more than one grade level. In this case we have designated the appropriate levels. Some activities are only appropriate for one specific grade level. Again, teachers could modify the imagery suggestions, making the experience more appropriate for a particular grade level. Teachers should also encourage students to develop their own imagery exercises.

D. SUB-AREA

For every activity listed under the basic four academic areas -- Language Arts, Science, Social Studies and Math -- we have identified an academic sub-area. The sub-areas serve as a means to classify and categorize the content of the academic activities.

E. SUGGESTED TIME

Length of time for a particular exercise is difficult to suggest. Some teachers emphasize certain areas of study more than other areas. Some of us would like students to be more familiar with certain content, and are thus inclined to lengthen a particular exercise. Therefore, you must consider these variables when you decide how long a specific exercise should last. The activities are flexible. They can be five minutes or thirty minutes in duration. As the one administering the imagery exercise, you control the suggestions (verbal commands). Some suggestions may require a pause of as long as a few minutes in order to allow the imager sufficient time to scan all of the important details and to experience imagination.

Understand that time is very arbitrary and requires individual preference. We have given you a suggested length of time for each imagery exercise, and perhaps you may wish to follow it as an initial point of reference. Remember, time seems much longer for the reader than the imager. So, experiment with different lengths of time.

F. IMAGERY DESCRIPTION

A brief description of each activity is provided in order to give you a general idea of the nature of the content. Although short, it does focus on the main area covered.

G. IMAGERY EXERCISE

The imagery exercises are presented in the same format as were the instructional and relaxation imagery exercises, i.e., short statements which are the basic oral suggestions administered by the teacher during the activity. There are 15 to 30 suggestions per exercise. All of the exercises begin with the suggestion, "sit comfortably and relax." The last two suggestions of each exercise are:

> "See yourself slowly returning to the classroom."
> "When I count to ten, open your eyes."

The length of each particular developmental imagery exercise is determined by the duration of each pause. At the end of each suggestion, you must pause. The pauses can be 15 - 30 seconds or a few minutes, depending on how much time you want your students to image. Certain lines have asterisks (*) at the end, suggesting a 2 - 3 minute pause.

NOTE: *No matter how slowly you are going, you're probably going too fast!*

Remember, as students learn to image and allow their imaginations to take over, they are bombarded by images. Time flies when you image. Fifteen minutes may seem to be no more than five, so don't be reluctant to try long pauses. The students will fill the time with plenty of high quality images.

The basic reason for the suggested time periods is to keep a certain degree of *focus* on the academic content. Your objective is to have students learn about and experience the subject matter in the form of visualizations. These visualizations provide the learner with new perspectives, new emotional feelings and greater cognitive awareness.

We reiterate, teachers should *practice* giving the instructional and relaxation exercises before administering the subject-related developmental imagery exercises. It's very important that you express yourself in an even flow, with poetic tone, easily and effortlessly. It takes practice, so move slowly!

H. VARIATIONS

One of our objectives is to have teachers explore and develop a variety of imagery related experiences for their students. Therefore, to help in the conceptualization, we have included some variations or alternatives to the suggested activity which may trigger some additional ideas.

I. FOLLOW UP ACTIVITIES

Most educators will agree that learning should be multi-dimensional and should involve the learner in different types of activities (some for mastery, some for reinforcement, others for motivation). Because of the nature of imagery, follow up activities can very easily be developed. Imagery evokes imagination; imagination needs expression; expression needs an outlet. For many of the exercises, creative writing would be ideal. Other exercises might be appropriate for some form of artistic construction. One of the side effects created by imagery is that students tend to do more inquiring, which is fantastic for teachers who are progressive in their teaching style.

We have included at least two possible follow up activities for each imagery exercise. Obviously, you could generate many more.

If you have studied the basic characteristics and elements of the imagery process presented in Chapter 1 and have taken sufficient time to practice administering the instruction exercises, you should be ready to move on to the academic-related developmental imagery activities in the next several chapters.

If you have reached this point and still remain uncomfortable about the technique, perhaps you need to reread Chapters 1 and 2 and discuss and explore the content with some friends. We also recommend that you *try* the imagery exercises yourself, either by having someone read them to you or by putting the suggestions on a tape.

SAMPLE EXERCISE WITH DESIGNATED PAUSES

The following sample exercise has suggested pause times for each imagery line of verbal suggestion. Try it according to the designated time schedule. Begin to learn the importance and nature of correct pausing.

SAMPLE EXERCISE

NO: **18**   TITLE: BUILDING THE GREAT WALL OF CHINA

ACADEMIC AREA: SOCIAL STUDIES   **GRADE LEVEL**: Intermediate
SUB-AREA: World History   **SUGGESTED TIME**: 16 mins.

IMAGERY DESCRIPTION:

Students will experience the building of the Great Wall. They will feel the stone, mix the cement and help place the large stone blocks. They will acquire a good idea of its size, strength and distance as they observe it from different perspectives.

IMAGERY EXERCISE:

● RECOMMENDED TIME FOR PAUSING:

Sit comfortably and relax	
You are in a horse-drawn wagon approaching the construction site of the Great Wall of China	30 sec.
You are a peasant laborer working on the Wall	30 sec.
Feel the hot sun as you climb up a hill to the site	30 sec.
Look at the huge stone blocks that have been placed in the ground as a foundation	30 sec.
Look around and see thousands of people working, from hill to hill, for miles and miles*	2 mins.
See yourself dragging a huge stone, by rope	30 sec.
As you pull...feel the pressure on your arms, back, legs	30 sec.
Feel the sweat running down your face	30 sec.
See the blisters on your hands	30 sec.
Watch others lifting these heavy stones into place	30 sec.
See yourself sitting, talking to others, during a break	30 sec.
Listen to what they are saying*	3 mins.
Hear the shouts of soldiers, as they order you back to work	30 sec.
Watch the Wall slowly being built*	2 mins.
See the Great Wall for as far as you can see	30 sec.
Notice its size	30 sec.
See yourself walking on the Great Wall	30 sec.
Feel the emotion and excitement	15 sec.
See yourself returning to the classroom	15 sec.
When I count to ten, open your eyes	

VARIATIONS:

Students could participate in the building of any significant structure(bridges, roads, monuments, pyramids, etc.). They could participate as workers, designers, supervisors, etc.

FOLLOW UP ACTIVITIES:

Construct a model of the Great Wall of China. Research specific facts about the Wall and prepare an oral report.

3. Imagery in Language Arts

NO: 19   **TITLE:**   BUTTERFLY BALLET

ACADEMIC AREA: LANGUAGE ARTS   **GRADE LEVEL:** Primary/Intermed.

SUB-AREA: Creative Writing   **SUGGESTED TIME:** 15 mins.

IMAGERY DESCRIPTION:

Students will begin observing a butterfly in a field and, later, become a butterfly, experiencing things with the music.

MATERIALS NEEDED: Instrumental recording.

IMAGERY EXERCISE:

Sit comfortably and relax
See yourself in a large field on a sunny day
BEGIN TAPE SOFTLY
Feel the grass under your bare feet
Smell the wild flowers
See their color
Watch them sway in the breeze
Feel your hair blowing
Observe a butterfly landing on a stem
Watch the pulsing wings
Examine the delicate patterns and colors
Look closer to see the veins fanning out to the edge of each wing
Watch it flutter…and fly
Chase it*
Become a butterfly and join it
Feel the sun
Ride upward on warm air currents*
Experience the inside of a cloud
Feel its moisture on your wings
Fly down to a flower
Taste the sweet nectar
Feel your heart pounding
See yourself returning to the classroom
When I count to ten, open your eyes

VARIATIONS:

Change the animal or allow student to choose any animal he/she wishes (e.g., bird, tiger, shark, etc.). Student becomes an object rather than an animal (e.g., ball, pencil, kite, etc.).

FOLLOW UP ACTIVITIES:

Design new patterns for butterfly wings. Build kites with butterfly shapes and fly them. Make a list of nouns that name all of the things seen and verbs describing all of the things done.

NO:**20**   TITLE: BUBBLES

ACADEMIC AREA: LANGUAGE ARTS   **GRADE LEVEL:** Primary/Intermed.

SUB-AREA: Creative Writing   **SUGGESTED TIME:** 15 mins.

IMAGERY DESCRIPTION:

Students become bubbles and follow themselves while listening to the music.

MATERIALS NEEDED: Recording featuring light, quick melodies (Handel, Air from Harpsichord Suite in E Major, Music In Today's Classroom, Harcourt, Brace Jovanovich)

IMAGERY EXERCISE:

Sit comfortably and relax
Feel yourself becoming very light
You are a bubble
Examine your shape and color
Touch your delicate walls
Begin to move with other bubbles
BEGIN TAPE, PLAY TO END
Bump...float...turn
Rise and fall with the music
Change colors
Enjoy your life as a bubble
Play
Take something for a ride in you
Smell interesting odors as you pass them
Examine textures of different objects
Float
Pop and come back again
Split and become lots of little bubbles
Join to make one big bubble again
TAPE ENDS
See yourself returning to the classroom
When I count to ten, you will open your eyes

VARIATIONS:

Students may become anything light (feathers, snowflakes, seeds, etc.) or small (molecules, sand on the beach, etc.).

FOLLOW UP ACTIVITIES:

Use real bubbles or balloons and move them to the music. Draw the distorted view of a scene as if pictured through a bubble (use pot lids to get the effect). Design a "floating city." Write a story about how it came to be.

NO: **21**   TITLE: IMAGES

ACADEMIC AREA: LANGUAGE ARTS   GRADE LEVEL: Primary/Intermed.

SUB-AREA: Creative Writing   SUGGESTED TIME: 15 mins.

IMAGERY DESCRIPTION:

Using a simple formula, students will write short poems about images they see while flying on a magic carpet.

IMAGERY EXERCISE:

> **Sit comfortably and relax**
> **You're getting onto a beautiful magic carpet**
> **You're taking off...up...up...up**
> **Fly over one of your favorite vacation places**
> **Notice how clear everything is**
> **Let's create some images**
> **Look below and find something...an object**
> **Now give that object color**
> **Have it do something**
> **Place it somewhere funny**
> **Now write what you saw in a soft white cloud just above you**
> **Now continue your journey and create more images**
> **Remember the formula! Find an object, give it color, have it do something and place it somewhere**
> **Don't forget to write your finished poems in the little white clouds**
> **Now see all your poems floating by...one-by-one**
> **See your magic carpet slowly coming back**
> **See yourself returning to the classroom**
> **When I count to ten, open your eyes**

VARIATIONS:

Using the same formula, students could write images about feelings (happy, sad, anger, frustration, etc.). They would describe a feeling, give it color and action and place it somewhere.

FOLLOW UP ACTIVITIES:

Write or draw your images on paper. Make a model of one of the images. Using the formula create some images for objects in the classroom. Have each student present at least one of their images.

ACADEMIC AREA: LANGUAGE ARTS   GRADE LEVEL: Primary/Intermed.

SUB-AREA: Creative Writing   SUGGESTED TIME: 10 mins.

IMAGERY DESCRIPTION:

Students will imagine that they are creating different sounds by tapping on household objects, their bodies and later in a store downtown.

MATERIALS NEEDED: Recording of steel drums (Native Steel Drum Band, Music In Today's Classroom, Harcourt Brace Jovanovich)

IMAGERY EXERCISE:

Sit comfortably and relax
See yourself at home with nothing to do
Try the TV...and the radio
Hook up your tape recorder
Hear the click as you push "record"
Tap on a glass, hear it ring
Record it
Find other things that make noise when you tap on them
Go wild
Tap everything you see
BEGIN TAPE, PLAY TO END
Tap in the kitchen...in the refrigerator...on the pots and pans...
and dishes
Go into every room of the house
Try your body...your head...feet
Go outside...and tap on an animal
Go into a store
Watch shoppers staring as you enjoy each aisle
TAPE ENDS
See yourself returning to the classroom
When I count to ten, open your eyes

VARIATIONS:

Students could be natives in a jungle beating out a message and receiving the answer. Students could be dribbling a basketball all over...on many surfaces, inside and out.

FOLLOW UP ACTIVITIES:

Create a "Tapping Tape" like the one heard. Experiment with metal objects making your own "Steel" drums. Mime "A Boring Day at Home!' Make metal mobiles that play in the breeze. Brainstorm all of the things that could be tapped.

NO:**23**   TITLE: LITTER LEGEND

ACADEMIC AREA: LANGUAGE ARTS   GRADE LEVEL: Primary/Intermed.

SUB-AREA: Creative Writing   SUGGESTED TIME: 10 mins.

IMAGERY DESCRIPTION:

Students will become a piece of litter bouncing along the highway to the sounds of a recording

MATERIALS NEEDED: Recording featuring Percussion (Lou Harrison,
Suite for Percussion, Music In Today's Classroom, Harcourt, Brace
Jovanovich)

IMAGERY EXERCISE:

Sit comfortably and relax
See yourself as an empty food container
Notice your bright colorful lettering
Smell the lingering odor of food that was once inside you
Taste it
BEGIN TAPE, PLAY TO END
Feel yourself being crushed...and tossed out of a car window
Bounce along the highway as the car disappears
Come to rest along the shoulder of the highway
Watch as things continue to pass you
Feel something pick you up
Examine them as they examine you
Feel yourself traveling to a new place
Enjoy the adventure you are about to have...
TAPE ENDS
See yourself returning to the classroom
When I count to ten, open your eyes

VARIATIONS:

Students could be a piece of rock as it is eroded away from a
mountain top. Students could be soap bubbles going down the
drain. Students could be a ball which bounces away from the
game.

FOLLOW UP ACTIVITIES:

Make a time line showing the life of a food wrapper, including
the adventure. Tape an interview with a piece of litter. Use
musical phrases for responses. Write a ballad, "The Legend of
Litter."

46

NO: **24**   TITLE: MUSICAL MOTOR

ACADEMIC AREA: LANGUAGE ARTS   GRADE LEVEL: Primary/Intermed.
SUB-AREA: Creative Writing   SUGGESTED TIME: 10 mins.

IMAGERY DESCRIPTION:

   Students will become an engine and move through a fantasy
   while they listen to a recording.

MATERIALS NEEDED: Recording featuring Percussion (Carlos Chavez,
   Toccata for Percussion, Music in Today's Classroom, Harcourt,
   Brave Jovanovich)

IMAGERY EXERCISE:

> **Sit comfortably and relax**
> **See yourself as a motor inside of something**
> **Scan your surroundings**
> **See where you are and what you can do**
> **Feel your metal parts**
> **Smell the oil that helps you move smoothly**
> **Listen to yourself being started up**
> *BEGIN TAPE, PLAY TO END*
> **Watch your parts moving in harmony**
> **Notice their sizes and shapes**
> **Examine their colors**
> **See different-sized gears turning**
> **Feel your power**
> **Move at different speeds**
> **Watch your machine perform**
> **Listen to what people are saying about you**
> **Do something different from other motors**
> **Shut yourself off**
> **See yourself returning to the classroom**
> **When I count to ten, open your eyes**

VARIATIONS:

Begin with the students' playing the percussion instruments by jumping on them like trampolines.
Suggest that the student is the motor of a household appliance, racing car, etc.

FOLLOW UP ACTIVITIES:

Draw a design of the engine you were. Build a model with
moveable parts from junked objects. Write a story from the
engine's point of view. Make a tape of various engines; try
to duplicate their sounds with instruments.

ACADEMIC AREA: LANGUAGE ARTS   GRADE LEVEL: Primary/Intermed.

SUB-AREA: Creative Writing   SUGGESTED TIME: 15 mins.

IMAGERY DESCRIPTION:

Students will become scientists in the laboratory, inventing something new and unusual.

MATERIALS NEEDED: Instrumental recording.

IMAGERY EXERCISE:

Sit comfortably and relax

See yourself in a white laboratory coat

BEGIN TAPE SOFTLY

Note the wires...flasks...instruments and chemicals in your laboratory

Feel the smooth steel and glass equipment as you construct a maze of tubes for your invention

Choose a jar, open it, smell it, and examine the color and texture

Read the label

Pour some into a large beaker and watch it flow

Mix other unusual substances with it

Smell their odors, change their colors

Watch it bubble, listen to it

Follow it through the maze of tubing

Touch and smell it

Feed some to a laboratory animal

INCREASE VOLUME

Watch how it affects the animal's size...sounds...movement ...color...and abilities

Observe the animal doing something weird

Bottle the secret substance and label it

Put it in a safe place

See youself returning to the classroom

When I count to ten, open your eyes

VARIATIONS:

Put restrictions on laboratory equipment (i.e., only electrical items, etc.). Rather than transforming an animal, build an invention and test it to see if it works.

FOLLOW UP ACTIVITIES:

Write about the imagery experience. Change the ending so you test the formula. Dress a stuffed animal to show how it changed. Write the story from the laboratory animal's point of view. Research how animals are used in laboratory experiments.

NO: **26**   TITLE: SPACE VISITORS

ACADEMIC AREA: LANGUAGE ARTS   GRADE LEVEL: Primary/Intermed.

SUB-AREA: Creative Writing   SUGGESTED TIME: 15 mins.

IMAGERY DESCRIPTION:

Students will meet creatures from outer space. They will work with them and help repair the creature's damaged space ship.

IMAGERY EXERCISE:
Sit comfortably and relax
See yourself at home in your own bed
Listen to an unusual sound outside
Quietly, investigate with a flashlight
Hear the sound again getting louder
Feel your heart pounding in your chest
Observe space creatures moving out of a damaged space ship
Notice their size and color*
Hear the blinking lights of the ship
Try to communicate with them
Listen to the strange sounds they make
Observe their facial gestures
Examine the texture of their bodies
See their footprints
They are trying to tell you something
They need your help...*
Get them to follow you
Hide them in a safe place
Watch them doing things that amaze you*
Find out what they eat
Take them to your favorite place
Help them repair their ship
Decide whether you want to go with them
Hear the rumble of the engines as the ship leaves Earth
See yourself returning to the classroom
When I count to ten, open your eyes

VARIATIONS:

Aliens could be just like Earth people except for one thing, e.g., features upside down, talk backwards, etc. Students could do different things with the space creatures (play ball, eat, go to the movies, etc.).

FOLLOW UP ACTIVITIES:

Write a story about how you escaped or why you decided to go along. Make a model of the space ship. Write a nonsense poem about how the aliens looked and what they could do. Research real U.F.O.'s.

NO: **27**   TITLE: DEAR SANTA

ACADEMIC AREA: LANGUAGE ARTS   **GRADE LEVEL:** Primary

SUB-AREA: Letter Writing   **SUGGESTED TIME:** 10 mins.

IMAGERY DESCRIPTION:

Students will write a letter to Santa on a giant piece of paper. They will walk on the paper, moving to the appropriate positions for writing a letter.

IMAGERY EXERCISE:

> **Sit comfortably and relax**
> **You're standing on a large sheet of paper**
> **Notice the lines and spaces**
> **Jump from one line to another**
> **See yourself lifting up a giant magic marker**
> **Feel its weight and notice its color**
> **Take it with you to the top right side of the paper**
> **Now with your marker...write the word December**
> **See yourself begin with a large capital D***
> **See the word December** *SPELL FOR YOUNGER STUDENTS*
> **Now put a 3 for the third day of December, and a comma**
> **See yourself writing 1984**
> **Now take your marker and walk over to the left side of the paper**
> **Take one giant step in from the edge and write Dear Santa with a comma***
> **Hop down to the line under the comma and begin your letter to Santa**
> **Fill the page with lots of words and pictures***
> **You're now at the bottom of the page**
> **Let's close the letter with "Thank you"**
> **Remember to sign your name**
> **Now look again at all the places you visited on your page**
> **See yourself returning to the classroom**
> **When I count to ten, open your eyes**

VARIATIONS:

Older students could write the body rather than draw. Any letter can be written this way, e.g., thank you note, etc. Students could become the ink, paper, etc.

FOLLOW UP ACTIVITIES:

Practice writing an actual letter. Draw a picture of the imaginary letter to Santa. Construct a large sheet of paper and walk through the steps in writing a letter.

NO: **28**   TITLE: DAISY DIAGRAMS

ACADEMIC AREA: LANGUAGE ARTS   GRADE LEVEL: Primary/Intermed.

SUB-AREA: Parts of Speech   SUGGESTED TIME: 5 mins.

IMAGERY DESCRIPTION:

Students will view a daisy with a noun in its yellow center and adjectives on the white petals.

IMAGERY EXERCISE:

      Sit comfortably and relax

      See yourself walking through a large field

      Hear insects and birds calling to each other

      Look down and see a large brown seed near your foot

      Feel your fingertips dig into the soil to plant it

      Listen to a rumble as the green sprout pushes up through magically to become a large daisy

      Touch the soft yellow center and see it open up and become a round viewing screen

      Watch as the word "daisy" appears on the screen

      Notice a dull pulsing light as words describing the daisy appear on each white petal

      Follow the light around the yellow center as the words are read to you

      Large daisy…magical daisy…beautiful daisy…yellow and white daisy…tall daisy…sweet smelling daisy

      All of the petals describe this daisy…a tall…large…beautiful…sweet smelling…yellow and white…magical daisy

      Plant another seed

      Watch it grow…and open

      Read the name of an object in its center

      Now see the words that describe the object on each of the petals*

      See yourself returning to the classroom

      When I count to ten, open your eyes

VARIATIONS:

Use verbs as the center and adverbs as the descriptive words. Use prepositional phrases as the descriptive petals. Use story characters from the Reading book.

FOLLOW UP ACTIVITIES:

Draw one or all of the daisies seen for a mural. Give partial daisy to be completed---only the petals or center filled. Take sentences apart and put into "daisy diagrams".

ACADEMIC AREA: LANGUAGE ARTS   GRADE LEVEL: Primary/Intermed.

SUB-AREA: Parts of Speech   SUGGESTED TIME: 5 mins.

IMAGERY DESCRIPTION:

Students will have an opportunity to generate action words on their personal mini-computers.

IMAGERY EXERCISE:

Sit comfortably and relax
You're in front of your computer
You will view many scenes today
Set the program...for action
Listen to the noises you make as you see yourself moving...in the morning...at night...in your bedroom...kitchen...on stairs*
See yourself moving...over something...through something... under something*
See yourself like an animal...like a machine...like a bug...like a rock
See yourself in a tree...in water...up high in the air...on a bike... skateboard
See an animal...hear it...give it color
See a machine...feel its parts...put it somewhere...hear its engine
Now see a color...watch it move...in the air
Give it shape...texture...sound...move it fast
Slow it down...watch it stop and disappear
See yourself returning to the classroom
When I count to ten, open your eyes

VARIATIONS:

Use with nouns, adjectives, etc. Observe only animals of the sea or plants or vehicles, etc. Paint action pictures. Take movies of action scenes.

FOLLOW UP ACTIVITIES:

Tell a short story, acting out all of the verbs. Mime all actions that one animal can do. Find verbs with almost the same meaning. Make a collage or crossword puzzle with verbs only.

NO: **30**   TITLE: A PUMPKIN'S PUNCTUATION PROGRAM

ACADEMIC AREA: LANGUAGE ARTS   GRADE LEVEL: Primary

SUB-AREA: Punctuation   SUGGESTED TIME: 10 mins.

IMAGERY DESCRIPTION:

Students will carve a face onto a pumpkin, using the shapes of the period, exclamation point, question mark, and comma for facial features.

IMAGERY EXERCISE:

Sit comfortably and relax
See yourself in the middle of a pumpkin patch on Halloween night
Find the biggest pumpkin you've ever seen
Touch the smooth, hard, orange pumpkin
To carve a face, you'll need to use your special laser-beam wand
Feel the lightness of the wand*
Cut two round periods for the eyes
Make them small...and round
Use a long exclamation point for the nose
See it long and very straight with a round period at the bottom
Question marks make good ears
Make a big rounded curve on top...then down...and a period underneath
Do the other ear in the same way
Make scary teeth with lots of commas
Now look at your pumpkin and all the features you gave it*
See yourself returning to the classroom
When I count to ten, open your eyes

VARIATIONS:

Paint a giant Easter egg, Halloween mask, etc. Use something other than a laser-beam wand.

FOLLOW UP ACTIVITIES:

Decorate a pumpkin using only punctuation marks as features. Decorate a pumpkin as in the Exercise and Pin on sentences or phrases corresponding with the punctuation marks.

ACADEMIC AREA: LANGUAGE ARTS   **GRADE LEVEL:** Primary

SUB-AREA: Punctuation   **SUGGESTED TIME:**   10 mins.

IMAGERY DESCRIPTION:

Students will view a TV show featuring friendly monsters. When the monsters talk, you can see punctuation marks floating from their mouths.

IMAGERY EXERCISE:

> **Sit comfortably and relax**
> **See yourself seated in front of your TV**
> **Tune in to Monster's Punctuation Program**
> **Watch a big, ugly, friendly monster come onto the screen***
> **Give him color...and lots of hair**
> **See his mouth opening and beginning to yell at another monster with big feet**
> **Feel his anger as big exclamation points pour out of his mouth as he asks**
> **See the exclamation points fading to become periods as he states his answer**
> **Watch the monsters talk...continue to see different punctuation marks coming from their mouths***
> **Watch big, colorful commas coming from the monster's mouth as he counts the horns on his head**
> **One, two, three, four...see the commas**
> **Now see a lot of monsters talking***
> **See yourself returning to the classroom**
> **When I count to ten, open your eyes**

VARIATIONS:

Use dinosaurs, animals or cartoon characters instead of monsters. Watch yourself speaking with a friend and see punctuation marks floating out as you speak.

FOLLOW UP ACTIVITIES:

Using cartoon strips, write new conversation determined by facial and body language. Have students take the roles of punctuation marks. Students must interact with each other using only one kind of punctuation.

ACADEMIC AREA: LANGUAGE ARTS   **GRADE LEVEL:** Primary

SUB-AREA: Punctuation   **SUGGESTED TIME:** 10 mins.

IMAGERY DESCRIPTION:

Students will become armed with quotation mark shooters and trap words as they are spoken by various characters.

IMAGERY EXERCISE:

> **Sit comfortably and relax**
> **See yourself sitting on a beautiful horse**
> **Feel his soft mane and velvet-smooth neck**
> **You are the Quotation Mark Kid**
> **Feel the weight of your gun holsters**
> **Load the guns with quotation-mark bullets***
> **You are ready to shoot at some wild words as they are spoken**
> **See the Marshall standing in front of the jailhouse**
> **Hear him say "Howdy, Kid"**
> **Watch the words come out of his mouth and into the air**
> **Quick! Draw your left shooter and fire a set of marks in front of "Howdy"**
> **Take your right shooter and hit some marks after the word "Howdy"**
> **See a dangerous-looking bad guy**
> **Say something tough to him**
> **See your words in the air**
> **Shoot quote marks around your words**
> **See other words in the air needing marks**
> **Shoot some more marks***
> **See yourself returning to the classroom**
> **When I count to ten, open your eyes**

VARIATIONS:

Change or add more characters to the story. Have students use a rope to lasso words in a rodeo.

FOLLOW UP ACTIVITIES:

Write a script for the Quotation Mark Kid. Illustrate how the "Kid" shot marks in the air. Make a list of words or sayings needing quotation marks.

NO:**33**   TITLE: DICTIONARY 500

ACADEMIC AREA: LANGUAGE ARTS   GRADE LEVEL: Primary/Intermed.
SUB-AREA: Reference Skills   SUGGESTED TIME: 5 mins.

IMAGERY DESCRIPTION:

Students will race little cars through a dictionary, making pit stops at certain words.

IMAGERY EXERCISE:

> Sit comfortably and relax
> You're in a shiny, new racing car
> See its colors and fancy design*
> See a large number on the hood
> You're in the "Dictionary 500"...get ready
> Your first stop is the word "fuel"
> As you speed watch the "a" words becoming a blur...the b's...c's...d's
> Hear yourself screeching to a halt as you almost enter the "g" section
> Back up slowly to the word "fuel"
> Read its meaning..."gasoline"
> Fill up your tank and pull out for your next destination..."tire"
> That's a long way down the dictionary
> Better use your word jumping skill
> Quick, hop over the m's, n's, o's, p's and q's
> Start reading those guide-words signs
> You're into the "t's"...read the signs
> See "tan", "tape"...keep moving ahead
> You're there...coast in at "tire" and look at the definition
> Continue your race stopping at the "z" or last section of the race*
> See yourself crossing the finish line and returning to the classroom
> When I count to ten, open your eyes

VARIATIONS:

Substitute other vocabulary words. Concentrate on only one dictionary skill. Have the students walk through the dictionary.

FOLLOW UP ACTIVITIES:

Make up a dictionary game. Brainstorm other ways students can use the dictionary. Make a dictionary with pictures and illustrations.

NO: **34**   TITLE: USING THE CARD CATALOG

ACADEMIC AREA: LANGUAGE ARTS   GRADE LEVEL: Intermediate

SUB-AREA: Reference Skills   SUGGESTED TIME: 10 mins.

IMAGERY DESCRIPTION:

Students will learn about the card catalog system used by school libraries. They will observe the differences among the cards and the type of information written on the cards.

IMAGERY EXERCISE:

Sit comfortably and relax
You're sitting at a mini-computer
Notice the large screen and hundreds of buttons
Press and program for "Library Card Catalog System"
See the numeral 582 as a card appears
Notice its sparkling colors
See the author's last name first
See the printed book title changing colors
See the publication date flashing
Next. . . see a title card made of wood
Burn a book title into the wood
Watch it as it flames and smokes
Don't forget to burn a numeral on the left
The last type of card is the subject card
See the subject card as a large piece of chocolate cake
Take a can of whip cream and write a subject. . . author's name.
. . publication title. . . publisher. . . and date
Now see all three types of cards
Notice how the position of information varies on each
Press "End" and return to the classroom
When I count to ten, open your eyes.

VARIATIONS:

The cards could be presented in many different ways, using colors, textures, etc. Students could build, paint or photograph cards. They could take an imaginary trip through the library.

FOLLOW UP ACTIVITIES:

Visit the library and study the different type cards. Write a paragraph describing how to use the card catalog for someone who has never used it before. Create a bulletin board of card catalog information.

NO: **35**   TITLE: ORAL REPORT

ACADEMIC AREA: LANGUAGE ARTS   GRADE LEVEL: Intermediate

SUB-AREA: Speaking Skills   SUGGESTED TIME: 5 mins.

IMAGERY DESCRIPTION:

Students will imagine themselves making an oral report to
their class. They will become aware of many details and
feel what it is like to stand in front of other people and
speak.

IMAGERY EXERCISE:

> **Sit comfortably and relax**
> **You're ready to give a report to the class**
> **Notice how nicely you are dressed**
> **See your combed hair and shiny face**
> **Feel the confidence as you walk to the lecturn**
> **Take a deep breath**
> **Feel relaxed, calm and comfortable**
> **Look at your report**
> **Notice all the information**
> **Begin to share it with the class***
> **Show some diagrams of important features of your report**
> **See positive reactions from the students**
> **See a smile on the teacher's face**
> **Notice how clear your speech is and how much information you
> have given**
> **See how interested everyone is in your report**
> **Hear the applause as you conclude your excellent presentation**
> **Feel the confidence and success**
> **See yourself returning to the classroom**
> **When I count to ten, open your eyes**

VARIATIONS:

Students could see themselves making other types of oral
presentations to other classes, an assembly,etc. Specific
content could be included such as facts, graphs, illustrations,
questions, etc.

FOLLOW UP ACTIVITIES:

Make a successful oral report to the class.

ACADEMIC AREA: LANGUAGE ARTS   **GRADE LEVEL:** Primary/Intermed.
SUB-AREA: Spelling   **SUGGESTED TIME:** 5 mins.

IMAGERY DESCRIPTION:

Students will begin a routine writing of the weekly spelling list and watch their ordinary pencil change to many other writing implements. Teacher should substitute actual list words and spell each one for the students where indicated.

IMAGERY EXERCISE:

Sit comfortably and relax
See yourself at your desk, preparing to practice writing your weekly spelling list
See the lines and spaces
Hold your pencil in front of you...notice the color and little nicks along the sides
Examine the eraser...and point
Hear your teacher speaking the first list word
SAY WORD
Spell it on the first line *SPELL WORD*
Notice the thin, gray pencil letters
Listen to the next word *SAY*
Feel a change in the pencil
The pencil is becoming a fancy pen
Let the ink letters flow smoothly
As you spell *SPELL*...see their color
Get ready for a new word...and color...as your pen becomes a fat marker *SAY*
Smell the ink as you write large bold letters *SPELL*
The paper will never be big enough for the next word *SAY*
Write this with a large paint brush
Pick your favorite wall *SPELL*
See yourself returning to the classroom
When I count to ten, open your eyes

VARIATIONS:

Eliminate spelling each word after pronouncing it as practice for the weekly test. Limit writing implements to only one or two others each time.

FOLLOW UP ACTIVITIES:

Try to show some or all words as they might be written in the Exercise. Brainstorm for new ways to write words and illustrate it happening. Write words in an unusual way and see if others can guess how it was done.

NO: **37**   TITLE: SCRABBLE SPELL

ACADEMIC AREA: LANGUAGE ARTS   GRADE LEVEL: Primary/Intermed.
SUB-AREA: Spelling   SUGGESTED TIME: 10 mins.

IMAGERY DESCRIPTION:

After introducing the weekly spelling list, students will pre-
select the easiest and most difficult word to spell on a large
scrabble board.

IMAGERY EXERCISE:

Sit comfortably and relax
See yourself standing on a large gameboard
Step on the squares and trace one with your toes
Hear blocks of wood being dumped onto the board
Feel their smooth surfaces with carved letters
Climb up to the top of the pile and feel them shifting
Scan the letters...find the first letter of the easiest word in this week's list
Carry the letter over to a blank square
Listen as you slide it into place
Make the sound of that letter softly
Continue to choose blocks as you spell the easy word*
Have the blocks touch so you can read them going across
Pronounce it each time you add a letter
When it is spelled, go back and trace each letter
Move your finger in the carved grooves
See something that reminds you of that word, floating by in a cloud
Say the word and write it in the air with a magic wand
Now do the same thing in spelling the hardest word from this week's list
See yourself returning to the classroom
When I count to ten, open your eyes

VARIATIONS:

Spell only one word each time. Teacher chooses a word(s) and
spells aloud during Exercise.

FOLLOW UP ACTIVITIES:

Use a scrabble board to spell list words. Write words, cut a-
part and glue blocks back together to spell. Draw meaning
clouds or balloons for words.

60

ACADEMIC AREA: LANGUAGE ARTS   **GRADE LEVEL:** Intermediate

SUB-AREA: Types of Literature   **SUGGESTED TIME:**   10 mins.

IMAGERY DESCRIPTION:

Students will become contestants on a game show in which they must decide whether a certain story or scene is non-fiction or fiction. If they make the correct choice, a buzzer will ring indicating that they have scored points.

IMAGERY EXERCISE:

> **Sit comfortably and relax**
> **See yourself on a live TV Game Show**
> **Notice the audience….stage…lights**
> **See the game show host…introducing you**
> **Notice the scoreboard and two buzzers**
> **test the non-fiction buzzer on the left**
> **See the buzzer on the right…for fiction**
> **feel the tension in your finger tips as you prepare to play the game**
> **Remember!…buzzer after each question**
> **Question 1: See a space ship taking a trip to another planet with pink people**
> **Press your button…if you selected fiction you received 25 points**
> **Question 2: Observe as a man called Abraham Lincoln becomes President of the United States**
> **Great! You scored another 25 points for selecting non-fiction**
> **Continue playing…just see the scene and press your buzzer**
> **See yourself winning lots of points**
> **See yourself returning to the classroom**
> **When I count to ten, open your eyes**

VARIATIONS:

Select scenes from stories the class has read, substituting or adding them. Make the buzzer true-false and test comprehension of one story read by the class.

FOLLOW UP ACTIVITIES:

Write your own sample questions. Act out the show. Make two lists, one for non-fiction and one for fiction. Change situations so that you can now move them to the other column. Rewrite one story making it from fiction to non-fiction.

ACADEMIC AREA: LANGUAGE ARTS   **GRADE LEVEL:** Primary/Intermed.

SUB-AREA: Word Study   **SUGGESTED TIME:** 5 mins.

IMAGERY DESCRIPTION:

Students will see flowers with root words as their seeds, affixes as their nourishment and different word forms as they bloom.

IMAGERY EXERCISE:

Sit comfortably and relax

See yourself in a large dirt area that has just been plowed

Notice the straight rows of soil, ready for planting

Smell the rich peatmoss...feel its moisture

Take out your packet of "word seeds" and open it

Pour the little brown specks into your palm and choose the one that says "wish"

Bend over, put it into the soil and sprinkle the special fertilizer "affixes" on top

See "ing"..."ed"..."es" and "ful" being covered by the dirt as you smooth your hand over the surface

Watch as a large plant, full of buds, begins growing

Whisper the root word "wish" as the roots soak up the affixes

Smell the sweet fragrance as words begin to bloom...wishing...wished...wishes...wishful

Look far into the center of the last bud and make a wish

See it coming true inside the flower

See yourself returning to the classroom

When I count to ten, open your eyes

VARIATIONS:

Use only nouns or verbs, etc. Use only specific affixes for all words.

FOLLOW UP ACTIVITIES:

Draw one or all of the plants seen, sharing the last flower's picture. Create new plants from given seeds. Create the bag of fertilizer when given the blooms.

ACADEMIC AREA: LANGUAGE ARTS   **GRADE LEVEL:** Primary/Intermed.

SUB-AREA: Word Study   **SUGGESTED TIME:** 10 mins.

IMAGERY DESCRIPTION:

Students will form new compound words using the word "house" and depict each one with a picture on a screen.

IMAGERY EXERCISE:

Sit comfortably and relax
See yourself in front of your mini-computer
Program it for "house" and be ready to change each house as the word clues change
"Doghouse" is the first word
Make it just the right size and shape for the dog who lives in it
Paint his name on it, using your favorite color*
"Treehouse"...put it up into a tree
Take the dog out...put something you would have in your treehouse*
Don't forget a way to get up there, too
"Dollhouse"...get it out of the tree
Put tiny furniture in it and have a member of the doll family in each room*
"Firehouse"...hear the sirens, see the trucks and equipment
Don't forget to slide down the pole
"Beachhouse"...feel the hot sun and sand on your bare feet
See yourself returning to the classroom
When I count to ten, open your eyes

VARIATIONS:

Begin with another word and build.

FOLLOW UP ACTIVITIES:

Draw and label new compounds with house. Draw compounds for others to guess the words shown. Make a collage of compounds with words and pictures.

NO: 41   **TITLE:**   PAC MAN ATTACK

ACADEMIC AREA: LANGUAGE ARTS   **GRADE LEVEL:** Primary/Intermed.
SUB-AREA: Word Study   **SUGGESTED TIME:** 10 mins.

IMAGERY DESCRIPTION:

Students will view Pac Man as he gobbles prefixes and suffixes and changes words. Teachers may wish to introduce the words used before the Exercise is used.

IMAGERY EXERCISE:

Sit comfortably and relax
You're in front of an exciting video game
See the word "weightlessness" on your screen flashing and making sounds*
See a multi-colored Pac Man eating its way toward the word
Hear it chomping as "ness" is gobbled up
See "Weightless" still remaining
See Pac Man eating the s's and the "le"
See the word "weight" remaining
Have a new word enter..."unbelievable"
Watch Pac Man first eat the prefix "un"
Now see him eat the suffix "able"
Have Pac Man continue to eat parts of your own special word*
Notice how fat Pac Man is getting
Squeeze him...see the word parts coming from his mouth
See these word parts in different colors
Hear them making weird sounds*
See Pac Man sleeping by a tree
Listen to his...zzzz's
See yourself returning to the classroom
When I count to ten, open your eyes

VARIATIONS:

Use other words, e.g., only those with a prefix, change y to i, etc. Run the game in reverse with Pac Man adding endings to root words.

FOLLOW UP ACTIVITIES:

Make a list of words that only Pac Man would enjoy (suffixes). Create a Pac Man cartoon where he eats up all sorts of word parts. Brainstorm other ways to add or take away prefixes and suffixes.

ACADEMIC AREA: LANGUAGE ARTS   **GRADE LEVEL:** Primary
SUB-AREA: Word Study   **SUGGESTED TIME:** 5 mins.

IMAGERY DESCRIPTION:

Students will follow Mrs. Saw and Mrs. Seen as they shop. Mrs. Saw shops alone, while Mrs. Seen needs a helper.

IMAGERY EXERCISE:

Sit comfortably and relax
See yourself hiding behind the soup can display at your local grocery store
Your mission is to spy on two shoppers...Mrs. Saw and Mrs. Seen
Here comes Mrs. Saw now
See the word "SAW" on her shirt
She is alone with her shopping cart
Mrs. Saw saw potatoes...and put them into her cart
She also saw bread...milk...and eggs
Mrs. Saw saw the cashier and paid for the food
You saw her pick up her bags and leave just as Mrs. Seen was coming in
Mrs. Seen is not alone -- she never is alone
Look at her helper behind her
Notice "Has," her helper...see "HAS" written on his strange costume
Mrs. Seen has seen the potatoes but can't lift the bag
Notice Has lifting the sack off the shelf and into the cart easily
Mrs. Seen has seen beans and apples
Mrs. Seen has seen her car being loaded with bags, thanks to "Has"
See yourself returning to the classroom
When I count to ten, open your eyes

VARIATIONS:

Use other verbs that take "helpers." Have two helpers (have and has) instead of one.

FOLLOW UP ACTIVITIES:

Write about one of the shoppers and draw an illustration. Write a new story about Mr. Saw and Mr. Seen.

NO: **43**	TITLE:	SHORT "A"	

ACADEMIC AREA:	LANGUAGE ARTS	GRADE LEVEL:	Primary
SUB-AREA:	Word Study	SUGGESTED TIME:	5 mins.

IMAGERY DESCRIPTION:

Students will visualize a scene with sounds and objects that remind them of the short "a" sound. Teacher may wish to emphasize short "a" words.

IMAGERY EXERCISE:

Sit comfortably and relax
See yourself holding a glass with your favorite drink
Smell it...taste it...drink it all, enjoying every swallow
Peek into the glass, at the bottom
See the letter "a" printed there
Hear a tiny voice making the "a" sound
Put it close to your ear and hum along with the tune
Watch the tracks made by the ant
She's writing the letter "a" with her little tracks
Look inside the letter "a" and see a fat apple
Hear an ax chop the apple in half
Examine the inside of the apple
See a black seed...look closer...it's not a seed
It's the nose of a cat
Watch her arch her back...and chase a rat into a funny hat
Listen to "baaa" coming from the hat
Hear it getting louder as you watch a lamb leap out of the hat
Smell and feel the grass
Hear "Mary Had a Little Lamb" being sung with only the sound of "a"
See yourself returning to the classroom
When I count to ten, open your eyes

VARIATIONS:

Any vowel or consonant sounds may be explored this way.

FOLLOW UP ACTIVITIES:

Class sings the "a" sound to "Mary Had a Little Lamb" or other tunes. List all of the words you remember with the short "a" sound. Draw some. Make more. Create a diorama, "The Land of Short 'a!"

NO: **44**   TITLE: THE OPPOSITE BOX

ACADEMIC AREA: LANGUAGE ARTS   **GRADE LEVEL:** Primary/Intermed.

SUB-AREA: Word Study   **SUGGESTED TIME:** 10 mins.

IMAGERY DESCRIPTION:

Students will create imaginary scenes that depict the opposite from the actual event or situation.

IMAGERY EXERCISE:

Sit comfortably and relax

You have just received a "magical box"

By pressing a special button you have the power of making things opposite from what they really are

Just point the box toward an object and press the button marked "opposite"

Point it at a light that is on and press

See the light go out

See a friend laughing

Point the box at her and see her begin to cry

See your mother or father yelling

See what happens when you push the button

Take your magical box outside and make things opposite from what they are

Enjoy the fun*

Change day to night

See people looking puzzled*

See a new school bus

Make it an old dumpy one

Finally, give all the people with sad faces happy faces

See yourself returning to the classroom

When I count to ten, open your eyes

VARIATIONS:

Substitute or add other opposites. Focus on specific types of word opposites (untie-tie, nonsense-sense, etc.).

FOLLOW UP ACTIVITIES:

Choose one change and write about it in a nonsense poem. Take a serious problem and write why you would change it. Draw before and after pictures using opposites. Draw a scene or figure, splitting down the middle to accent opposites.

ACADEMIC AREA: LANGUAGE ARTS   GRADE LEVEL: Primary

SUB-AREA: Word Study   SUGGESTED TIME: 5 mins.

IMAGERY DESCRIPTION:

Students will watch a circus train as cars are being loaded and hang a sign that indicates singular and plural on each car.

IMAGERY EXERCISE:

> **Sit comfortably and relax**
> **See yourself in charge of loading a train full of circus animals and people**
> **See your big black engine...smell the smoke coming out of the smokestack**
> **Watch each car being loaded...then hang a sign telling what is in that car**
> **Look at the red car with one clown**
> **See his funny face and hair**
> **Hang a sign that says "Clown"**
> **Wait, here come two more clowns into the red car**
> **Paint an "s" and make the sign say "Clowns"***
> **Look at the green car and see 3 elephants**
> **Hang up the "Elephants" sign on the green car**
> **Oh, no...3 elephants is too many**
> **Put two little elephants in the blue car**
> **Cross out the "s" in elephants to make the green car say "Elephant"**
> **Hang a sign that says "Elephants" on the blue car with the 2 little ones***
> **Paint more signs**
> **Now see the train beginning to move out**
> **See yourself returning to the classroom**
> **When I count to ten, open your eyes**

VARIATIONS:

Use other plural types (e.g., "es", "ies"). Put them in cages instead of cars.

FOLLOW UP ACTIVITIES:

Make a train with appropriate signs. Each student adds a car. Given a filled train, students write "s" on some or cross out "s" to correct.

NO: **46**   TITLE: CHANGING SENTENCES

ACADEMIC AREA: LANGUAGE ARTS   GRADE LEVEL: Primary/Intermed.
SUB-AREA: Written Expression   SUGGESTED TIME: 10 mins.

IMAGERY DESCRIPTION:

Students will use   a mini-computer   to write and rewrite sentences
correctly as they describe changing scenes. Teacher should
read hyphenated sentences very slowly.

IMAGERY EXERCISE:

Sit comfortably and relax
You're at a microcomputer
Program it for sentence writing
See a picture of John fishing
Print-out John-is-fishing
Put John in a boat, color it blue
Rewrite your sentence
John-is-fishing-in-a-blue-boat
Make the boat rock in rough water
Now...print out the sentence*
Put Bob in the boat and give him a fishing pole
Print-out the sentence
Bob-and-John-are-fishing-in-a-blue-boat-that-rocks-on-the-water*
Keep changing the scene
Have your computer print-out the correct sentence for each scene...remember the period*
Make up funny and strange sentences*
Have your computer print-out a sentence having each word a different color
Press END...and return to the classroom
When I count to ten, open your eyes

VARIATIONS:

Make sentences simple or complex according to grade level.

FOLLOW UP ACTIVITIES:

Write as many sentences as you can remember imaging. Brainstorm
a list of nouns/participles/verbs to substitute in this
imagery exercise. Create illustrations for new sentences.

ACADEMIC AREA: LANGUAGE ARTS   **GRADE LEVEL:** Primary

SUB-AREA: Written Expression   **SUGGESTED TIME:** 5 mins.

IMAGERY DESCRIPTION:

Students will experience the free flowing nature of cursive writing from the perspective of the pencil. They will feel the gliding motion of each stroke in the formation of letters.

IMAGERY EXERCISE:

Sit comfortably and relax
See yourself being gently fastened to a golden yellow pencil
You're in position and ready for a ride
Feel a giant hand picking up the pencil
You are now on a large sheet of paper
Look up and see the giant finger tips tightly grasping the pencil
Feel the beginning movement as a big fancy swooping H is made
Hear the scratching as the huge point is dragged along the paper
Feel yourself being swept around as a curvy E is made
Feel yourself shooting up…around…and down as the pencil loops two huge L's
Finally feel a fast sweep around as a circle is formed for the letter O
As the pencil lifts off the paper look closely at the word "Hello" written in cursive style
Notice how all the letters are connected
See yourself returning to the classroom
When I count to ten, open your eyes

VARIATIONS:

Use just one letter and make it in color. Include music with the Imagery Exercise. Become the paper, the ink, crawl around the letters. Use paints, textures, sound, movement, etc.

FOLLOW UP ACTIVITIES:

Have students describe what was imaged. Have them practice making the letter or word that was used in the Imagery Exercise. Have students select music to represent each letter written cursively.

TITLE: FUNNY PHRASES

ACADEMIC AREA: LANGUAGE ARTS **GRADE LEVEL:** Primary/Intermed.
SUB-AREA: Written Expression **SUGGESTED TIME:** 20 mins.

IMAGERY DESCRIPTION:

Using a mini-computer, students will view several common phrases, e.g., "eating like a bird," which they must then literally portray on the screen.

IMAGERY EXERCISE:

Sit comfortably and relax
You're in front of your mini-computer
Set the program for Funny Phrases
Create a scene for each phrase...exactly as the words are read...not what we really mean when we say them
Have fun...see a person who is "all thumbs"
Hear someone saying "buzz off"
Create a picture of your buzzing off*
Make it funny and detailed
Here are some more:
"Smart cookie"...*
"Killing time"...*
"Eating like a bird"...*
"Cool it"...*
"Losing your marbles"...*
"Take a hike"...*
Make some new phrases
Enjoy creating funny scenes*
See yourself returning to the classroom
When I count to ten, open your eyes

VARIATIONS:

Use other idioms or compound words. Use proverbs, e.g., the early bird catches the worm. Use tongue twisters.

FOLLOW UP ACTIVITIES:

Draw two scenes for each phrase, showing figurative and literal interpretations. Create some new idioms of your own. Keep a record of phrases used by people you know.

ACADEMIC AREA: LANGUAGE ARTS

GRADE LEVEL: Intermediate

SUB-AREA: Written Expression

SUGGESTED TIME: 10 mins.

IMAGERY DESCRIPTION:

Students will view a tree as it seems to display human characteristics.

IMAGERY EXERCISE:

> Sit comfortably and relax
> You're walking in a beautiful forest
> Smell the fresh air and the wind blowing
> Hear a whispering noise...coming from a large tree ahead
> Listen closely...to the wind in the trees
> Watch tree branches move...like arms
> They bend...and reach like fingers
> Listen to the noise they make
> Observe other trees nearby as they appear to be communicating
> with each other
> Look inside the tree
> Smell the sap and notice the colors
> Feel the soft, white pulp
> Touch the rough bark at the base
> Feel the tree's mood
> Give the tree a voice and a name
> Listen to the tree describe its experiences*
> See yourself leaving the forest and returning to the classroom
> When I count to ten, open your eyes

VARIATIONS:

Begin with another object (machine) or another setting, e.g., shell in the ocean.

FOLLOW UP ACTIVITIES:

Write a poem personifying a tree. Draw and compare trees and people. Write a ballad, "The Song of the Trees." Create a myth that is part human and part tree.

NO: **50**   TITLE: THE SENTENCE BUILDER

ACADEMIC AREA: LANGUAGE ARTS   **GRADE LEVEL:** Primary/Intermed.

SUB-AREA: Written Expression   **SUGGESTED TIME:** 20 mins.

IMAGERY DESCRIPTION:

Students will become carpenters and build sentences using wooden boards, paint, nails, etc. They will also include pictures for the sentences being constructed.

IMAGERY EXERCISE:

Sit comfortably and relax
You are a carpenter with an apron around your waist
Feel the weight and the nails inside and the hammer on your belt
See yourself standing in front of a large wall
Find a lot of different size pieces of board
You are going to build a sentence*
Open your favorite color paint...smell it
Dip your brush in and paint the word "Puppy" on a piece of board
Nail the board with "Puppy" on it onto the wall
Puppy is the subject
See a picture of a puppy above your painted word
Let's describe the puppy...funny...little...happy...cute...cuddly
Select a word that describes your puppy and paint it on another piece of board
Nail it on the wall in front of "Puppy"
The subject is getting bigger...keep building
Use green paint and a small piece of board for the word "A"
Make sure it is a capital "A"
Put it in front of the word that describes "Puppy"
Read your 3 words
Your subject is complete
Now think of action words that tell what puppies can do...run...play...bark...chase
Paint what your puppy can do on a board*
Nail that verb up after the word "Puppy"
Now you have 4 words...read them

VARIATIONS:

Students could use other types of materials for building a sentence (clay, wire, finger paint, sticks, etc.). Students could use a mini-computer or video game for developing sentences.

FOLLOW UP ACTIVITIES:

Write your sentence on paper. Illustrate what your puppy was doing in the Imagery Exercise. Select a different animal or theme and have students image themselves creating a story.

ACADEMIC AREA: GRADE LEVEL:

SUB-AREA :   SUGGESTED TIME:

IMAGERY DESCRIPTION:

See...THE SENTENCE BUILDER **50**

IMAGERY EXERCISE:

**Look at your action word again
You can describe the action word
Tell where the puppy is doing it
Tell how the puppy is doing it
Paint these new words onto a long board and nail it at the end
of your sentence***

**Now paint a big round period at the end
See your puppy doing what your sentence says
Look closely at all your painted words
See yourself returning to the classroom
When I count to ten, open your eyes**

VARIATIONS:

See...THE SENTENCE BUILDER

FOLLOW UP ACTIVITIES:

See...THE SENTENCE BUILDER

NO: 52   **TITLE:**   WRITING BOOK REPORTS

ACADEMIC AREA: LANGUAGE ARTS   **GRADE LEVEL:** Primary/Intermed.

SUB-AREA: Written Expression   **SUGGESTED TIME:** 10 mins.

IMAGERY DESCRIPTION:

Students will take a plane and visit a favorite scene from a story they have read. They will also create a title for that scene.

IMAGERY EXERCISE:

Sit comfortably and relax
You have just finished reading a great book
Think about your favorite scene from the book
Let's visit where that scene takes place and see the characters
Get into a special sky-writing plane
Take off and start your trip*
You're now over a scene just like that from the book
Scan the view below for characters and setting
Listen with your special radio to what is happening beneath you
Watch the story carefully to the end of the scene
Think of a special title for the scene
Now press a sky-writing button and write this title in the sky
Land safely and admire your work
See yourself returning to the classroom
When I count to ten, open your eyes

VARIATIONS:

Focus on climax scene, funny scene, etc. Focus on character or setting only.

FOLLOW UP ACTIVITIES:

Rewrite the scene. Create a 3-D scene. Write an account of what you saw from the air. Visit other scenes from your book or other books.

4. Imagery in Math

ACADEMIC AREA: MATH   **GRADE LEVEL:** Primary

SUB-AREA: Sets, Numbers and Numera- **SUGGESTED TIME:** 10 mins.
                tion

IMAGERY DESCRIPTION:

Students will be given an opportunity to think about numbers while developing and using a number line. They will experience addition using their number line and be encouraged to think of different uses for the number line.

IMAGERY EXERCISE:

Sit comfortably and relax
See a number line made of chocolate candy
Smell it...touch it
See the chocolate numbers along the line going up to number 20
Now see Pac Man coming to the first number of your number line
See Pac Man looking very hungry as he examines the long chocolate number line
Listen to Pac Man asking you how many numbers he can eat
Tell him how far he can go
Watch him eating your number line*
See him stopping at a certain number
Notice how many numbers are left on your line
Now see two chocolate number lines with two Pac Men
Pac Man A can eat up to number 10
Pac Man B can eat up to number 12
Now watch the Pac Men eat their numbers
Notice how many more numbers Pac Man B ate than Pac Man A
Now have your number line change to a peppermint candy line...to a marshmallow line
See all the numbers on your number lines
Now see yourself eating part of your candy number line
See yourself returning to the classroom
When I count to ten, open your eyes

VARIATIONS:

Students could paint a number line using arrows to indicate movement. Students could become a number line, watching movement along the line.

FOLLOW UP ACTIVITIES:

Draw a chocolate number line showing Pac Man eating certain numbers along the line. Draw several number lines and have car races; indicate their finishing position by placing an X by a number. Write a story of how Pac Man becomes "Blob Man" after eating up numbers on a number line.

ACADEMIC AREA: MATH   **GRADE LEVEL:**   Primary

SUB-AREA: Sets, Numbers and Numera-   **SUGGESTED TIME:**   5 mins.
                 tion

IMAGERY DESCRIPTION:

Students will design and construct tens-boxes. They will
see themselves manipulating blocks and forming tens-boxes.
They will experience counting single blocks and tens-blocks.

IMAGERY EXERCISE:

Sit comfortably and relax
See a table filled with little wooden blocks
Pick them up and feel them
Feel the weight, shape and hardness of the blocks
See an empty plastic tray
See yourself putting 10 of these blocks into the tray
You now have a tens-box
Count the ten blocks in your box
See yourself coloring each block
See yourself making two more tens-boxes
Look at your three tens-boxes
Make each tens-box a different color
Give each tens-box a name
Count all the blocks in your three tens-boxes
Notice how many little wooden blocks you have
Now see yourself writing that number on a large sheet of paper
Use paint, make it big, and put it on the floor
Now place your three tens-boxes around the sheet of paper
Take a picture of what it looks like
See it clearly
Now see yourself coming back to the classroom
When I count to ten, open your eyes

VARIATIONS:

Students could see themselves building little blocks of
tens-boxes. Students could see various combinations of
tens-boxes. They would paint, draw or construct tens-
boxes. They could become either a block or tens-box.

FOLLOW UP ACTIVITIES:

Have students practice manipulating individual blocks and
tens-boxes for addition and subtraction. Have students draw
various tens-boxes on newsprint or oak tag.

ACADEMIC AREA: MATH   **GRADE LEVEL:** Primary

SUB-AREA: Sets, Numbers and Numera- **SUGGESTED TIME:** 5 mins.
tion

IMAGERY DESCRIPTION:

Students will see various sets of things in which additional elements will be added forming larger sets. Animals will be used to reinforce the concept of addition within sets.

IMAGERY EXERCISE:

> **Sit comfortably and relax**
> **See yourself entering a large zoo**
> **Smell the air as you begin to see animals in large cages**
> **Listen to the sounds all around you**
> **See a set of four monkeys in a cage where there are trees and running water**
> **Look at the monkeys playing***
> **Notice their color...see their tails**
> **Look closely at their eyes**
> **Listen to them as they move freely about the cage**
> **See the zookeeper opening up a side door**
> **See another monkey being let into the cage**
> **Notice the color of this new monkey**
> **Listen to the monkeys greeting the new monkey**
> **Notice how friendly they are**
> **Notice how many monkeys there are now in the set**
> **Count them**
> **Give each one a name**
> **Have the monkeys play a game**
> **See yourself feeding them**
> **See the monkeys with clothes on**
> **See the monkeys riding bikes**
> **See yourself leaving the zoo and returning to class**
> **When I count to ten, open your eyes**

VARIATIONS:

Other animal sets could be used. More than one element could be added to the set. An element could be taken away from the set. Students could become an element of the set.

FOLLOW UP ACTIVITIES:

Describe the experience by writing about the reaction of the monkeys when a new monkey was added to the cage. Illustrate by drawing a picture of the monkeys welcoming their new monkey. Create other sets adding new elements.

NO:**56**   TITLE: EMPTY SET

ACADEMIC AREA: MATH   GRADE LEVEL: Primary
SUB-AREA: Sets, Numbers and Numera- SUGGESTED TIME: 5 mins.
            tion

IMAGERY DESCRIPTION:

Students will be exposed to a set of birds that suddenly flies away, leaving the set empty. Their attention will be drawn to the fact that the set became empty.

IMAGERY EXERCISE:

Sit comfortably and relax
See yourself walking through the woods on a nice, sunny day
See the tall trees
Notice all the wild flowers growing everywhere
Hear the birds singing
See the tall trees
Notice all the wild flowers growing everywhere
Hear the birds singing
See the sun shining through the trees
Listen to the leaves blowing in the wind
Notice a group of birds taking a bath in a little pond
Count them
See them splashing their wings
See them drinking the water
Look at the color of these birds
Watch the birds having fun in the water
Hear a loud noise in the distance
See the birds spring up into the air
Watch them fly away
Look back at the pond where the set of birds had been bathing
Notice the set is now empty -- the birds are gone
See yourself leaving the woods and returning to the classroom
When I count to ten, open your eyes

VARIATIONS:

Other animals could be used in demonstrating how a set could become empty. Students could see other sets of things such as fish, cars, boats, or toys and experience the set becoming empty.

FOLLOW UP ACTIVITIES:

Draw 2 illustrations (1) a full set of birds (2) an empty set. Create other illustrations where a set becomes empty. .Write a story of how a set became empty.

ACADEMIC AREA: MATH

GRADE LEVEL: Primary

SUB-AREA: Sets, Numbers and Numera- **SUGGESTED TIME:** 5 mins.
tion

IMAGERY DESCRIPTION:

Students will relate multiplication operations to the joining of equivalent sets, to arrays and to the number line.

IMAGERY EXERCISE:

Sit comfortably and relax
See 3 sets of 6 birds flying in the sky
Listen to the sounds of the birds
See the 6 birds in each set
Now paint a multiplication sentence for the 3 sets of 6 birds
Paint your answer to the multiplication sentence
See your answer in color
Have it move...talk
See yourself at a zoo
Visualize 4 sets of 3 monkeys
Then visualize a multiplication sentence
See your answer
Now look up into a night time sky
See an array of flashing colored lights
See 4 rows of 6 flashing lights
Take a magic flashlight and write a multiplication sentence in the dark sky
See the answer flashing in a strange color
Now create your own equivalent sets making a multiplication sentence for it*
See yourself returning to the classroom
When I count to ten, open your eyes

VARIATIONS:

You could have students create their own sets of objects or things. Have students write multiplication sentences using different media. They could become an element of a set.

FOLLOW UP ACTIVITIES:

Design some posters showing different sets and arrays. Have students create imagery exercises for other operations (Addition, Subtraction). Illustrate the joining of equivalent sets on 3 x 5 cards.

NO: **58**   **TITLE:**   WORD NAMES

ACADEMIC AREA: MATH   **GRADE LEVEL:** Primary

SUB-AREA: Operations and Properties **SUGGESTED TIME:** 10 mins.

IMAGERY DESCRIPTION:

Students will experience writing the word names for standard numerals.

IMAGERY EXERCISE:

> Sit comfortably and relax
> You're in a sky-writing plane
> Sit down in the soft leather driver's seat
> Notice the switches and dials in front of you
> Look out the window and see the propellor and wings
> Look next to you and find a special control for writing in the sky
> When you are up in the air all you have to do is push this control (forward)
> Out of the plane will come a stream of white smoke
> Now get ready to take off
> Feel the vibrations as the engine begins to roar
> Feel the plane taking off up...up...into the blue sky
> See yourself going through the clouds
> Look below and notice how small everything is
> Now get ready to write some numbers in the sky
> Push the control forward and write the word name for numeral 3
> Have the plane fly and make the word name for numeral 3
> See the white smoke writing the word three
> Now take your plane lower
> Look up and see the word you have just made
> Notice how large it is
> Watch it float like a cloud
> Now do some more sky writing
> Write the word names for other numerals*
> You're coming back and landing the plane
> See yourself returning to the classroom
> When I count to ten, open your eyes

VARIATIONS:

Students could see themselves writing word names through different means, such as painting, drawing, etc. Students could become a pen or pencil and see themselves actually writing the word names for numerals.

FOLLOW UP ACTIVITIES:

Students could write about their experience of writing word names through sky writing. Students could draw what the sky writing looked like from above, from the ground, from the plane.

ACADEMIC AREA: MATH   **GRADE LEVEL**: Primary

SUB-AREA: Operations and Properties   **SUGGESTED TIME**: 5 mins.

IMAGERY DESCRIPTION:

Students will be given several large numbers by their own names requiring them to write the standard numeral name using video electronics.

IMAGERY EXERCISE:

>**Sit comfortably and relax**
>**See yourself in a huge video game room**
>**Notice all the equipment and screens**
>**Listen to the sounds...see the flashing lights**
>**See yourself at the controls of a video game**
>**Press start...see your screen light up**
>**This special video game allows you to write or draw most anything**
>**Let's practice writing standard numerals**
>**Use different size type and colors**
>**Make them big...small...funny**
>**See the word name for 48**
>**Make the word name dance...sing...talk**
>**See the numerals in large green print**
>**Make your screen as large as you want**
>**Now listen to some more numbers**
>**See the numerals appearing on your large screen: 600, 722, 817**
>**See yourself writing the standard numeral names**
>**See them in all different sizes and shapes**
>**See all the numerals flashing on your screen**
>**See yourself returning to the classroom**
>**When I count to ten, open your eyes**

VARIATIONS:

Students could use other means for writing numerals. The procedure could be reversed by having the students see the word name and then being asked to print out the numerals.

FOLLOW UP ACTIVITIES:

Have contests for writing out standard numerals. Draw pictures or illustrations for large numbers. Create your own video game for writing standard numerals.

ACADEMIC AREA: MATH   GRADE LEVEL: Primary

SUB-AREA: Operations and Properties SUGGESTED TIME: 10 mins.

IMAGERY DESCRIPTION:

Students will have to tell time through manipulating, constructing and building clocks and parts of clocks. They will be instructed to move the hands of the clock to certain designated times.

IMAGERY EXERCISE:

> Sit comfortably and relax
> You're in an art room, ready to make your own clock
> First look up on the wall and see the school clock
> Look closely, see the shape, size, color
> Notice the two hands
> Look at the number 12 at the top of the clock
> Look at each black number and silently count and say 1 o'clock, 2 o'clock, 3 o'clock...12 o'clock
> Notice how the numbers go around in a circle
> Now look closely at the two hands
> Look at the small hand which is the hour hand and see where it's pointing
> Now look at the larger hand
> Notice where that is pointing
> Notice the little lines between the numerals representing all the minutes
> Gather materials to build your own clock
> Make yourself a great big clock
> Put in all the 12 numerals
> Put in the two hands
> Color it, paint it, do whatever you like
> Enjoy making your own clock
> Make your clock read 4 o'clock
> See yourself putting the little hand toward the 4 and the big hand toward the 12
> Now make 5 o'clock...6 o'clock
> See yourself returning to the classroom
> When I count to ten, open your eyes

VARIATIONS:

Students could be instructed to build or draw clocks using a variety of materials. They could be one of the clock's hands or one of the clock's numerals.

FOLLOW UP ACTIVITIES:

Make a chart showing different styles of clocks (big, small, fancy, unique, etc.). Have the clocks read many different times. Make a list of all the uses of clocks or why telling time is so important. Research time telling through the ages. Find out how the military services , airlines (pilots),etc., tell time.

NO: **61**   TITLE: SUBTRACTING NUMBERS

ACADEMIC AREA: MATH   GRADE LEVEL: Primary

SUB-AREA: Operations and Properties   SUGGESTED TIME: 5 mins.

IMAGERY DESCRIPTION:

Students will experience simple subtraction by taking away parts of a set. Familiar objects will be used to reinforce and stimulate the concept of subtraction.

IMAGERY EXERCISE:

> **Sit comfortably and relax**
> **See yourself at a circus**
> **See the clowns**
> **Notice the large animals**
> **Listen to the ring master welcoming everyone**
> **Listen to the noise...feel the excitement**
> **See the children holding balloons**
> **Notice all the different colors**
> **See yourself holding two balloons filled with helium in each hand**
> **See the color of the two balloons in your left hand**
> **See the color of the balloons in your right hand**
> **Feel the string tug as the four balloons try to fly away**
> **See yourself lose the grip of the two balloons in your left hand**
> **Watch the two balloons float away up...up**
> **Watch them getting smaller, smaller**
> **See the balloons reaching the top of the circus ceiling**
> **Hear them pop**
> **Notice how many balloons you have left in your right hand**
> **Look at them, count them**
> **See yourself getting in your car and leaving the circus**
> **See yourself coming back to the classroom**
> **When I count to ten, open your eyes**

VARIATIONS:

Students could be holding other kinds of objects and find themselves losing part of them, e.g., ice cream, lollipops, etc. Students could see different sets of things and visualize part of the set being taken away.

FOLLOW UP ACTIVITIES:

Draw a sequence of pictures illustrating the balloon experience. Students could draw various sets of things then subtract parts of the set through crossing out, putting X's, etc. Write a short story (like the circus story) illustrating something being subtracted.

ACADEMIC AREA: MATH   **GRADE LEVEL:** Primary/Intermediate

SUB-AREA: Operations and Properties   **SUGGESTED TIME:** 5 mins.

IMAGERY DESCRIPTION:

Students will solve ordinary problems through the use of imaginary specified facts in order to gain greater meaning. They will learn how to focus on the critical aspects of a problem.

IMAGERY EXERCISE:

Sit comfortably and relax
See 15 children coming into your house for your birthday party
Look at their faces
Notice the clothes they're wearing
See yourself talking to them
It's time to sit down and have the birthday cake
Mother has arranged it so that 5 children can sit at each table
Notice how many tables are needed for the children
See yourself seating the children
Now see all the children seated
Notice how happy everyone is as they begin to sing "Happy Birthday"
Look at the children singing
Enjoy this pleasant moment
See yourself returning to the classroom
When I count to ten, open your eyes

VARIATIONS:

Different quantities could be used. Different circumstances within the environment could be explored.

FOLLOW UP ACTIVITIES:

Draw a picture of the children at your birthday party. Increase the complexity of the problem, e.g., add more children. Write your own birthday image.

ACADEMIC AREA: MATH   GRADE LEVEL: Intermediate

SUB-AREA: Sentences and Problem   SUGGESTED TIME: 5 mins.
           Solving

IMAGERY DESCRIPTION:

Students will be given a word problem which requires them to use the four problem-solving steps (Tell, Show, Solve, and Answer).

IMAGERY EXERCISE:

Sit comfortably and relax

You're opening an envelope

See a word problem written on a yellow 3 x 5 card

Read what it says:

> **Bill has 25 picture cards of National League baseball players, 22 picture cards of American League baseball players and 35 picture cards of National Football League players. How many picture cards does Bill have in all?**

See yourself using the word problem solving steps

First tell about the facts

See the card numbers again, (repeat problem)

Now show the equations used for solving the problem

See the equation, 25   22   35

Now compute and solve the problem*

See your answer

And finally give the answer in a sentence

See the sentence

Bill had a total of 82 cards in all

See the 82 cards lying on a table in 3 piles, one pile for each league

See yourself returning to the classroom

When I count to ten, open your eyes

VARIATIONS:

Problems requiring other computational steps could be given. The sentence problem could be presented through different media.

FOLLOW UP ACTIVITIES:

Write a script for a sentence's problem and put on a 3 x 5 card. Make a list of the different ways to imagine a sentence problem.

ACADEMIC AREA: MATH   **GRADE LEVEL:** Primary

SUB-AREA: Sentences and Problem   **SUGGESTED TIME:** 5 mins.
               Solving

IMAGERY DESCRIPTION:

Students will be given a story problem where they have to
visualize certain details in order to respond correctly.
They will be required to compute using addition then subtraction.

IMAGERY EXERCISE:

> **Sit comfortably and relax**
> **Your pet dog has just given birth to six little pups**
> **See the little pups next to their mom**
> **Look at their little noses**
> **See their little tails wagging**
> **Listen to their little cries and moans**
> **Notice the different colors of the pups**
> **Listen to your mom saying that she will be giving four of the
> pups away**
> **Look at the four pups she will be giving to your relatives**
> **Notice how many pups will be left**
> **Look at the ones that will stay at your house**
> **Give the pups, who will be staying at your house, names**
> **See yourself holding one of the pups**
> **Feel the pup's soft fur and little paws**
> **Feel the pup lick your hand**
> **See yourself returning to the classroom**
> **When I count to ten, open your eyes**

VARIATIONS:

Any kind of pets or personal things or objects could be used
as the basis for a story problem. Facts could be rearranged
according to the student's level.

FOLLOW UP ACTIVITIES:

Make up your own little story problem. Illustrate the imaged
story problem. Bring pictures of your pets to school. Make
up some images involving pets.

NO: **65**   TITLE: MONEY

ACADEMIC AREA: MATH   GRADE LEVEL: Primary

SUB-AREA: Sentences and Problem   SUGGESTED TIME: 5 mins.
            Solving

IMAGERY DESCRIPTION:

Students will be exposed to different combinations of coins. They will see these coins in imaginary ways. The coin values will be reinforced through repeated coin images.

IMAGERY EXERCISE:

> **Sit comfortably and relax**
> **See a penny and notice its color**
> **Feel it and hold it in your hand**
> **Notice someone's face on the penny**
> **See 1979 written on the penny**
> **Have it become as large as you would like**
> **Now see 3 large pennies**
> **Have the pennies do something**
> **See a toy bank filled with hundreds of pennies**
> **Shake the can...listen to the pennies banging around**
> **Now see a nickel which represents 5 cents**
> **Notice thc color and shape of the nickel...have it do something**
> **Now see 3 nickels which represent 15 cents**
> **Now see a dime which is 10 cents**
> **See the color and shape of the dime**
> **See 3 dimes...make the dimes larger**
> **Now see one penny, one nickel and one dime**
> **Notice how much money you have**
> **That's right...16 cents**
> **See a set of coins which equals 20 cents**
> **See yourself making up new sets of coins equaling different values***
> **See yourself returning to the classroom**
> **When I count to ten, open your eyes**

VARIATIONS:

To familiarize students with coins and their values, you can continue to use a multi-sensory approach suggesting that the students do different things with the coins.

FOLLOW UP ACTIVITIES:

Draw the coins. Make up a money game. Make play money. Create a bank to be used in the classroom.

ACADEMIC AREA: MATH   **GRADE LEVEL:** Intermediate
SUB-AREA: Relations and Functions   **SUGGESTED TIME:** 5 mins.

IMAGERY DESCRIPTION:

Students will be provided opportunities for developing the meaning of a fractional number. Different shaped figures will be presented in which students must identify fractional parts.

IMAGERY EXERCISE:

> **Sit comfortably and relax**
> **See yourself relaxing on the grass**
> **See a huge blimp floating in the sky**
> **See a large glass screen in the blimp's underneath section**
> **Begin to see shapes flashing on the screen**
> **See a large square divided into four equal parts**
> **See 3 of the parts red**
> **See 1 part green**
> **Next see a circle flashing on the screen**
> **See 5 equal parts**
> **Make 1/5 a color**
> **Make 2/5 another color**
> **Finally make the remaining 2/5 another color**
> **See the different parts and colors**
> **Next see a beautiful octagon**
> **See 3/8 as a certain texture**
> **See 1/8 as a food**
> **See 4/8 as different things that make you laugh**
> **Now see all the eight parts of your octagon**
> **Now create a whole and divide in some way***
> **Watch the blimp slowly float into the distance**
> **See yourself returning to the classroom**
> **When I count to ten, open your eyes**

VARIATIONS:

Students could imagine fractional parts of a set or a number line. Students could see themselves making parts to fit into whole shapes. The screen could be created on another type of vehicle or thing.

FOLLOW UP ACTIVITIES:

Draw pictures of imagined shapes and objects. Draw a blimp with a screen and have different shapes flashing. Illustrate the various images seen on the blimp's screen.

ACADEMIC AREA: MATH   **GRADE LEVEL:** Primary

SUB-AREA: Relations and Functions   **SUGGESTED TIME:** 5 mins.

IMAGERY DESCRIPTION:

Students will be asked to visualize parts of a whole. Different objects will be used to reinforce the process of breaking things down into parts. Again a multi-sensory approach will be used to increase the quality of the imagery.

IMAGERY EXERCISE:

Sit comfortably and relax

See yourself sitting at your kitchen table

See a large delicious apple pie in front of you

Smell it

Feel its crust

Now see yourself cutting the pie in half

Now cut the pie into four equal parts

Serve the pie to your mother, father and sister or brother

Each person including yourself gets one quarter or ¼ of the pie

Go outside and look up at the moon

Change the way the moon looks

See half of the moon

See ⅓ of the moon

See yourself drinking ⅓ of a can of coke

See yourself giving the remaining ⅔ of the can of coke to a friend

Paint a large circle

Take a pencil and divide it into fourths

See yourself painting each part a different color

See yourself returning to the classroom

When I count to ten, open your eyes

VARIATIONS:

Use different objects. Have students do different things with parts of a whole. Use different shapes as wholes. Have students become fractional parts. Have students become a food being fractionalized.

FOLLOW UP ACTIVITIES:

Make a chart illustrating different fractions. Use clay or paint and have students construct fractional parts. Write a short story and have something in the story become fractionalized.

NO:**68**   TITLE: MULTIPLY WITH DECIMALS

ACADEMIC AREA: MATH   GRADE LEVEL: Intermediate

SUB-AREA: Relations and Functions   SUGGESTED TIME: 5 mins.

IMAGERY DESCRIPTION:

Students learn the rule for placing the decimal point in the product. They will imagine several problems, compute and correctly place the decimal in the product.

IMAGERY EXERCISE:

Sit comfortably and relax
See yourself in front of your own personal mini-computer
See the screen
See all the keys
Press the on button
Find the keys for the numerals
Ready
Print out the following multiplication problem
Solve and correctly place the decimal
5.2 x 1   pause...see 5.2
5.2 x .1   pause...see .52
5.2 x 10   pause...see 52
5.2 x .01   pause...see .052
Make up some more problems
Practice correctly placing the decimal in the product
Press a button and have all your finished problems appear
Spell out on the screen END
See yourself returning to the classroom
When I count to ten, open your eyes

VARIATIONS:

Students could use their computers for the purpose of dividing with decimals. Students could draw, paint or construct multiplication problems involving decimals.

FOLLOW UP ACTIVITIES:

Keep a record of all the problems created by the student on his/her imaginary computer. Write a list of math activities that could be used on the imaginary computer.

ACADEMIC AREA: MATH   **GRADE LEVEL:** Primary
SUB-AREA: Geometry and Measurement   **SUGGESTED TIME:** 10 mins.

IMAGERY DESCRIPTION:

Students will locate different shapes found in our community as they see themselves flying freely on top of a
magic balloon. They will be directed toward certain places
but will be free to see and visit different things and
places. They will see many different shapes, colors, sizes
of objects found around us.

IMAGERY EXERCISE:

> **Sit comfortably and relax**
> **See yourself climbing on top of a giant balloon**
> **Feel the balloon**
> **Feel the balloon taking off and slowly rising up into the soft air**
> **See yourself flying slowly over your town**
> **Notice how clear everything is**
> **Now begin to see things that are square***
> **Have your balloon come lower**
> **Move about town and discover everything that is square**
> **Notice the different colors of square things**
> **Notice the different sizes of square things**
> **See how people use square objects**
> **Now take your balloon into someone's house**
> **See everything that is square**
> **See yourself going into different rooms**
> **See yourself leaving the house and going back up into the air**
> **Feel the wind blowing**
> **Look once more at all the things that are square**
> **Now see yourself returning to the classroom**
> **When I count to ten, open your eyes**

VARIATIONS:

Have students locate things that are circular, rectangular
or triangular. Have students become something that is circular or rectangular. They could shape themselves into a
square.

FOLLOW UP ACTIVITIES:

Make a list of all the things or objects found during the
imaginary experience. Create a mural showing the variety of
things found in our environment that are square. Research
the field of Architecture or Commercial Art and find out the
importance of squareness.

NO: **70**   TITLE: MAKING DIFFERENT SHAPES

ACADEMIC AREA: MATH   GRADE LEVEL: Primary/Intermed.

SUB-AREA: Geometry and Measurement   SUGGESTED TIME: 10 mins

IMAGERY DESCRIPTION:

Students will see themselves making different shapes. Through actual manipulation, they will gain a better appreciation for differences and similarities among shapes. A multi-sensory approach will be used to heighten the experience of constructing different shapes.

IMAGERY EXERCISE:

Sit comfortably and relax
See yourself in a licorice factory
See all different colored licorice
Notice the different sizes
Notice licorice hanging on the walls and the ceiling
See a large table where you can make different shapes
Fill your room with all licorice candy
See yourself taking some licorice and making a circle
Make different size circles with the licorice
Use different colors
Smell the licorice
Feel the licorice and notice its texture
Now make a square with the licorice
See yourself eating the square made of licorice
Now make rectangles of different sizes
See yourself making a gigantic triangle
Make a fat triangle
Make a thin triangle
Look around the room, notice all the shapes you have made*
Invite your friends in to see your licorice shapes
Take pictures of all your shapes
See yourself leaving and returning to the classroom
When I count to ten, open your eyes

VARIATIONS:

Students could make shapes using other foods or materials such as clay. They could paint the different shapes. They could become licorice and feel themselves being shaped and twisted.

FOLLOW UP ACTIVITIES:

Make a chart showing different shapes. Make a list classifying things according to shape. Draw a picture of all the shapes created at the licorice factory.

ACADEMIC AREA: MATH   GRADE LEVEL: Primary

SUB-AREA: Geometry and Measurement   SUGGESTED TIME: 10 mins.

IMAGERY DESCRIPTION:

Students will visualize themselves using objects that are of various lengths. They will begin to see and feel differences. They will understand the importance of measurement and how it is used regularly in our environment.

IMAGERY EXERCISE:

Sit comfortably and relax
See yourself looking at your hand
Notice the size of your fingers
See the thumb which is a little more than an inch
See your largest finger which is about 2 inches
See yourself in your bedroom looking at objects that are smaller than 2 inches*
See yourself writing with a 5 inch pencil
Notice how long the pencil is
See the color of this 5 inch pencil
See the shape
Look at the point
Now see yourself brushing your teeth with a 5 inch toothbrush
See yourself writing with a three inch pencil
Now see yourself writing with a small 2 inch pencil
Feel how small the pencil is
See a delicious milk shake in a 6 inch glass
Notice how big the glass is
Find other things in the house that are the same size as the 6 inch glass
See yourself drawing something that is 2 inches...5 inches...10 inches
See yourself returning to the classroom
When I count to ten, open your eyes

VARIATIONS:

Students could become an inch and compare different things. Students could become a six inch ruler and imagine all the reasons why someone would use a ruler of this size.

FOLLOW UP ACTIVITIES:

Make a chart   showing several objects of different sizes. Make a list of things that are approximately 6 inches in length. Measure the length of different objects found in the classroom. Create a story about Mr. or Mrs. Inch.

NO: **72**   TITLE: MEASUREMENT-FEET, YARDS

ACADEMIC AREA: MATH   GRADE LEVEL: Primary
SUB-AREA: Geometry and Measurement   SUGGESTED TIME: 10 mins.

IMAGERY DESCRIPTION:

   Students will explore the various uses for a 3 foot wooden
   yardstick. They will learn how some people are very dependent
   on the yardstick. They will see the yardstick being used in
   different occupations.

IMAGERY EXERCISE:

   Sit comfortably and relax
   See yourself as a 3 foot wooden yardstick
   Notice how tall you are
   See all the numbers on you
   See each little inch marked from 1" to 36"
   Notice your color
   Feel how heavy you are
   Notice how you can bend
   Now see yourself being used to measure a floor
   Feel yourself being laid on the floor
   Notice how large the floor is
   See yourself being used to measure the height of the ceiling
   See yourself being placed on the wall until you touch the ceiling
   See a builder using you to measure wood
   See your parents using you to measure a large box
   Feel a pencil being run along your body and stopping at the 24 inch line
   See yourself being used for other jobs*
   Notice where the carpenter keeps you at night
   Notice the closet where mom keeps you
   See yourself standing next to your little sister who is just about 3 feet or a yard tall
   See yourself leaving and returning to the classroom
   When I count to ten, open your eyes

VARIATIONS:

   Students could be a one foot ruler. Students could be a
   number on a ruler or yardstick. Students could be a certain
   size box noticing how much they can hold or how much can be
   put into the box.

FOLLOW UP ACTIVITIES:

   Draw a yardstick. List all the uses of the yardstick. Illustrate a workman using a yardstick in building a house.

95

ACADEMIC AREA: MATH   **GRADE LEVEL:** Primary

SUB-AREA: Geometry and Measurement   **SUGGESTED TIME:** 10 mins.

IMAGERY DESCRIPTION:

Students will observe how a thermometer registers the temperature. Students will visit different climates and observe the changes in temperatures. They will observe how the temperature varies during a single day.

IMAGERY EXERCISE:

Sit comfortably and relax
See a giant thermometer hanging on the side of a building
Look closely at the glass tube filled with red mercury
Notice the numbers written to the left of the glass tube
Look at the very top…see the number 120 , meaning 120 degrees
Now slowly follow the numbers 115-110-105-100-95-90
See yourself going down to zero
Notice that the numbers below zero begin with minus 1 and continue minus 2, 5, 10, 15, 20, 25
The hottest the thermometer can read is 120 above 0
The coldest the thermometer can read is 25 below 0
Notice how the red mercury starts at the bottom of the thermometer and goes up the glass tube to a certain number
Notice where the mercury is today
See the mercury at a certain number
See yourself in Florida in August
Feel the heat of the sun
Find a thermometer and notice where the mercury is
See yourself in Alaska in December
Feel the cold temperature
Find a thermometer and notice where the mercury is
Visit a few more places and record the temperature
See yourself returning to the classroom
When I count to ten, open your eyes

VARIATIONS:

Students could become a thermometer and feel themselves change all during the day or they could be the red mercury and feel themselves rising and falling during the day.

FOLLOW UP ACTIVITIES:

Construct a thermometer (paper, wire, paint, glass, etc.). Record the temperatures for a week (a.m. and p.m. temperatures). Research the changes in temperatures in different countries. Compare and contrast.

ACADEMIC AREA: MATH   **GRADE LEVEL:** Primary

SUB-AREA: Geometry and Measurement   **SUGGESTED TIME:**   15 mins.

IMAGERY DESCRIPTION:

Students will have an opportunity to experience the use of liquids in measurement. They will visualize themselves pouring specified amounts of liquid into various containers. They will taste the liquid, feel it, and observe the liquid in different shaped containers.

IMAGERY EXERCISE:

Sit comfortably and relax
See yourself in an orange juice packaging factory
Notice all the different size containers
Pick up a pint container of juice
Taste the juice
Feel its coolness as you swallow it
See hundreds of pint containers
Notice the colors of the containers...read the labels
See some empty gallon containers
Begin to fill the gallon container
Begin emptying the pint containers into the gallon container
Watch it being filled
Keep track of all the pint containers you are using
Notice how many pint containers you had to use in order to fill the gallon container
Count them*
See eight empty pint containers...see the gallon container filled with fresh orange juice
Notice how heavy the gallon container is
Now fill a quart container with orange juice
Again use the juice in the pint containers
Put the quart and gallon containers in a bag and take them home
See yourself returning to the classroom
When I count to ten, open your eyes

VARIATIONS:

Use different liquids, containers and locations to illustrate liquid measurement. Have the students be a container and feel themselves being filled.

FOLLOW UP ACTIVITIES:

Construct various containers (pint, quart, gallon, etc.). Build different shape containers. Draw a chart illustrating different liquid measurements.

ACADEMIC AREA: MATH   GRADE LEVEL: Primary/Intermed.

SUB-AREA: Geometry and Measurement   SUGGESTED TIME: 15 mins.

IMAGERY DESCRIPTION:

Students will have an opportunity to convert from one unit of measure to another unit of measure. They will observe the use of measurement in a most practical manner.

IMAGERY EXERCISE:

Sit comfortably and relax

See yourself visiting a construction site

Notice a large house being built

See yourself talking to the builders about different units of measure

See the carpenter cutting a 5 foot board

Think of how many inches that represents

Hear the workman tell you that the house is 33 feet tall

Look at the height of the house

Imagine how many yards tall the house is

See the concrete worker pouring 12 gallons of water into a wheel barrel filled with cement mix

Imagine how many quarts that is

See yourself carrying an 8 pound box of nails

Feel the weight of the box

Imagine how many ozs. the box weighs

See a truck dumping dirt to be used as fill

Listen to the dirt falling out of the truck and crashing to the ground

See yourself asking the driver how much dirt was just dumped

Hear the driver tell you 5 tons and 814 lbs.

Imagine how many lbs. of dirt was dumped

See yourself waving goodbye to the workers...coming back to class

When I count to ten, open your eyes

VARIATIONS:

Students could visit other places where people are using various units of measure. They could become a large scale or ruler. They could see themselves interviewing people who use measurement on a daily basis.

FOLLOW UP ACTIVITIES:

Make a list of all the materials used on a construction site that require measurement. Construct a mural illustrating these materials. Write a short story about the importance of measurement.

NO: 76   **TITLE:**   WEIGHING THINGS

ACADEMIC AREA: MATH   **GRADE LEVEL:** Primary

SUB-AREA: Geometry and Measurement   **SUGGESTED TIME:** 5 mins.

IMAGERY DESCRIPTION:

Students will experience the weights of different objects. They will become a scale in order to fully appreciate the differences in weights.

IMAGERY EXERCISE:

Sit comfortably and relax
See yourself as small as a scale
Notice your size, shape, color
Feel what you are made of
See numbers on you
See the numbers 1 through 10
Your scale can measure things up to ten pounds
See the little hand on your face point to a number when something is being weighed
Begin to feel objects on you
See a book on you
Have your little hand point and tell us how heavy the book is
See other objects on you
Notice how heavy these objects are
See something on you that weighs a pound
See something on you weighing 5 pounds
Now see something 10 pounds
Notice the difference in these weights
Continue to see yourself weighing different things*
See yourself returning to the classroom
When I count to ten, open your eyes

VARIATIONS:

Students could see themselves as a scale in a vegetable market, at an airport, post office, etc.

FOLLOW UP ACTIVITIES:

Weigh several objects and record their weight. Make a list of things that have similar weight. Design a scale. Go to the supermarket and observe the different weights of various products.

NO: 77   **TITLE:**   GEOMETRIC TERMS AND IDEAS

ACADEMIC AREA: MATH   **GRADE LEVEL:** Primary/Intermediate

SUB-AREA: Geometry and Measurement   **SUGGESTED TIME:** 10 mins.

IMAGERY DESCRIPTION:

Students will have an opportunity to review basic geometry terminology and concepts. This will provide a better foundation for further work with geometric ideas.

IMAGERY EXERCISE:

> Sit comfortably and relax
> See yourself in the center section of a large empty movie theater
> In front of you, see a giant screen
> On your lap is a special control box which allows you to make special pictures and sound effects
> Try it out...enjoy
> Practice drawing some geometric terms
> Make a drawing for the term *point*
> See many points on the giant screen
> Create a *line segment* which has two end points
> Give it sound...color
> Have it move...dance
> See many line segments
> See people walking on your line segment
> Now see yourself making rays which have one end point
> Now create angles which are rays with the same end point
> See yourself creating rays which are parts of a circle and have 2 end points
> Now see all the geometric ideas you have created
> Bring all of them back on your screen
> Notice all the colors, shapes, sizes
> Listen to the sounds as they move around on your screen
> See yourself returning to the classroom
> When I count to ten, open your eyes

VARIATIONS:

Students can imagine themselves constructing congruent segments. Make a chart illustrating various geometric terms.

FOLLOW UP ACTIVITIES:

Students can imagine themselves constructing congruent segments of different lengths. Make a chart illustrating various geometric terms.

ACADEMIC AREA: MATH   **GRADE LEVEL:** Intermediate

SUB-AREA: Geometry and Measurement   **SUGGESTED TIME:** 15 mins.

IMAGERY DESCRIPTION:

Using the formula for finding the volume of a rectangular prism, students will determine how many cubic inches are in a specified rectangular prism.

IMAGERY EXERCISE:

> **Sit comfortably and relax**
> **See yourself at your mini-computer**
> **Press start and ready**
> **Diagram a rectangular prism**
> **Notice the 3 sides showing**
> **Notice the cubic units within the prism**
> **Now make your units one inch**
> **See the length 3" -- width 4" -- height 5"**
> **See all the cubic inches in your prism**
> **Notice the lines separating the cubic units**
> **You're using the formula, l x w x h**
> **Determine the volume of your rectangular prism**
> **Print your answer on your screen**
> **Notice how many cubic inches the volume is**
> **Create another rectangular prism**
> **Put in your own dimensions for length, width and height**
> **Find the volume of different size rectangular prisms***
> **See a truck container...see large boxes being loaded**
> **Decide on the length, width and height of the container**
> **Decide on the size of the boxes**
> **Determine how many boxes can be loaded**
> **Push your "Storage" key for later retrieval**
> **See yourself returning to the classroom**
> **When I count to ten, open your eyes**

VARIATIONS:

Students could become a cubic unit and describe being put into a rectangular prism. Students could be a truck and feel themselves being loaded with cubic units (boxes).

FOLLOW UP ACTIVITIES:

Design and construct a rectangular prism. Write several problems where other students need to determine the volume of your rectangular prisms. Find the actual volume of a truck container, a swimming pool, or a large garbage container.

ACADEMIC AREA: MATH   **GRADE LEVEL:** Intermediate

SUB-AREA: Geometry and Measurement   **SUGGESTED TIME:**   10 mins.

IMAGERY DESCRIPTION:

Using their imaginary mini-computers, students will practice writing proportions. They will be presented sentences stating that two ratios are equivalent. This will prepare students for subsequent work on problem solving using proportions.

IMAGERY EXERCISE:

> **Sit comfortably and relax**
> **See yourself in front of your mini-computer**
> **See the screen**
> **Feel the keyboard**
> **Press the get ready button**
> **Press clear and start**
> **Type out the word proportions**
> **Now listen to the following sentences describing proportions**
> **When you hear the proportions, print out the equation using ratio fraction format**
> **Listen: 4 to 2 is equivalent to 2 to 1**
> **Now see it on your screen**
> **You decide the size, shape and color of the type**
> **Next: 9 to 7 is equivalent to 18 to 14**
>   **1 to 5 is equivalent to 10 to 50**
> **Now make up your own proportions***
> **See all the proportions on the screen**
> **Make up a word problem with a proportion**
> **Solve and answer the problem**
> **See all the proportions you have created on your screen**
> **Notice the variety**
> **Feel the confidence in doing proportions**
> **Turn off your mini-computer and return to class**
> **When I count to ten, open your eyes**

VARIATIONS:

Students could be asked to name a missing term in a proportion. They could create objects, pictures, symbols for the purpose of illustrating proportions.

FOLLOW UP ACTIVITIES:

Make up proportions with missing terms. Write problem statements with proportions. Design charts using illustrations for visual presentation of various proportions. Have a contest for solving proportions with missing terms.

ACADEMIC AREA: MATH   **GRADE LEVEL:**   Intermediate

SUB-AREA: Geometry and Measurement   **SUGGESTED TIME:**   5 mins.

IMAGERY DESCRIPTION:

Students will be given an opportunity to construct an equilateral triangle.

IMAGERY EXERCISE:

Sit comfortably and relax

See yourself sitting at a table with large drawing paper, a compass and straightedge

See yourself beginning to construct an equilateral triangle

First see yourself constructing a line segment of a particular length

Write in the Letters A and T indicating your two points

With your compass tip on A draw an arc through T

With the same compass setting see your compass tip on T drawing another arc that intersects the first

This intersection is N

Now with your straightedge connect A to N and T to N

See NAT as an equilateral triangle

Construct another equilateral triangle

Go through the same process again*

Now look at all your completed equilateral triangles

Notice the differences in size

Give each of them a name and color

See yourself returning to the classroom

When I count to ten, open your eyes

VARIATIONS:

Students could imagine themselves constructing an Isosceles triangle. Students could become a compass and see themselves doing different measurements.

FOLLOW UP ACTIVITIES:

Illustrate the imagined equilateral triangle. Write the steps involved in constructing equilateral triangles.

ACADEMIC AREA: MATH   **GRADE LEVEL:** Intermediate

SUB-AREA: Geometry and Measurement **SUGGESTED TIME:** 10 mins.

IMAGERY DESCRIPTION:

Students will learn about <u>perimeter</u> through measuring a polygon. They will imagine polygons having different shapes, sizes and dimensions.

IMAGERY EXERCISE:

> **Sit comfortably and relax**
> **See yourself swimming in a 4 sided polygon shaped pool**
> **Notice the size of this pool**
> **Feel the coolness of the water**
> **Swim around and enjoy***
> **Determine the length of each of the four unequal sides of the pool**
> **Swim to each side**
> **Imagine a distance for each side**
> **See it in feet**
> **Leave a sign indicating the length of that particular side**
> **See the number clearly on your sign**
> **Now swim to the other 3 sides and determine the lengths**
> **Leave a sign at each side**
> **Now swim to the center of the pool and look at the four signs**
> **Find the *perimeter* of the pool which is the sum of the lengths of its sides**
> **When you have the correct perimeter swim over to the diving board and paint the number underneath the board**
> **See yourself leaving the pool and returning to the classroom**
> **When I count to ten, open your eyes**

VARIATIONS:

Students could see polygons of different shapes, sizes and lengths. They could draw or construct polygons.

FOLLOW UP ACTIVITIES:

Draw a picture of your swimming pool. Make a list of all the things you can think of that are polygon shaped.

NO: **82**   TITLE: DESIGNING AND READING ROAD MAPS

ACADEMIC AREA: MATH   GRADE LEVEL: Intermediate
SUB-AREA: Statistics and Graphing   SUGGESTED TIME: 20 mins.

IMAGERY DESCRIPTION:

Students will construct and practice reading maps with printed mileage tables. They will learn how to do scale drawing and how distances can be found by making a direct measurement on the map. They will also use a ratio to convert the measured distance to the actual distance.

IMAGERY EXERCISE:

Sit comfortably and relax
You're sitting in front of your mini-computer
See the screen, press clear and start
Design and diagram a road map
Show the distance between two cities
Use one color line for interstate highways
Use another color for state or local roadways
Put in little dots indicating towns on the route
On the bottom of your screen, print out a scale for miles, e.g.,
1"   10 miles
Now see yourself constructing the map
Check your map using your scale
See if your distances are correct
Add anything you'd like to your map
See the colors of your map
See all the connecting lines
Notice the symbols and highway signs
Look closely at one of your highway signs
Notice how clear everything is
Take pictures of your map
If you'd like, clear the screen and design a new map*
Press the button "Storage" -- you can retrieve your map any time
Turn off your mini-computer and return to the classroom
When I count to ten, open your eyes

VARIATIONS:

You could give the students certain geographical areas with the names of cities and their respective distances and then have them design a map using a specified scale. You could suggest various dimensions and features to be included in the map drawing.

FOLLOW UP ACTIVITIES:

Select one of the maps designed and constructed on the mini-computer and reproduce it on large oak tag. Have students figure out distances using each others' maps and scales for measurement. Study various maps and compare features, symbols, details, scales, etc.

ACADEMIC AREA: MATH   **GRADE LEVEL:** Intermediate

SUB-AREA: Statistics and Graphing   **SUGGESTED TIME:** 10 mins.

IMAGERY DESCRIPTION:

Students will have an opportunity to organize a set of data through a frequency graph. They will learn that interpretation of the data depends to a large degree on how it is organized and presented visually.

IMAGERY EXERCISE:

> **Sit comfortably and relax**
> **See yourself making a frequency graph**
> **See the lines of a right angle**
> **Notice the size of your right angle**
> **See yourself planning a grade distribution for your class**
> **On the left or vertical extension of your right angle write in numbers 1 through 10**
> **See the numbers spaced equally along your line**
> **Next to your numbers, vertically write the words (number of students)**
> **Now go to the bottom or horizontal extension of your right angle**
> **From left to right see the numbers 75-80-85-90-95-100**
> **Your graph is ready for the data**
> **On the left is Number of Students**
> **On the bottom is Grade Scores**
> **Now listen to the number of students that received certain grades**
> **Three students received a grade of 75**
> **Put dots on the graph above the 75**
> **See the vertical dots going up your graph**
> **Plot the grades for the rest of the class**
> **Now see your completed frequency graph**
> **See yourself returning to the classroom**
> **When I count to ten, open your eyes**

VARIATIONS:

Students could use different types of frequency graphs, e.g., bar graph, for organizing data that interests them. They could become the data, feeling themselves being placed on the graph. They could create graphs electronically.

FOLLOW UP ACTIVITIES:

Conduct an in-class survey and present the data on a frequency graph. Construct a large frequency graph on newsprint. Find out how frequency graphs are used in business and industry.

NO:**84**   TITLE: SCALE DRAWING

ACADEMIC AREA: MATH   GRADE LEVEL: Intermediate
SUB-AREA: Statistics and Graphing   SUGGESTED TIME: 15 mins.

IMAGERY DESCRIPTION:

Students will be given an opportunity to learn the value and
practical use of ratio-scale drawings. They will learn how to
design, construct and read a scale drawing.

IMAGERY EXERCISE:

     Sit comfortably and relax
     Take pictures of each room of your house
     Take pictures of different angles
     Go to your private workroom
     Hang them all on the wall
     Notice how clear the pictures are
     Now take a big piece of drawing paper and construct a scale
     drawing or floor plan of your house
     Decide on a scale to be used as a ratio
     Now determine the size of each room
     First, the actual size, then the scale size
     When you have the scale size, begin to draw the room
     Leave openings for doorways
     See yourself drawing and connecting the rooms on the floor plan
     Label each room
     See windows, closets, stairs, etc.
     See yourself finishing all the detail in your floor plan*
     Check your scale again to make sure you have used proper ratios
     Now see the completed scale drawing
     Notice its size, color...shape of the rooms
     See yourself hanging the drawing on the wall
     Put a frame around the drawing
     See yourself returning to the classroom
     When I count to ten, open your eyes

VARIATIONS:

Students could use other mediums for doing a scale drawing such
as paint, wood, blocks, wire, clay, etc. Students could have
imagined themselves taking pictures from above their rooms, then
adding the proper scale to the picture.

FOLLOW UP ACTIVITIES:

Find a book in the library that has actual scaled floor plans.
Ask a neighbor to show you his floor plan. Reconstruct the
imagined scale drawing. Do an actual scale drawing of your
house using actual measurement and scaling.

5. Imagery in Science

NO: 85   TITLE: HIDE & SEEK WITH THE ANIMALS

ACADEMIC AREA: SCIENCE   GRADE LEVEL: Primary

SUB-AREA: Animal Life   SUGGESTED TIME: 15 mins.

IMAGERY DESCRIPTION:

Students will seek out animals with protective coloration in a game of hide and seek. Animals emphasized are those found in a pond environment.

IMAGERY EXERCISE:

Sit comfortably and relax
See yourself being "it" in a game of hide & seek
Hear yourself counting to twenty...eyes covered for counting
Scan the countryside for hidden animals*
See a tree frog napping on a green leaf
Notice the way he blends in
Feel his smooth skin
Look for the brown-horned toad on them
Touch his bumpy back
Watch as a leaf seems to fly away...a butterfly
Observe the changing colors of a chameleon as he scurries from a brown branch to a green leaf
Watch him blend in and disappear
Search the dry grass for the peeping pheasant chicks
Note their brown shades of color
See the mother pheasant sitting completely still as you pass by
Peer into a pool of water and observe the pond floor where tiny animals hide*
See something moving in the mud*
Watch as a turtle suddenly becomes rocklike
Find one more hiding animal and see its color
Watch it as it moves
See yourself returning to the classroom
When I count to ten, open your eyes

VARIATIONS:

Focus only on one type of animal (insects, fish, mammals, birds, etc.). Add more animals to the Exercise. Focus on another environment (jungle, forest, desert, etc.).

FOLLOW UP ACTIVITIES:

Make an animal scrapbook, showing how each protects itself. Choose an animal to be. Write a story about how your color helped you to escape danger. Create a new animal with unique, built-in protection. Write a nonsense poem about it.

NO: **86**   TITLE: FEATHERED FANTASY

ACADEMIC AREA: SCIENCE   GRADE LEVEL: Primary

SUB-AREA: Animal Life   SUGGESTED TIME: 15 mins.

IMAGERY DESCRIPTION:

Students will experience transformation of body structure from a human being to a bird. Then they will raise their young after watching them hatch.

IMAGERY EXERCISE:

Sit comfortably and relax

See yourself sitting on the edge of a nest, high in the tree branches

Feel the rough straw and twigs between your clawed-toes as you squeeze tightly to hold on

Raise your wings and feel how light the hollow bones make them feel...Fly*

Examine your feathers and see the brilliant colors and patterns

Smooth them down with your hard, pointy beak

Count the eggs in your nest and notice their color and size

Watch as they begin to crack...jiggle...and hatch*

Remove the broken eggshells from the nest

Listen as the fuzzy, blind chicks call for something to eat

Feel yourself glide away to search for food

See yourself and your mate making many trips to find bugs...seeds...and other food

Aim at the opened mouths, dropping bits of food at the red targets

Feel the nest becoming crowded as your babies grow and sprout feathers*

Hear them flapping their wings as they try to fly away

See yourself returning to the classroom

When I count to ten, you will open your eyes

VARIATIONS:

Rewrite the Exercise, substituting key words, so that children become a reptile, amphibian, or fish.

FOLLOW UP ACTIVITIES:

Make a time line of the growth stages of birds. Research the species of bird they saw during the Exercise. Create a puppet play showing birds giving advice to and disciplining their babies.

NO: **87**   TITLE: THE GREAT ESCAPE

ACADEMIC AREA: SCIENCE   GRADE LEVEL: Primary

SUB-AREA: Animal Life   SUGGESTED TIME: 15 mins.

IMAGERY DESCRIPTION:

Students will become a chicken embryo and experience the development from the second to the twenty-first day. They will begin as cells dividing, breathe and feel their heartbeat, develop wings, legs and feathers and, eventually, hatch.

IMAGERY EXERCISE:

Sit comfortably and relax
See yourself as an undeveloped baby chicken inside a large, dark, warm and wet chicken egg
You are very, very tiny and not yet a chicken*
Feel yourself growing as your cells divide again and again
Breathe the oxygen coming through little holes in your shell
Listen to your heart as it begins to beat
Examine your blood vessels which are like little tubes
Stretch out your wings and see their color and size and shape*
Look at your legs...and feet
Feel the soft feathers starting to grow all over you
You are getting crowded in the shell
Hear yourself chirp for the first time
Feel the bump on your beak...it's your egg tooth
Use it to escape from the crowded egg
Scratch...pound...push...scrape...wiggle*
Smell the fresh air coming in through the cracks
Listen as noises become louder
Pull your wet, feathered body out onto the warm straw nest
See yourself returning to the classroom
When I count to ten, you will feel rested and happy

VARIATIONS:

By deleting a few key words, children may become any kind of bird, not just a chicken.

FOLLOW UP ACTIVITIES:

Design a model of the inside of an egg from which a chick would not want to hatch. Write a monologue that a chick might have as he emerges and sees the world for the first time. Act it out, constructing an egg from boxes or paper bags.

ACADEMIC AREA: SCIENCE   GRADE LEVEL: Primary
SUB-AREA: Animal Life   SUGGESTED TIME: 15 mins.

IMAGERY DESCRIPTION:

Students will become a salamander and experience hibernation at the bottom of a pond. They will focus on the slowing down of body functions as well as the change from fall to winter to spring.

IMAGERY EXERCISE:

> **Sit comfortably and relax**
> **See yourself as a beautiful salamander**
> **Notice your colorful spots and smooth skin**
> **Scan your home along a pond**
> **See the signs of fall...changing leaves...cooler air***
> **Feel yourself getting sleepy**
> **Swim to the pond bottom**
> **Feel the soft, warm mud**
> **Dig into it and become very relaxed***
> **Listen to your heartbeat slowing down...your breathing soft**
> **Notice other pond creatures in the mud around you**
> **Hear the water above you beginning to freeze**
> **See the hard, white surface forming**
> **Listen to the silence of winter**
> **Enjoy a dream and sleep till spring***
> **Observe the sunlight above...becoming brighter...and warmer**
> **Hear the last bits of ice melting**
> **Try to move**
> **Slowly emerge from the mud**
> **Feel the warmth of the water**
> **Stretch...and swim to the surface**
> **Scan the surroundings for signs of spring***
> **See yourself returning to the classroom**
> **When I count to ten, open your eyes**

VARIATIONS:

Students could become another hibernating animal in a different habitat. More detail about other pond inhabitants may be inserted.

FOLLOW UP ACTIVITIES:

Compare and contrast how different animals survive the winter. Write about your dreams while hibernating. Draw a picture of what the world looks like from the bottom of a pond. Research the other animals that winter in a pond.

NO: **89**   TITLE: BORN TO BE KING

ACADEMIC AREA: SCIENCE   GRADE LEVEL: Primary/Intermed.
SUB-AREA: Animal Life   SUGGESTED TIME: 20 mins.

IMAGERY DESCRIPTION:

Students will hatch as a Monarch caterpillar on a milkweed plant. They will experience the larva stage, then spin a cocoon and emerge as an adult butterfly searching for food.

IMAGERY EXERCISE:

Sit comfortably and relax
See yourself inside a tiny white egg...the size of a head of a pin
Your egg is hanging on the underside of a leaf
Feel yourself breaking out of the soft shell*
Count your eight pairs of feet along the yellow, black and white stripes of your body
Move your head and feel your black horns
Taste the milkweed
To you, it's delicious...keep munching
Feel the leaf bend under your weight as you grow
Keep munching and hear the leaf crunch as you chew
You are too big for your skin -- wiggle out of it
Now you are a larvae...3,000 times bigger than when you hatched
Feel yourself hanging upside down from a branch
Slowly spin a mat of silk...cover your entire self
Feel yourself change colors...grow...become a butterfly*
Burst from the hardened pupae case
Come out and feel your wet wings unfolding
See the black and orange and white colors
Feel yourself leaping into the air...fly*
Land on a beautiful flower and smell its sweetness
Roll out your proboscis (pro-BOS-cis) and suck up the tasty nectar
You will now change from a butterfly back to yourself
When I count to ten, you will open your eyes

VARIATIONS:

Follow the metamorphosis of a different species of butterfly or moth. Have students observe the change as the milkweed plant instead of the caterpillar.

FOLLOW UP ACTIVITIES:

Using nutshells, grains, cereals, match sticks, etc., make models of various stages of development. Students enact the pupae stage by "wrapping up" in strips of cloth or paper and break free to take their first flight. Write a story or poem about the change or the first flight.

NO:**90**   TITLE: MOVING MONARCHS

ACADEMIC AREA: SCIENCE   GRADE LEVEL: Intermediate/Upper

SUB-AREA: Animal Life   SUGGESTED TIME: 15 mins.

IMAGERY DESCRIPTION:

Students will migrate to Mexico as a Monarch butterfly does in the fall after laying its eggs. They will observe land features they pass over, as well as temperature changes of different regions.

IMAGERY EXERCISE:

Sit comfortably and relax
See yourself as a graceful, orange and black Monarch butterfly
Land on a milkwood leaf to lay your last egg
Feel yourself pressing against the underside of the leaf to deposit the tiny white egg
Smell the signs of Autumn in the air
Notice the color changes and the cooler breezes
The magnetite in your body tingles, points the way: your compass
Begin a long flight south, to a place you've never seen before
Feel the excitement as you fly
Look down and listen as you pass over
cities...forests...swamps...rivers...and other strange places*
Feel the intense heat and smell the sweat of Mexican farmers working in the fields
Listen to the tools striking the hard soil
Climb higher and higher, 10,000 feet, to the mountains
Inhale the cooler, thinner air
See the treetops touching to form a canopy of shelter
Feel the tree branches bending beneath the weight of a million Monarchs like you*
See orange and black cover everything...enjoy and relax
You will end your dormant winter in the Mexican mountains and return to the classroom
When I count to ten, open your eyes

VARIATIONS:

Have students follow a similar migration route as a bird. Reverse the Exercise and have them make their way north to lay their eggs in the spring.

FOLLOW UP ACTIVITIES:

Plot a possible migration route on a map. Research the places that would be passed over en route. Compare and contrast Insect and Bird Migration. Compare and contrast Moths and Butterflies. Write a short story about the day you swallowed a piece of magnetite.

ACADEMIC AREA: SCIENCE   GRADE LEVEL: Intermediate

SUB-AREA: Animal Life   SUGGESTED TIME: 15 mins.

IMAGERY DESCRIPTION:

Following a brief discussion, students will experience the ways that a hydra moves, reproduces and attacks its prey, tiny water animals. Showing a photo before the exercise is recommended. Students should be aware that the hydra is a very tiny water animal.

IMAGERY EXERCISE:

Sit comfortably and relax

See a large aquarium full of clear fresh water

Notice the colors and textures of the rocks, plants and fish

Move past these inhabitants to the stones at the tank bottom

A hydra is using its sticky disks to cling to a rock

Gracefully the brown tentacles bend and somersault

Watch the graceful ballet-like movements*

High above, hydra eggs float on the surface, waiting to hatch

An old hydra grows new tentacles to replace the ones that have broken off in battle

Feel the water ripple as a tiny water flea scurries blindly toward the hydra*

See his large antenna searching for water-plants to eat

Observe the collision and see the hydra's nerve network sending a message to its stinging cells

Listen to the struggling flea and the threadlike tentacles piercing its body to inject paralyzing poison

Watch the limp flea, forced through the hydra's mouth hole to the sac-like stomach

See the footlike base contract and extend sluggishly, as the hydra moves away

You will move past the plants and the fish, out of the aquarium and return to the classroom

When I count to ten, you will open your eyes

VARIATIONS:

Observe a different microscopic animal as it searches for food and reproduces. Have the students become the hydra.

FOLLOW UP ACTIVITIES:

Research the nine-headed monster of Greek mythology which was destroyed by Hercules, the Hydra. Create a comic strip, including conversation or a silent movie with appropriate background music that depicts the Imagery Exercise experience. Examine and record movements of a hydra, using a microscope.

ACADEMIC AREA: SCIENCE   GRADE LEVEL: Primary/Intermed.

SUB-AREA: Dinosaurs   SUGGESTED TIME: 10 mins.

IMAGERY DESCRIPTION:

Students will step out of a time machine to spy on various dino-
saurs. Pronunciation of each dinosaur is included:
Brontosaurs (bron-toe-SAWR-us), Tylosaurus (Tile-o-SAWR-us),
Archelon (ARK-uh-lon), Tyranosaurus (tie-ran-o-SAWR-us),
Triceratops (try-SER-uh-tops).

IMAGERY EXERCISE:

Sit comfortably and relax

See yourself stepping from a time machine to an uncivilized place

Notice the tall trees and unusual plants

Feel the earth shake as a huge body appears

Notice the small head and long, long neck

See him eating from treetops

Watch as Brontosaurus wades into the bay*

Peer into the water

Feel the swish as Tylosaurus whips her tail and paddles through the water

Notice her jaws like those of an alligator

Archelon swims by, a sea turtle bigger than a car

Feel his wrinkled skin and rough shell*

Move back to land...and a later time

Hear the roar of Tyrannosaurus, King of the meat-eating monsters

Notice his sharp teeth...muscular tail...and clawed toes

Watch as he battles Triceratops, the three-horned monster

Observe how he uses the bone shield on his head*

Feel the earth shake as one crashes defeated to the ground

See yourself passing through 70 million years back to the present

See yourself returning to the classroom

When I count to ten, open your eyes

VARIATIONS:

Different dinosaurs could be substituted or added, placing
emphasis on one environment (sea) or type (flying dinosaurs).

FOLLOW UP ACTIVITIES:

Duplicate a dinosaur skeleton with wire armature and cover with
paper maché to paint.   Do a scale drawing of a dinosaur.
Create your own "perfect" dinosaur--one that could have avoided
extinction. Build it.

NO: **93**   TITLE: GIANT PUZZLE

ACADEMIC AREA: SCIENCE   GRADE LEVEL: Intermediate
SUB-AREA: Dinosaurs   SUGGESTED TIME: 20 mins.

IMAGERY DESCRIPTION:

Students will find, wrap, crate, and rebuild a dinosaur, like one found in Dry Mesa, Colorado.

IMAGERY EXERCISE:

>Sit comfortably and relax
>See yourself on a high plateau in Colorado
>Look at the view
>Cover your eyes as you feel dust blowing in the wind
>Feel your muscles begin to ache as you dig carefully and slowly with picks and air guns
>Hear the sound of your small tool hitting something hard
>Uncover, clean and coat each giant bone with shellac*
>Feel the weight as you cover the eight foot shoulder blade with burlap soaked in plaster
>Wrap each piece this way
>Hear the roar of the crane lifting the bones to the crates
>Travel on the truck back to the museum
>Sort the huge bones and notice the shape and size of each
>Decide where each bone fits
>Build the dinosaur
>Imagine the five-story tall dinosaur munching on tree tops
>See the color and texture of his skin
>See him move his head...feet...and tail
>Hear him communicate with others of his kind
>Now see the skeleton once again...in the museum
>See yourself returning to the classroom
>When I count to ten, open your eyes

VARIATIONS:

Students could be one of the giant bones, finally reunited with the rest of the skeleton.

FOLLOW UP ACTIVITIES:

Visit a museum. Interview a dinosaur bone. Find out what really happened to the dinosaurs. Research and hypothesize about dinosaur extinction. Compare and contrast dinosaurs to today's reptiles. Using only a few bones, try to recreate with illustrations the animal they came from.

116

ACADEMIC AREA: SCIENCE   GRADE LEVEL: Primary/Intermed.

SUB-AREA: Earth's Core   SUGGESTED TIME: 10 mins.

IMAGERY DESCRIPTION:

Students will dig to the center of the Earth as a giant shovel. They will become aware of the different composition of each layer as they reach the core.

IMAGERY EXERCISE:

Sit comfortably and relax
See yourself as a giant digging tool
Examine your parts
Begin digging through the Earth's crust
Smell the dirt and rock
Notice the colorful layers and different textures
Listen to the crust heave and tremble
Feel the great heat within
Watch the melted rock mixing with hot gases
Note the pressure building at the base of a volcano
Examine the different materials as you continue to pass through them to the core*
Feel the pull of gravity becoming stronger
Notice how soft the core is
Enjoy it
Look up through the shaft you've made
See the sky, 900 miles up
Slowly see yourself returning to the classroom
When I count to ten, open your eyes

VARIATIONS:

Students could dig through another planet or the moon to discover similarities to the Earth. Students could continue digging to the other side of the Earth.

FOLLOW UP ACTIVITIES:

Make a model of an underground city and life-support systems. Write a poem comparing the Earth and its layers to a kind of fruit. Create an accurate model of the Earth's layers using appropriate materials for hard and soft sections.

ACADEMIC AREA: SCIENCE

SUB-AREA: Ecology

GRADE LEVEL: Intermed./Upper

SUGGESTED TIME: 10 mins.

IMAGERY DESCRIPTION:

Students will discover the effects of an oil spill on plant and animal life along the Chesapeake Bay. The focus will be upon rescuing wild birds, cleaning and feeding them, and eventually releasing them back to the wild.

IMAGERY EXERCISE:

Sit comfortably and relax

See yourself strolling along the Chesapeake Bay

Smell the salt air as it mixes with the odor of oil

Feel the slimy, black coating on the marsh grass, shells and sand

Hear the water lapping against a beached oil barge

Examine the water's edge where fish of all sizes and kinds have washed ashore*

Listen to the flapping wings of an oil-covered swan as it struggles to hide from you

Feel the excitement as rescue workers capture the terrified birds with large nets and place them in burlap sacks

Follow them to the cleanup center

Hear a duck gasping for air as his nostrils are cleared

Feel the warm suds as you help to lower a goose into a detergent bath

Squeeze gently to remove the oil

See feathers becoming white and soft as hair dryers dry them*

Hear the corn mixture being devoured by hungry birds

See yourself returning to the classroom

When I count to ten, open your eyes

VARIATIONS:

Students could become the oil-covered birds that are being rescued. Students could aid the rescue of another animal caught in an oil slick.

FOLLOW UP ACTIVITIES:

Contact the U. S. Fish and Wildlife Service to ask about rescue procedures after an oil spill. Write a script for an interview with an animal that has experienced being caught in an oil slick. Draw "before" and "after" scenes of an oil spill. Visit or write to an area that has recovered from an oil spill.

NO:**96**   TITLE: ECOSYSTEMS

ACADEMIC AREA: SCIENCE   GRADE LEVEL: Primary/Intermed.

SUB-AREA: Ecology   SUGGESTED TIME: 10 mins.

IMAGERY DESCRIPTION:

Students will build the appropriate environment for a given animal. They will include such things as food sources, care of young, natural enemies, climate and other plant and animal life sharing the ecosystem.

IMAGERY EXERCISE:

>**Sit comfortably and relax**
>**See your favorite animal**
>**Measure its size**
>**Note how it feels to touch it**
>**Watch it breathe**
>**Examine its face**
>**Put it in its natural environment**
>**Follow along as it searches for food***
>**Watch how much it eats**
>**Feel the temperature of the surroundings**
>**Observe the plant life...and other animals that live here***
>**Watch them interact with your animal**
>**See it care for its babies**
>**Watch them grow...and play...and learn**
>**See the animal's worst enemy coming into focus**
>**Observe how it protects itself and survives**
>**Put it into an unnatural environment**
>**Watch it adapt...or escape from here**
>**See yourself returning to the classroom**
>**When I count to ten, open your eyes**

VARIATIONS:

Suggest a specific animal rather than the students' selecting. Suggest a general category (e.g., sea animal, desert animal).

FOLLOW UP ACTIVITIES:

Build a diorama of your animal's ecosystem. Compare and contrast ecosystems of fresh and salt water animals. Write about the animal in the unnatural environment in a nonsense poem. Illustrate it.

ACADEMIC AREA: SCIENCE   **GRADE LEVEL:** Intermediate

SUB-AREA: Ecology   **SUGGESTED TIME:**   15 mins.

IMAGERY DESCRIPTION:

Students will be part of a team of eagle experts, climbing trees and banding eaglets. They will observe eating habits and remove unhatched eggs for study.

IMAGERY EXERCISE:

Sit comfortably and relax

See yourself at the base of a large, tall tree

Check your compass bearings and map

Strap on the pole climbers...safety belt with harness and fix your lines around the tree

Feel your spikes gripping the rough bark...and pine needles against your face

Climb to a nest 75 feet above

Observe the young eaglets inside the twig nest*

Climb in slowly and hear the parents screeching as they circle overhead

Scoop up an egg that should have hatched and drop it into your sack

Smell the uneaten fish and bones scattered about

Count the chicks

Gently attach an aluminum leg band to each one

Feel the soft tufts of down the eaglets have plucked out to make room for new feathers*

Scan the nest for rabbit bones...goose feathers...and other scraps of food*

Look at the view around you

Begin your long, slow climb to the bottom

See yourself returning to the classroom

When I count to ten, open your eyes

VARIATIONS:

Students could become the young eaglets or the parent eagles observing the banding of their young. A different endangered bird or animal species could be tagged.

FOLLOW UP ACTIVITIES:

Research the effects that DDT has had on the eagle population. Why is banding important? What other ways does man threaten the eagle? Compare and contrast the African Bateteur, the Madagascar Serpent Eagle, the Philippine Eagle and the American Eagle. Research Indians and their relationship to eagles.

NO: **98**   TITLE: EAGLE VS. AIRPLANE

ACADEMIC AREA: SCIENCE   GRADE LEVEL: Intermediate

SUB-AREA: Ecology   SUGGESTED TIME: 15 mins.

IMAGERY DESCRIPTION:

Students will observe the illegal hunting of eagles by a small plane, rescuing the injured eagle. The setting is the Chilkat River in Alaska, a winter haven for the bald eagle.

IMAGERY EXERCISE:

Sit comfortably and relax

See yourself along the banks of the wild Chilkat River in Alaska

Scan the frost-covered cottonwood trees, full of roosting bald eagles

Hear the flapping wings and air wooshing as one bird swoops to stab a spawning salmon with its talons*

Watch it rise, noting the yellow and black eyes searching for a place to devour its catch

Hear the buzz of a plane in the distance

Watch it approaching the eagle site

Observe as it picks out a gliding eagle and slowly closes in on him*

Hear the screeching of the bird as it rises and dips to escape the plane's pursuit

Feel a chill as a long, steel barrel is poked through the plane window

Listen to the roar of the gun echoing through the forest

Feel the excitement...and fear...as you rush to the falling animal

Hear yourself whispering encouragement

Calm the injured bird

Feel its weight as you wrap...lift it...and carry it to safety

See yourself returning to the classroom

When I count to ten, open your eyes

VARIATIONS:

Students could become the hunted eagle. Students could observe the illegal hunting of another endangered species.

FOLLOW UP ACTIVITIES:

Write to the National Wildlife Federation, 1412 16th Street, NW, Washington, D. C., 20036, for information on endangered species. Prepare a display for the school. Make a copy of the Great Seal of the United States. Research its origin and the symbols used.

ACADEMIC AREA: SCIENCE   **GRADE LEVEL:** Primary/Intermed.

SUB-AREA: Ecology   **SUGGESTED TIME:** 10 mins.

IMAGERY DESCRIPTION:

Students will become part of a mountain and experience the erosion process. They will experience temperature changes that crack the rock and wash down to a river in a rainstorm. Following the river, they will come to rest on the ocean floor.

IMAGERY EXERCISE:

>Sit comfortably and relax
>See yourself high on a mountain top
>You are part of the earth
>Examine your color and texture*
>Feel yourself expanding in the sun's heat
>And contracting in the cool night air
>Listen as a crack begins to separate you from the rest of the mountain
>Feel rain trickling over you and into your crack
>Hear the crack widen
>Feel yourself tumbling away and down the mountain rolling to the river far below
>Plunge into the fast-moving rapids
>Feel pieces of you being bumped and scraped as you are carried along by the current*
>Taste the salt as you move from fresh to ocean water
>Feel yourself slowing down
>Move with the tides...back and forth
>Notice how the plant and animal life is changing as you enter the sea
>Settle to the ocean floor
>Scan what's around you
>See yourself returning to the classroom
>When I count to ten, open your eyes

VARIATIONS:

Students could become part of a desert rock formation being eroded by wind. Students could be the water that causes the erosion.

FOLLOW UP ACTIVITIES:

Make a photo essay of area sights showing erosion. Contact local agencies to see what is being done about it. Write a story or poem about a land form being eroded by water, wind or plant life.

NO:**100**   TITLE: FOSSIL DIG IN JERUSALEM

ACADEMIC AREA: SCIENCE   GRADE LEVEL: Intermediate

SUB-AREA: Fossils   SUGGESTED TIME: 15 mins.

IMAGERY DESCRIPTION:

Students will discover fossils in the large stone piles of Jerusalem. They will examine and guess the origins of what they find. The Exercise will focus on sea fossils.

IMAGERY EXERCISE:

> **Sit comfortably and relax**
> **You're climbing over ancient stone piles near Jerusalem where palaces once stood**
> **Feel the intense heat and dryness**
> **Touch the rough surface of a small rock**
> **It was the coiled shell of an ammonite (AM-uh-nite)**
> **Try to imagine its colors and shape**
> **Smell the salt that still lingers**
> **Scan the rocks again**
> **Choose one that interests you**
> **Examine every detail of the impression***
> **Picture the bone or shell before it was buried in the ocean floor**
> **See the creatures that once lived within it**
> **Watch it move...and search for food**
> **See it die...sinking to the bottom**
> **Feel the pressure of clay and sand as it covers the body and squishes into the shell cavities**
> **Watch as minerals soak into the shell**
> **Feel the dryness as the sea takes millions of years to become a desert***
> **Hold the stone copy of the shell**
> **Examine it from a new angle**
> **See yourself returning to the classroom**
> **When I count to ten, open your eyes**

VARIATIONS:

Students could become the fossil and speak to the finder about where they came from and how they lived.

FOLLOW UP ACTIVITIES:

Take a "fossil hunt" to New York City. Using magnifying glasses, examine marble or limestone buildings such as Tiffany's, Saks Fifth Avenue, Macy's and the Tishman Building closely. Make fossils with plaster and shells. Have a fossil dig for another class. Visit a museum.

ACADEMIC AREA: SCIENCE   GRADE LEVEL: Primary

SUB-AREA: Matter   SUGGESTED TIME: 15 mins.

IMAGERY DESCRIPTION:

Students will become a super hero, "Magnet-Man," to learn the properties of magnets. They will be made aware that iron objects can be picked up by a magnet, through cloth and in water as well.

IMAGERY EXERCISE:

> Sit comfortably and relax
> Hear yourself saying the magic word "loadstone"
> Suddenly your body is becoming hard and smooth -- a magnet
> See your North and South Poles
> Test your strength by touching something with iron on it
> Hear it clink as it sticks to you*
> Move around the classroom and see paper clips and thumb tacks coming toward you*
> Pick up some other things
> Go outside and test your strength
> A carpenter on the roof dropped all of his nails
> Help him
> See your friend lose his toy car in the muddy pool of water
> Use your power in the water to get the car out
> Look Out! There's a mean-looking character who may have a weapon hidden in his cape
> Your strength works right through the cloth...frisk him
> You have one last mission for today
> Santa Claus has lost his way home
> Use your magnetism to help him
> Find the North Pole and guide him back
> Watch Santa slowly disappear
> See yourself returning to the classroom
> When I count to ten, open your eyes

VARIATIONS:

Students could view Magnet-Man (or Magnet-Woman) coming into their classroom to teach for the day. The Exercise could be a comedy of problems that being a magnet creates.

FOLLOW UP ACTIVITIES:

Write about a new adventure of Magnet-Man (e.g., Magnet-Man at the Tool Shop). Act it out. Test properties with real magnets. Make a model of Magnet-Man from small boxes or real magnets. Make a cartoon strip of one episode from the Imagery Exercise. Write a limerick about Magnet-Man.

NO:**102**   TITLE: GOING IN CYCLES

ACADEMIC AREA: SCIENCE   GRADE LEVEL: Primary/Intermed.

SUB-AREA: Matter   SUGGESTED TIME: 10 mins.

IMAGERY DESCRIPTION:

Students will become a water molecule and change from a solid to a liquid and gas. They will be aware of how temperature determines the movement and form of the molecules.

IMAGERY EXERCISE:

Sit comfortably and relax
You are a molecule of water
Examine your 2 hydrogen and 1 oxygen atoms
Feel yourself becoming very hard and cold
You are a chunk of ice, hanging onto a tree branch
See yourself pack shoulder-to-shoulder with other molecules*
Try to move...feel your stiffness
See yourself sparkle in the sunlight
Feel its warmth...begin to melt
Become a drop of water splashing to the ground
Watch other drops joining you to form a big puddle
Flow with each ripple and move freely
Feel the Earth's warmth increasing beneath you*
Try to escape it
Rise into the air...up...up...totally free
Become part of a cloud...float...rise
Look down at the Earth
Feel yourself become cooler, heavier and wet
Fall and crystalize into a snowflake...see your delicate pattern*
Float down to some place interesting
As you melt again, notice that you still have the same hydrogen and oxygen atoms
See yourself returning to the classroom
When I count to ten, open your eyes

VARIATIONS:

Students could be the sun causing temperature changes, so that water must freeze, evaporate, etc. Students could be a tree, watching the same molecules going round and round.

FOLLOW UP ACTIVITIES:

Make a water cycle diagram (cut snowflakes, plastic bags for drops, etc.). Write a story about a water molecule who refused to change from one form to another. Research other substances that change forms as water does. Test them. Record findings.

125

ACADEMIC AREA: SCIENCE   GRADE LEVEL: Intermediate
SUB-AREA: Matter   SUGGESTED TIME: 10 mins.

IMAGERY DESCRIPTION:

Students will follow the word "hello" into a telephone trans-
mitter to a receiver at the other end. They will see sound
change to pulses of electricity and back to sound.

IMAGERY EXERCISE:

Sit comfortably and relax
Hear yourself speaking the word "hello" into a telephone
**Watch the word leave your mouth and strike a disk of metal
inside the phone**
Feel the sound vibrations changing to pulses of electricity*
Examine their size and shape
Note their colors
Watch the pulsing movements as they go
Travel along the wires to your friend's house*
See the pulses entering the receiver
Notice their pattern and rhythm
Watch them change as they pass through the coils
Observe that the shape and color are disappearing
Hear the word "hello" being spoken into your friend's ear
Follow your friend's voice back along the same path
See yourself returning to the classroom
When I count to ten, open your eyes

VARIATIONS:

Students could follow radio sound waves from the station trans-
mitter to a radio at home. Students could follow a transmission
from Earth to a space vehicle.

FOLLOW UP ACTIVITIES:

Draw and label a diagram of sound waves changing over the phone.
Research the contributions of Bell and Marconi. Write about a
word that got "stuck" in the lines. Make and test your own
phone. Visit a radio or TV station.

ACADEMIC AREA: SCIENCE   **GRADE LEVEL:** Intermediate

SUB-AREA: Matter   **SUGGESTED TIME:**   10 mins.

IMAGERY DESCRIPTION:

Students will become the nucleus of an atom. They will experience being split and starting a chain reaction. Students will
become aware that the nucleus contains protons and neutrons,
while electrons are smaller and orbit the nucleus.

IMAGERY EXERCISE:

> **Sit comfortably and relax**
> **See yourself as the nucleus of an atom**
> **Feel your protons**
> **Count them**
> **Observe their shape and color**
> **Notice their positive charges**
> **Now examine your neutrons clustered with the protons**
> **Feel the compactness of your parts***
> **Listen to the tiny electrons orbiting around you**
> **Count them as they fly by**
> **Note their negative charges**
> **See yourself with thousands of other atoms exactly like you***
> **Mingle with them**
> **Feel the impact of a proton bullet splitting you**
> **Observe your parts as they fly into other atoms…and split them**
> **See this happen again and again**
> **Feel the energy and heat building**
> **Release the power**
> **Watch where it goes**
> **See yourself returning to the classroom**
> **When I count to ten, open your eyes**

VARIATIONS:

Students could become the proton bullet that causes the chain
reaction.

FOLLOW UP ACTIVITIES:

Build a model of the atom you became during the Exercise, as well
as atoms of hydrogen, oxygen, etc. Research nuclear reactors.
Keep a current events notebook about some in the U. S. Debate
the pros and cons of having nuclear plants.

ACADEMIC AREA: SCIENCE   GRADE LEVEL: Primary/Intermed.

SUB-AREA: Matter   SUGGESTED TIME: 10 mins.

IMAGERY DESCRIPTION:

Students will observe Benjamin Franklin carrying out the "Kite" experiment. They will see him and his son with a kite and Leyden Jar during a thunderstorm in 1752.

IMAGERY EXERCISE:

Sit comfortably and relax

See yourself traveling back in time more than 200 years, to 1752

Examine your colonial clothing and surroundings*

Hear horse-drawn carriages in the street

Feel the cobblestones under your shoes as you walk

Listen to a clap of thunder as a storm begins

Feel the raindrops

Watch people running for cover as the sky darkens

Smell the smoke of a burning barn, struck by lightning

Watch as a man and his son come out of their house with a kite and a jar

Observe the silk kite rising into the dark, windy sky*

Watch as a flash of lightning follows the string to a key near his hand

Hear the cry of surprise as the shock almost knocks the man over

See him smile and speak to the boy as the key is held near a strange jar (Leyden Jar)

Look into the jar

Listen to what they are saying*

See yourself returning to the classroom

When I count to ten, open your eyes

VARIATIONS:

Students could see themselves conducting the experiment as Franklin did. Students could see themselves talking to Benjamin Franklin about the experiment.

FOLLOW UP ACTIVITIES:

Design and build your own kite. Research kite experiments done by Marconi, Wright Brothers and Bell. Write about an adventure you could have on a kite. Draw a cross section of a home including as many Franklin inventions as you can.

ACADEMIC AREA: SCIENCE   **GRADE LEVEL:** Intermediate

SUB-AREA: Plant Life   **SUGGESTED TIME:** 10 mins.

IMAGERY DESCRIPTION:

Students will become chloroplasts and aid the photosynthesis process. They will split water molecules, watch new compounds forming and see the release of oxygen into the air.

IMAGERY EXERCISE:

Sit comfortably and relax
Put yourself inside a leaf
See your body become disc-shaped and green
Feel yourself absorbing the Sun's energy...and trapping it*
Listen to water rising through the plant's stem
Use your energy and split the water molecules as they flow into the leaf
Now watch new compounds forming...and mixing*
See their colors and shapes
Listen to the sounds they make
Watch where they go
Taste the new sugar that's forming
Smell it...touch it
Observe how the plant uses it to grow
Watch oxygen molecules escape to the air
Feel yourself working more slowly
Hear the plant's factory shutting down*
Notice that the sun is setting
Feel the night air...becoming cooler
Stop working and enjoy your rest
See yourself returning to the classroom
When I count to ten, open your eyes

VARIATIONS:

Students could view the process through a high-powered microscope. Students could take a tour through a leaf factory, the guide being a chloroplast, water molecule, etc.

FOLLOW UP ACTIVITIES:

Draw a diagram of the photosynthesis process. Act out the process having people play the parts of oxygen, hydrogen, carbon, etc. Use sound effects to describe the process. Draw and explain the process as a factory assembly line.

ACADEMIC AREA: SCIENCE   **GRADE LEVEL:** Primary

SUB-AREA: Plant Life   **SUGGESTED TIME:** 15 mins.

IMAGERY DESCRIPTION:

Students will become a seed, starting at a point where they are being tossed to the ground. They will be encouraged to experience everything that is happening in their environment as well as the growth stages.

IMAGERY EXERCISE:

> **Sit comfortably and relax**
> **You are a grass seed**
> **Notice your color...size...shape**
> **Feel yourself being tossed to the ground and covered by dirt**
> **As you lie in the ground, notice all around you**
> **Explore all that is inside of you***
> **Notice changes in temperature and weather conditions**
> **Absorb the water**
> **Use the minerals**
> **Feel yourself emerging into the dirt***
> **Smell the dirt**
> **Feel the sun shining down on you**
> **Feel the water running over you**
> **Begin to see yourself becoming a blade of grass**
> **Watch the process slowly***
> **See how clear everything is**
> **Feel yourself grabbing hold of the earth as you slowly rise upward toward the sky**
> **Feel yourself branching out to form new seeds**
> **Watch them scattering in the wind**
> **See yourself slowly returning to the class**
> **When I count to ten, open your eyes**

VARIATIONS:

Students could become other forms of plant life beginning at the first stage of the growth process. Students could become the soil and experience the plant taking hold of and growing out of them.

FOLLOW UP ACTIVITIES:

Draw the images that they saw during the Exercise. Construct models depicting the various stages of growth that they imaged. Compare the different speeds of seed germination by observing various seeds on damp cotton as they sprout.

NO: **108**   TITLE: THE BIRDS, THE BEES, AND ME

ACADEMIC AREA: SCIENCE   GRADE LEVEL: Primary/Intermed.

SUB-AREA: Plant Life   SUGGESTED TIME: 10 mins.

IMAGERY DESCRIPTION:

Students will see pollination from the inside of a flower. They will watch pollen grains enter the pollen tube to fertilize the egg cells and become new seeds.

IMAGERY EXERCISE:

Sit comfortably and relax
See yourself inside a flower as it begins to open
Feel the sun's rays
See its brightness as the petals stretch and curl apart
Examine the inside of the flower closely*
Smell its fragrance
Climb to the top of the petal and look at the view
Hear the sound of a hummingbird approaching
Dodge the narrow beak as it searches for sweet nectar inside the flower
Feel powdery pollen grains dusting you as the bird moves away to other flowers*
Watch as some of the grains fall into the pollen tube
Listen as they tumble down the tube to the egg cell
Reach down in...feel the egg cells inside mixing with the pollen
Pull one out and examine it closely*
Watch it grow into a new seed
See yourself returning to the classroom
When I count to ten, open your eyes

VARIATIONS:

Students could ride on the back of the humming bird or butterfly to get into the flower and observe.

FOLLOW UP ACTIVITIES:

Cut apart a large flower and examine its parts. Plant a variety of seeds and record growth stages. Make a model or diagram of the parts of a flower. Observe and record the types of birds and insects that aid pollination.

ACADEMIC AREA: SCIENCE   **GRADE LEVEL:** Primary/Intermed.

SUB-AREA: Seasons   **SUGGESTED TIME:** 15 mins.

IMAGERY DESCRIPTION:

Students will experience fall and winter as a Maple tree. Focus will be upon leaves changing and dropping and the sap beginning to flow again in the spring.

IMAGERY EXERCISE:

> **Sit comfortably and relax**
> **Feel your feet sinking into the soil-like strong roots**
> **Watch as your legs and arms become brown...rough like tree bark**
> **Watch as your leaves begin to change from dark green to other colors**
> **Listen to the chlorophyll breaking down as you feel the nights getting cooler***
> **See yourself making sugar as your leaves turn with purple and red pigment**
> **Hear the migrating birds calling goodbye to you**
> **Watch your leaves dropping, one-by-one, to the ground***
> **Hear the scraping of rakes and crackling leaves**
> **Smell the tiny leaf piles burning**
> **Feel a coating of frost cover you and the dying flowers below as animals disappear**
> **Watch where they go to hibernate**
> **See the snow become deep and icicles forming everywhere**
> **Hear your rigid branches clicking in the wind**
> **Feel the snow melting into the ground as the days become longer**
> **Feel your sap beginning to run again**
> **See yourself returning to the classroom**
> **When I count to ten, open your eyes**

VARIATIONS:

Parts I and II may be used together, omitting the first four lines.

FOLLOW UP ACTIVITIES:

Write a conversation between a tree that doesn't want to be cut for firewood and your father. Select music that portrays the mood of each season. Make a time line for a Redwood tree, including historical events as well as tree growth.

ACADEMIC AREA: SCIENCE   GRADE LEVEL: Primary/Intermed.

SUB-AREA: Seasons   SUGGESTED TIME: 15 mins.

IMAGERY DESCRIPTION:

Students will experience spring and summer as a Maple tree. Attention will be upon tree processes, such as buds becoming leaves, seed-making, and leaf color changes due to the presence of chlorophyll. Other seasonal signs of weather and activities are also mentioned.

IMAGERY EXERCISE:

Sit comfortably and relax
Feel your feet sinking into the soil-like strong roots
Watch as your legs & arms become brown & rough like tree bark
Feel strong and proud, towering over familiar houses
Listen as buds burst open and grow into fresh green leaves*
Feel the warm sun...smell the clean breezes...hear a gentle rain tapping on your leaves
Observe a bird family building its nest*
Smell the new flowers beginning to bloom below you
Watch your winged seeds spinning to the ground
Feel your leaves becoming larger and darker green as chlorophyll makes food for you
Feel the ground tremble as a sudden crash of thunder roars
See the flashes of lightning
Feel the pounding rain
Feel yourself pushed by the wind as the birds huddle in their nest to protect their babies
See a rainbow appear as it becomes quiet and cool
Use your root system to drink in fresh water and minerals
Feel clean and refreshed
Enjoy the evening breeze and listen to the bull frogs
See yourself returning to the classroom
When I count to ten, open your eyes

VARIATIONS:

Students could become another deciduous tree or an evergreen, forming needles and cones.

FOLLOW UP ACTIVITIES:

Make a four-season collage using pictures and "nature items" gathered from outside. Compare and contrast the different types of Maple trees. Make a leaf collection, identifying and classifying leaves. Brainstorm activities associated with each season.

ACADEMIC AREA: SCIENCE   **GRADE LEVEL:** Intermediate

SUB-AREA: Space   **SUGGESTED TIME:**   15 mins.

IMAGERY DESCRIPTION:

Students will witness a moon landing as a stowaway in the Apollo Spacecraft. The adventure will begin at Cape Kennedy with the first, second and final rocket stages firing. They will observe the moon landing as well as the gathering of moon rocks.

IMAGERY EXERCISE:

> **Sit comfortably and relax**
> **See yourself hiding somewhere in the Apollo Spacecraft at Cape Kennedy, Florida**
> **Scan the Columbia command module...control panels...computers...food supply...and other equipment**
> **See three suited astronauts enter**
> **Watch as they take their seats and listen to final instructions**
> **Hear the slow countdown**
> **Hear a roar as rocket engines throw tremendous blasts of gas**
> **Feel their heat**
> **Feel yourself rising smoothly as the first stage...second stage...and final stage of the Saturn Rocket fire and fall away***
> **Watch as you orbit the Earth**
> **See land shapes and oceans**
> **Feel gravity pulling toward the Moon**
> **Orbit the Moon**
> **See things man has never seen before***
> **Land softly on the Moon's surface**
> **Observe two astronauts with large packs drifting effortlessly on the moon's surface**
> **Examine the things that are being collected**
> **See yourself slowly returning to the classroom**
> **When I count to ten, open your eyes**

VARIATIONS:

Read lines 1 - 4 and then play record or tape of actual countdown and conversation of the Moon landing by Armstrong, Collins and Aldrin.

FOLLOW UP ACTIVITIES:

Construct a moonscape with paper mache or plaster mixture and label craters. Keep a daily chart of moon phases. Write a story about a spacecraft that could not return to Earth. Research Newton's laws. Apply them to rockets and space travel.

NO:**112**   TITLE: JOURNEY THROUGH THE TELESCOPE

ACADEMIC AREA: SCIENCE   GRADE LEVEL: Primary/Intermed.

SUB-AREA: Space   SUGGESTED TIME: 15 mins.

IMAGERY DESCRIPTION:

Students will travel through a giant telescope to see planets, stars and other heavenly bodies. They will pass the planets of our solar system and discover a new one.

IMAGERY EXERCISE:

Sit comfortably and relax
See yourself inside a large observatory peering through a giant telescope
Feel yourself begin to float effortlessly through the lenses, up into the sky
Watch the moon passing by
Observe what's happening on each planet as you approach first Mars, the red planet...
Next Jupiter with many moons...
Then Saturn, count the rings...
Uranus...Neptune...Pluto
See an undiscovered planet
Count its moons
Examine the land
Watch as the stars form constellations...
See the Big Dipper...Scorpius, with its poisonous sting...and Orion, the great hunter...
Hear them clash as they battle
Follow the Milky Way on your return trip to Earth
Observe unusual objects traveling through the sky*
See yourself returning to the classroom
When I count to ten, open your eyes

VARIATIONS:

More emphasis could be placed on the planets by adding details to observe and greater imaging time. Other constellations could also be viewed.

FOLLOW UP ACTIVITIES:

Write about the Undiscovered Planet of our solar system. Make a model of the Undiscovered Planet. Research the legend of Orion and Scorpius. Research and diagram movements of the stars according to the time of year.

NO: **113**   TITLE: UP, UP AND AWAY

ACADEMIC AREA: SCIENCE   GRADE LEVEL: Intermediate
SUB-AREA: Weather   SUGGESTED TIME: 20 mins.

IMAGERY DESCRIPTION:

Students will ride a weather balloon to study six cloud types.
Each type is described in terms of physical features, height
and potential weather expected.

IMAGERY EXERCISE:

Sit comfortably and relax
See yourself attached to a large weather balloon
You have equipment with you to record what you see
Check it over*
As you leave the ground, feel the dampness of fog on your face
Notice the layers or sheets of (stratus) clouds
Protect your equipment from the drizzle, as you rise from 6,000
to 20,000 feet and higher
Feel the colder air...examine the icy-webbed (cirrus) clouds
Watch the long feathers of ice curl around your balloon
Reach out and touch the ice crystals as they move to form small
balls or flakes
These (cirro-cumulus) clouds look like rippled sand
See the sunlight sparkling through
Descend to (alto-cumulus) lower clouds
They look more rippled with gray and white groups
They are full of water drops
You are going up...up to the (cumulo-nimbus) large flat-topped
cloud masses
Enjoy the peace and beautiful view*
Finally see yourself heading down through the fluffy-white
cumulus clouds*
See yourself returning to the classroom
When I count to ten, open your eyes

VARIATIONS:

This may be read including the cloud names, if desired. Students
could ride in another vehicle (blimp, not air balloon, etc.) to
make observations.

FOLLOW UP ACTIVITIES:

Observe, record and predict weather according to cloud formations.
Compare your finds to actual reports. Stage a TV weather report
with dialogue between the weather balloon and the ground. Release balloons with stamped and addressed cards to determine
distance traveled and wind direction. Chart findings.

NO:**114**   TITLE: WHERE DOES THE FOOD GO?

ACADEMIC AREA: SCIENCE   GRADE LEVEL: Primary/Intermed.

SUB-AREA: Your Body   SUGGESTED TIME: 15 mins.

IMAGERY DESCRIPTION:

Students will follow a piece of food as it is digested for use by the body cells. They will follow the process from the initial saliva breakdown in the mouth, to the stomach, intestine, and blood system.

IMAGERY EXERCISE:

Sit comfortably and relax
See yourself in a digestion-proof capsule
Look through the protective clear walls to the food you are on
Smell its aroma
Note its texture
Feel yourself rising as a giant hand moves you toward the opening mouth
Hear the teeth slashing...and the tongue moving
Watch the flow of saliva
Feel the mashed food being swallowed
Ride with it to the stomach
See the juices squirting in from the stomach wall
Notice their colors*
Watch them breaking down the food even more
See each tiny food particle
Follow one that interests you down the long, curled intestine*
Observe more changes taking place
Pass with it into a blood vessel
Travel to a hungry body cell
Observe the cell using the food
See yourself returning to the classroom
When I count to ten, open your eyes

VARIATIONS:

Students could follow a particular type of food (starch, carbo-hydrate, etc.) and observe its unique breakdown and specific usage by the body.

FOLLOW UP ACTIVITIES:

Write a story about the fantasy experienced. Draw a diagram, tracing the stages of digestion. Mix different foods with your saliva. Compare how they begin to digest. Study food groups to determine how each is used differently by the body.

NO: **115**   TITLE: MOVING TO THE BEAT

ACADEMIC AREA: SCIENCE   GRADE LEVEL: Primary/Intermed.
SUB-AREA: Your Body   SUGGESTED TIME: 10 mins.

IMAGERY DESCRIPTION:

Students will follow blood cells through the circulatory system. They will begin at the lungs and carry oxygen to the body, returning with carbon dioxide. Emphasis will be upon the changing color of the blood.

IMAGERY EXERCISE:

Sit comfortably and relax
Listen to the beating of your heart
Feel the steady rhythm
See the blood being pumped
Focus on a red blood cell inside you
Examine its disk shape from every side
Watch as it pulls oxygen from the lungs
See its bright red color
Travel with it through your body*
Observe the brightness draining away as it feeds oxygen to a body cell
Watch the body cell using the oxygen
Feel its weight as it fills with carbon dioxide
Note its color getting deeper
Trace its path back to the heart
See the pumping motion
Hear it become louder
Feel it pulling the blood to it
Watch hundreds of cells moving by and back to the lungs
See yourself returning to the classroom
When I count to ten, open your eyes

VARIATIONS:

Students could become a white blood cell rushing to fight an infection. Students could become the red blood cell as it exchanges oxygen for carbon dioxide.

FOLLOW UP ACTIVITIES:

Build a model of the circulatory system. Write a diary for "A Day In The Life Of A Blood Cell". Record pulse rates after various activities. Create a travel brochure for someone traveling through the bloodstream. Give interesting names to the stops made along the route.

6. Imagery in Social Studies

NO:116   **TITLE:** A JOURNEY THROUGH THE POSTAL SYSTEM

ACADEMIC AREA: SOCIAL STUDIES   **GRADE LEVEL:** Primary

SUB-AREA: Our Neighborhood   **SUGGESTED TIME:** 10 mins.

IMAGERY DESCRIPTION:

Students will take a fantasy journey inside of a package being handled and shipped by the U. S. Postal Department. Their journey will include being weighed, priced, driven by truck, being thrown, etc. Each step of the process will be mentioned in order that students gain greater understanding of how our mail system works.

IMAGERY EXERCISE:

> **Sit comfortably and relax**
> **Feel yourself in a box that is being wrapped**
> **Feel the movement as you are being taped, tied, fastened and addressed**
> **Feel yourself being picked up and carried to someone's car**
> **Hear the engine of the car as you head toward the post office**
> **Feel yourself shifting as the car stops and starts at red lights**
> **You are now bouncing and swaying on a large scale**
> **Hear the postal clerk telling how much the package will cost for shipment**
> **Feel yourself being thrown into a large mail bag**
> **As you lie there quietly, feel the impact of other packages continuing to crush you**
> **Feel yourself being thrown into a large truck**
> **Listen to some voices of nearby truck drivers**
> **Hear the engines roar as you speed away**
> **Feel yourself being dumped out of your mail bag and onto a large table**
> **Feel yourself being tossed onto a metal rack**
> **Feel yourself being carried in a mail sack**
> **Feel the bouncing as the mail person walks along**
> **Hear a doorbell ring and someone say "thank you"**
> **See yourself returning to the classroom**
> **When I count to ten open your eyes**

VARIATIONS:

Students could be a letter or a package being shipped by air. They could be a postal worker for a day or a stamp where they could see everything. They could be a mail truck making deliveries.

FOLLOW UP ACTIVITIES:

Visit a post office, speak to the supervisor and take a tour. Write a diary of a mailed package. Write a short story describing what the adventure was like.

NO:117 **TITLE:** A LOOK AT OUR NEIGHBORS' OCCUPATIONS

ACADEMIC AREA: SOCIAL STUDIES **GRADE LEVEL:** Primary

SUB-AREA: Our Neighborhood **SUGGESTED TIME:** 10 mins.

IMAGERY DESCRIPTION:

Students will see themselves visiting several neighbors discussing many different occupations. They will listen to their neighbors describe the various kinds of responsibilities they have with their jobs. They will learn about work schedules, job locations, and traveling to work.

IMAGERY EXERCISE:

Sit comfortably and relax
See yourself making a list of questions that you will ask your neighbors concerning their occupations
See yourself phoning your neighbor to make an appointment for an interview
See yourself about ready to leave your house to visit several neighbors
See yourself visiting your first neighbor
Feel the soft couch as you sit and relax
Listen to your neighbors describe their occupations
Look at each face as they talk
See yourself asking them some questions about their jobs*
Now see yourself visiting other friendly neighbors
Again listen to what they have to say about their jobs
Hear them tell you what they like best and what they like least
Now go and visit some more neighbors
Listen to all the different kinds of jobs
Learn as much as you can*
See the neighbors enjoy talking to you
Notice how each neighbor talks differently about his work
See yourself saying thank you and goodbye to your last neighbor
See yourself returning to the classroom
When I count to ten, open your eyes

VARIATIONS:

Students could see themselves visiting their neighbors for other reasons. They could visit with other people. They could visit with people who have the same types of jobs. They could interview people at an unemployment agency.

FOLLOW UP ACTIVITIES:

Make a list of all the different types of jobs. Compare the jobs according to something that interests you, such as location, jobs that pay a lot of money, jobs involving working with a lot of people versus jobs where there is little interaction..

140

NO:**118**   TITLE: BUYING FOOD FOR THE FAMILY

ACADEMIC AREA: SOCIAL STUDIES   GRADE LEVEL: Primary

SUB-AREA: Our Neighborhood   SUGGESTED TIME: 10 mins.

IMAGERY DESCRIPTION:

Students will experience planning and purchasing food for the family for a one-week period. They will actively select foods for certain meal times. They will have to make sure that consideration is given for nutrition and good health foods.

IMAGERY EXERCISE:

Sit comfortably and relax
See yourself sitting at your kitchen table
See a large sheet of paper in front of you
See yourself visualizing all the different foods that your parents buy each week
See the colors and shapes of packages of the different variety of foods they most purchase
See types of meat...and fish
See vegetables
See desserts
Continue to see all the food your family needs each week
Now see yourself planning a menu for each day beginning with breakfast*
See yourself writing the types of food on your shopping list
Continue doing this until you have enough food for the week
See yourself at the supermarket
See yourself picking food items from the shelves
Feel the boxes and packages
Smell some of the food items
See your shopping cart filling up
Feel it becoming hard to push
Now see yourself in your house putting all the food away
See yourself returning to the classroom
When I count to ten, open your eyes

VARIATIONS:

Students could make a list of things that are needed for building something or make a list of things needed on a camping trip. Students could see themselves making a special meal.

FOLLOW UP ACTIVITIES:

Prepare an actual shopping list for your family, then compare it to your parent's list. Decide which foods are more healthy for you by rating the foods according to categories. Have students keep track of the food they eat for a week, then compare.

ACADEMIC AREA: SOCIAL STUDIES   **GRADE LEVEL:** Primary

SUB-AREA: Our Neighborhood   **SUGGESTED TIME:** 10 mins.

IMAGERY DESCRIPTION:

Students will take an imaginary journey in a soft white cloud. The trip will take them over cities and towns. As they float smoothly in the sky, their attention will be directed to the ground in order that they can observe the many different means of transportation used in today's world.

IMAGERY EXERCISE:

> Sit comfortably and relax
> See yourself lying comfortably on a small, soft, slow-moving cloud
> high above the ground
> Begin to notice what the ground looks like
> See beautiful trees and open fields
> See houses and buildings of all kinds
> Now begin to notice how people are traveling
> Look closely at the vehicles they are using
> Notice the different highways and roads
> Look at other ways people are traveling
> Listen to the sounds
> See the colors and shapes of the different vehicles
> Continue to float in the sky
> Listen to how quiet it is as you move slowly in the sky
> Now locate someone traveling in a very different way
> Watch closely
> Notice how people travel together
> Notice a large group of people traveling together
> Continue to observe people traveling*
> Enjoy the relaxed feeling you are experiencing
> Look again at all the different ways people are traveling
> See yourself floating back...back returning home
> See yourself returning to the classroom
> When I count to ten, open your eyes

VARIATIONS:

Students could identify with one type of transportation means, experiencing the different ways people are using it. Students could see themselves as travelers visiting many places.

FOLLOW UP ACTIVITIES:

List and diagram the different types of transportation vehicles you observed. Construct models of the various vehicles. Create a vehicle for travel in the future.

ACADEMIC AREA: SOCIAL STUDIES   GRADE LEVEL: Primary

SUB-AREA: Our Neighborhood   SUGGESTED TIME: 10 mins.

IMAGERY DESCRIPTION:

Students will have an opportunity of spending a day with a local municipality worker in charge of town cleanup and repairs. They will travel by truck and will visit different locations where cleaning up is needed. Students will get an idea of the ways people litter and the disrespect some people have for their town.

IMAGERY EXERCISE:

Sit comfortably and relax

See yourself in the front seat of a large garbage truck

Feel the bumps as you ride down the stree

Your first stop is a recreation park

Look around and notice the litter

See the types of things people have scattered

Listen to the town worker describe how people continue to litter

Next stop is a shopping mall

Look onto the streets

Notice the types of litter lying around

Continue your trip watching people litter as you ride around

Notice the different places people litter

Look at these different places

As you ride around town, notice the different kinds of containers the town has placed to dispose of garbage

Look at their shapes and size

See youself talking to the worker about ways to keep the streets clean

Listen to his suggestions

See yourself returning from your visit

When I count to ten, open your eyes

VARIATIONS:

Students might spend a day with other town departments: fire, police, etc. They could see themselves interviewing people about littering.

FOLLOW UP ACTIVITIES:

Develop a campaign to keep our streets clean. Use charts, TV and radio commercials. Make signs and posters. Take pictures of the different types of garbage dirtying up our streets. Write a newspaper article entitled, "Help Keep Our Streets Clean."

ACADEMIC AREA: SOCIAL STUDIES   GRADE LEVEL: Primary/Intermed.

SUB-AREA: Our Neighborhood   SUGGESTED TIME: 15 mins.

IMAGERY DESCRIPTION:

Students will see themselves living right in the heart of a large, present day American city. They will experience all the characteristics, life styles and problems found in big city living. They will travel through the city seeing the various types of buildings, structures, streets and bridges.

IMAGERY EXERCISE:

Sit comfortably and relax
You are living in an apartment house in the middle of a large city
See yourself waking up
As you lie quietly, listen to the city noise
See yourself coming outside and going for a walk
Watch the people going in and out of stores
Smell the black asphalt as they fill the hole
Listen to the cars, buses, and speeding taxi cabs
Sit for a moment and listen to some people talking
Look up and notice the hazy smoggy sky and tall buildings
See yourself getting onto a large bus
Notice all the exciting things happening
Next see yourself taking a subway train
See yourself jumping onto the train as the doors jam shut
See youself standing, holding onto a pole in the center of the train
Feel the train begin to move
Feel the bouncing and shaking
Hear the wheels screeching
Notice the lights flickering
See yourself rushing to get off the train
See yourself walking out of the subway and returning home
See yourself coming back to your classroom
When I count to ten, open your eyes

VARIATIONS:

Students could pretend that they are a bus or car that is traveling through the city. They could interview people, having them describe what it is like to live in a big city.

FOLLOW UP ACTIVITIES:

Write a short story entitled "A Visit To The City." Draw a mural depicting life in a big city. Make a list of all the fun things to do in a large city. Select a large city, then collect some research on its population and growth rate.

ACADEMIC AREA: SOCIAL STUDIES   GRADE LEVEL: Primary

SUB-AREA: Our Neighborhood   SUGGESTED TIME: 15 mins.

IMAGERY DESCRIPTION:

Students will experience being a movie camera that flies. Students will control the camera and have it take moving pictures of all the neat places in town where children can have fun. The students will decide what pictures to take and how to take the pictures.

IMAGERY EXERCISE:

Sit comfortably and relax
See yourself as a large movie camera
Notice all your switches and controls
Get ready to visit all the fun places in and around your town
When you get to a fun place press a button and begin taking pictures*
These pictures will be your own movie
Create music to go with your pictures
Zoom in close with your big camera lens
See colors and many different things
Notice how clear everything is
Listen to people having fun
Zoom in on different people
Watch people waving to you as you slowly film the crowd
Feel yourself being loaded with more film
Continue taking beautiful, clear pictures
See a video game center
Take pictures of children playing
See the excitement on their faces
Look up and take some beautiful pictures of the sky
Feel the enjoyment of having visited all your favorite fun places
See yourself returning to the classroom
When I count to ten, open your eyes

VARIATIONS:

They could make movies of other things or events. They could interview people while the movie is being made. They could create a car or motorcycle chase scene through the city.

FOLLOW UP ACTIVITIES:

Write a script for your movie. Make some pictures illustrating all the fun things to do. Make a list of all the fun places. Design a town and have lots of fun places included.

NO: 123   **TITLE:**   RULES FOR SAFETY

ACADEMIC AREA: SOCIAL STUDIES   **GRADE LEVEL:** Primary/Intermed.

SUB-AREA: Our Neighborhood   **SUGGESTED TIME:** 10 mins.

IMAGERY DESCRIPTION:

Students will see themselves as a   Safety Elf   who has come into someone's home to tell them all the different ways to practice safety. The Safety Elf will talk with boys and girls about the rules they must follow in their homes in order to avoid danger. The Safety Elf will point out different parts of the house where safety is needed.

IMAGERY EXERCISE:

Sit comfortably and relax
See yourself as a Safety Elf who teaches boys and girls how to avoid danger
Look at how you are dressed
See yourself flying down to a house where several children are waiting for you
See the children sitting there
See yourself sitting with the children
Begin to tell the children all the things they must do to avoid danger
Take the children to different rooms
Tell them about the things they must not do
See the children asking questions about safety
See yourself using colorful charts to show the children how to practice safety
See yourself giving the children little safety booklets
Read one of the booklets to the children
See yourself returning to the classroom
When I count to ten, open your eyes

VARIATIONS:

The   Safety Elf   could talk to students about safety in school, out of doors, in a car, etc. They could become a safety device and talk to children about how they could be used.

FOLLOW UP ACTIVITIES:

Make a list of rules for safety in the home. Make several illustrations which describe safety procedures used in the home. Write a newspaper story about the importance of safety in the home.

NO:**124**   TITLE: THE IMPORTANCE OF BANKING

ACADEMIC AREA: SOCIAL STUDIES   GRADE LEVEL: Primary

SUB-AREA: Our Neighborhood   SUGGESTED TIME: 10 mins.

IMAGERY DESCRIPTION:

Students will explore the different reasons for using our community banks. Through an actual survey consisting of asking bank customers their reasons for visiting the bank, students will gain knowledge and insight into the role of a bank. They will learn how important the bank is to our daily, personal and professional lives.

IMAGERY EXERCISE:

Sit comfortably and relax
See yourself in the front of your local bank
See yourself asking people questions just before they enter the bank
Listen to them discuss the reasons they bank
See yourself talking to an old person
Listen to how this person uses the bank
See a young person coming
Ask this person why she is going to the bank
Go inside the bank and walk up to a bank window
Stay there a few minutes
Listen to all the sounds
Watch what is happening
Feel free to ask the bank clerk questions
See people writing checks
Notice the different colors of the checks
See people carrying money
You're inside the bank's giant safe
See hundreds of safety deposit boxes
Look inside some of them
See what people put in there besides money
Look closely
See yourself returning to the classroom
When I count to ten, open your eyes

VARIATIONS:

Students could actually work as a bank clerk. They could be a pen observing what the pen is being used for. They could be a safety deposit box.

FOLLOW UP ACTIVITIES:

Make a chart showing the different reasons people use banks. Create your own bank in class with fake money, checks, loans, etc. Invite a bank clerk to come into class for a lecture.

NO:**125**   TITLE: THE LAWS WE LIVE BY

ACADEMIC AREA: SOCIAL STUDIES   GRADE LEVEL: Primary
SUB-AREA: Our Neighborhood   SUGGESTED TIME: 10 mins.

IMAGERY DESCRIPTION:

Students will have an opportunity to spend a day with a police officer in your town. They will ride in a police car, visit different places and listen to the police officer   describe specific laws relating to that location of town. Students will learn about many different types of laws and the way these laws are enforced.

IMAGERY EXERCISE:

Sit comfortably and relax
See yourself meet a nice police officer outside the police station
Notice how the officer is dressed
See yourself getting into the police car
Feel the car move as your tour of the town begins
Listen to the police person describe all the different road safety signs
Look closely at the signs as you drive
See yourself passing a school
Notice a sign indicating maximum speed for that street
Notice the different places where people *can* park and *cannot* park
Notice the signs concerning littering
Listen to the police officer telling you about other laws*
See yourself getting out of the police car and asking shoppers what they think about the laws of the town
Listen to what they have to say*
See yourself arriving back at the police station
See yourself returning to the classroom
When I count to ten, open your eyes

VARIATIONS:

Students could interview other professionals, e.g., firemen, public service, transportation workers, asking them about rules and regulations. They could see themselves as a police officer, a judge, a lawyer, etc.

FOLLOW UP ACTIVITIES:

Make pictures of different warning signs that motorists use while driving. Create your own town and make all the necessary laws. Survey some people in your community and find out what they think about the laws of their town.

NO:**126**   TITLE: THE LIFE OF A BULLDOZER

ACADEMIC AREA: SOCIAL STUDIES   GRADE LEVEL: Primary
SUB-AREA: Our Neighborhood   SUGGESTED TIME: 15 mins.

IMAGERY DESCRIPTION:

New construction is an important part of community development. This activity will take students through a day in the life of a large construction vehicle, a Bulldozer. They will become the Bulldozer and experience the variety of things the huge machine must do each day.

IMAGERY EXERCISE:

> **Sit comfortably and relax**
> **See yourself becoming a big yellow bulldozer**
> **Look at all your parts**
> **Lift your big plow**
> **Hear your big noisy engine**
> **See yourself puffing smoke as you climb onto a flat trailer truck**
> **Feel yourself backing off the truck onto the ground**
> **Notice the workmen telling you what to do first**
> **See yourself pushing dirt and rocks**
> **Feel the dirt going over your tracks**
> **Hear the gunning of the engine as the dirt becomes harder to push**
> **Continue to see yourself helping the workmen**
> **See yourself coming to a new place, a new job**
> **Again listen to the men instruct you as to what they want done in this area**
> **See all the colors of dirt, rocks, trees**
> **Feel the gasoline being put into you**
> **As you finish your last job feel the workmen washing you with a big hose**
> **Feel the water shooting at you**
> **Feel the dirt washing down you**
> **Feel the satifaction of having done a good day's work**
> **See yourself returning to the classroom**
> **When I count to ten, open your eyes**

VARIATIONS:

Students could become other types of equipment used in construction. They could see themselves as a construction worker. They could see themselves building a house, bridge, road, etc.

FOLLOW UP ACTIVITIES:

Draw an actual Bulldozer. Write a story entitled, "A Day In The Life Of A Bulldozer." Make a chart of the various kinds of jobs a bulldozer can do. Interview and observe a person who drives bulldozers.

ACADEMIC AREA: SOCIAL STUDIES   GRADE LEVEL: Intermediate

SUB-AREA: World History   SUGGESTED TIME: 15 mins.

IMAGERY DESCRIPTION:

Students will experience the methods used by persons dealing in the travel business during the 1700's. They will observe the various advertising strategies as well as listen to the announcements of new and exciting round trips to America. Students will learn about the various passenger accommodations, costs and length of trips.

IMAGERY EXERCISE:

Sit comfortably and relax

See yourself visitng a small building which houses a local travel agent in London, England, around 1750

As you walk into this building, notice the walls, windows, ceilings

Notice the posters hanging on the walls

Notice how the travel agent is dressed

Listen to the travel agent discussing the details of a new round trip to America

See yourself talking with the travel agent and asking her all about her business

Ask her anything you want

Listen to the travel agent discussing plans for future travel

Listen to her describe the different advertising strategies

Notice a family entering the store

Hear them asking the travel agent for information about a trip to America

Listen to the details as the travel agent speaks

Pick up a ticket

Look what is printed on the ticket

See yourself saying goodbye to the travel agent

See yourself returning to the classroom

When I count to ten, open your eyes

VARIATIONS:

Students could interview someone who has traveled extensively during that period of time. Students could go on a trip and experience the way travelers were treated.

FOLLOW UP ACTIVITIES:

Design a series of posters announcing trips to America during the 1700's. Write a trip itinerary specifying the daily activities for passengers. Research and report actual travel experiences during the 1700's. Create a photo album of someone's experiences.

NO: 128   **TITLE:** A DESERT CARAVAN

ACADEMIC AREA: SOCIAL STUDIES   **GRADE LEVEL:** Primary/Intermed.

SUB-AREA: World Geography   **SUGGESTED TIME:** 15 mins.

IMAGERY DESCRIPTION:

Students will experience what it is like to travel across an Arabian desert by camel. They will participate in a caravan and experience various changes in weather conditions. They will experience the intense heat and the importance of having plenty of water.

IMAGERY EXERCISE:

Sit comfortably and relax
You are at a desert city getting ready to mount a camel and join
a caravan
Notice how you are dressed
See people putting things onto the camel's back
See the color and the shape of the camel
Smell the odor as you stand there
Feel yourself climbing up onto the camel
Notice how high off the ground you are
Feel the hot, hot desert sun...the moisture in your hands
Feel the swaying as the camel walks in deep sand
See the desert hills and valleys...feel the hotness of the air
See the caravan stopping at a water hole
Feel the coolness of the water as you drink
Feel it running down your face and chest
Feel the wind starting to blow
See yourself covering your face with a cloth to protect your eyes
See it getting harder and harder to see
Listen to the swirling winds
Taste the dryness in your mouth
Feel the caravan moving slowly
See the sand storm ending...see a little town up ahead
See yourself returning to the classroom
When I count to ten, open your eyes

VARIATIONS:

Students could experience a caravan as a camel carrying heavy bags or people. Students could see themselves living in the desert and observing many caravans passing through.

FOLLOW UP ACTIVITIES:

Write a story about your desert caravan. Draw pictures capturing the details of hot, dry desert. Make the type of clothing you would wear on a desert caravan. Make a desert oasis with sand, water holes, camels, tents, etc.

NO:129   **TITLE:**   A VISIT TO A MEDIEVAL CASTLE

ACADEMIC AREA: SOCIAL STUDIES   **GRADE LEVEL:** Intermediate

SUB-AREA: World History   **SUGGESTED TIME:**   15 mins.

IMAGERY DESCRIPTION:

Students will explore the characteristics of castles in the Middle Ages. They will focus on the life style of the people who lived there and observe various traditions which took place, such as "The Making of a Knight." Students will learn about the construction and artistic features of castles and how castles were used as defense fortresses.

IMAGERY EXERCISE:

Sit comfortably and relax
See yourself walking across a draw bridge and into a large castle
Observe people moving about in the courtyard
Notice how people are dressed
See yourself walking into the great hall
Look closely at the thick gray stone walls and the high ceilings
Feel the dampness and cold
Notice the dark lighting
See the lady of the castle having dinner with family and friends
Listen to them telling stories and laughing
Smell the air
Allow yourself to visit the rest of the castle
See people gathered in a large room for the "Making of a Knight"
See a young squire bowing in front of the King and being touched by a sword
Listen to the words of the King
Watch the new knight putting on his armor
Notice the high towers
See the knights guarding the castle
See yourself crossing the draw bridge and leaving the castle
See yourself returning to class
When I count to ten, open your eyes

VARIATIONS:

Students could visit other medieval locations or places (a medieval house, a battle or siege on a castle, knights hunting, a great feast, musicians, games and events).

FOLLOW UP ACTIVITIES:

Recreate what you saw during your visit to the castle (draw, illustrate, design or build) certain features of castle life. Role play the "Making of a Knight." Have the class make medieval period clothing and create a short play. Illustrate how people lived within castles.

TITLE: A TRADING POST IN THE CANADIAN WILDERNESS--
                                    1880

ACADEMIC AREA: SOCIAL STUDIES   **GRADE LEVEL:** Primary/Intermed.

SUB-AREA: World History   **SUGGESTED TIME:**   20 mins.

IMAGERY DESCRIPTION:

Students will see themselves working in a trading post in the
Northern Canadian wilderness sometime around the 1880's. They
will observe articles being traded such as animal furs, skins,
meat, fish, gold, beads, clothing. They will talk with trappers,
fishermen, etc.

IMAGERY EXERCISE:

Sit comfortably and relax
See yourself inside a trading post in the Northern Canadian wil-
derness about 1880
Look around and notice the walls and ceiling
See a big fire roaring
See the person in charge of the post
Notice the goods and articles on shelves and tables
Look carefully at these items
See a trapper coming in from the cold
Look at his cold face...see snow and ice in his hair
Listen to the owner greet this person
Look at the large sack the man is carrying
Watch him dump the contents on the table
Listen to him describe his experiences
Listen to the trapper and the owner begin to trade
Observe the trading very carefully
Smell the coffee brewing over the fire
See it getting darker
Notice the large candles being lit
Sit on a bear skin rug next to the fire
Notice the owner's rifles and pistols
See yourself tired and about to fall asleep
See yourself returning to the classroom
When I count to ten, open your eyes

VARIATIONS:

Students could see themselves as a hunter who is visiting the
trading post. Students could see themselves building a trading
post, selecting items to be traded and sold.

FOLLOW UP ACTIVITIES:

Write a short story about the adventures of a hunter in the
Canadian wilderness. Draw a picture of an authentic trading
post. Construct a model of a trading post. Write to the
Canadian Historical Society for literature on trading post operations during the late 1800's.

ACADEMIC AREA: SOCIAL STUDIES   **GRADE LEVEL:** Primary/Intermed.

SUB-AREA: World History   **SUGGESTED TIME:** 20 mins.

IMAGERY DESCRIPTION:

This activity will provide the learner an opportunity to observe an ancient marketplace. They will see the variety of goods being sold as well as things people could eat. They will listen to the merchants advertising their products and making sales.

IMAGERY EXERCISE:

Sit comfortably and relax
See yourself visiting an ancient marketplace, Rome, 366 BC
It's a Saturday and the marketplace is packed
Listen to the sounds...see all the people
Notice how everyone is dressed
Feel the warmth of the summer sun
See yourself counting your spending money
Walk around for a while...enjoy everything
See youself purchasing something you like
Look at those people playing musical instruments
Listen to the merchants selling their products
Notice the different items they are selling
See yourself talking to other young people
See yourself going to a place where people eat
Buy something to eat...taste the food you have bought
Smell the air
Enjoy the sights as you walk freely throughout the marketplace
See yourself purchasing new clothing
See the colors...feel the texture
See different animals at the marketplace
Look around again and see all the different items being sold
Look at the detail of some of the items
See yourself coming back to the classroom
When I count to ten, open your eyes

VARIATIONS:

Students could visit other locations in the city of Rome (houses, government buildings, meeting places, sports' fields or stadiums, etc.). You could have the students participate in any number of normal daily activities.

FOLLOW UP ACTIVITIES:

Create an ancient marketplace with shops, musicians, merchants, etc. Have students make ancient looking products using clay, wheatpaste, etc.,which could be sold at market day. Write a paper comparing an ancient marketplace with a present-day mall.

ACADEMIC AREA: SOCIAL STUDIES   GRADE LEVEL: Primary/Intermed.
SUB-AREA: World History   SUGGESTED TIME: 25 mins.

IMAGERY DESCRIPTION:

Students will understand and appreciate the difficulties and hardships of travel during the early 1600's. They will become aware of the importance of cooperation and effort that people must give in order to make such a great trip.

IMAGERY EXERCISE:

Sit comfortably and relax
See yourself boarding the Mayflower
Notice the facial expressions of people saying goodbye
Feel the ship moving slowly out into the ocean
See yourself taking a tour of the ship
Visit the ship's storage area and see the food supply
Read the labels on the boxes of food
Listen to the Mayflower captain talking to his crew
Smell the salt in the air
Feel the ship rocking as the wind begins to roar
See large waves ripping against the ship's deck
Notice the people below deck talking in fear
It has been one month since you left port
Look again at all the passengers
Listen to what they are saying
Experience the trip for another three weeks
Hear the joyous shouts of the sighting of land
Notice the peoples' reactions as they leave for shore during a cold December day
Feel the relief of having arrived safely
See yourself coming back to class
When I count to ten, open your eyes

VARIATIONS:

Any voyage, expedition or long journey could be imagined by the students. Decide what aspects of the trip you wish to call to their attention.

FOLLOW UP ACTIVITIES:

Write a trip diary. Write a play. Draw a picture of the Mayflower. Interview a Mayflower passenger and write a newspaper article.

NO:**135**   TITLE: THE ROMAN SENATE: A DEBATE OVER TAXATION

ACADEMIC AREA: SOCIAL STUDIES   **GRADE LEVEL:** Intermediate

SUB-AREA: World History   **SUGGESTED TIME:**   15 mins.

IMAGERY DESCRIPTION:

Students will observe a real-life Roman Senate meeting during 440 BC. While sitting in the spectators' section of the Senate Hall, students will listen to the various representatives discussing their philosophies concerning the raising of funds through taxing the people. Among the speakers will be farmers, clergymen, and politicians.

IMAGERY EXERCISE:

Sit comfortably and relax
See yourself entering a large Senate Hall
Notice all the Senators sitting in rows
Look at their clothes
Notice the walls, ceiling, floor
Feel the wooden benches you are sitting on
Listen to the head of the Senate discussing the agenda for the day
Listen to the first speaker, a politician discussing the reason for needing more money
Next listen to a poor farmer telling how difficult it is to give more money
Listen to the Senators argue
Hear them shout
See the chairperson trying to maintain order
Hear one Senator describing a possible revolt by the poor if they are further taxed
Feel the dampness of this cold, poorly-lighted hall
See the Senators getting ready to vote
Listen to the chairperson read the results
Look at the expressions on the faces of the Senators as they leave the hall
See yourself returning to the classroom
When I count to ten, open your eyes

VARIATIONS:

Have students experience a Senate debate over other issues, e.g., declaring war, plans for building a new city, a trial, etc.
Have students interview a Senator, listening to a description of the role and function of the Senate.

FOLLOW UP ACTIVITIES:

Organize a classroom debate over the issue of taxation. Research and report actual proceedings of Senate activity. Draw a mural of what the Senate Hall looked liked.

ACADEMIC AREA: SOCIAL STUDIES   **GRADE LEVEL:** Primary/Intermed.

SUB-AREA: United States   **SUGGESTED TIME:** 10 Mins.

IMAGERY DESCRIPTION:
     Students imagine themselves visiting and taking a tour of the White House, Pennsylvania Ave., Washington, D.C.

IMAGERY EXERCISE:

Sit comfortably and relax
You are getting off a bus in front of the White House
It is a clear and beautiful day
Notice two U.S. Marine guards standing by the door
See yourself walking into the Great East Room
Notice the white and gold decorations and huge crystal chandeliers
Look around and see beautiful paintings of former Presidents
You are now in the Green Room
Notice the hand-tufted rug featuring the President's seal
Next...see yourself standing by a huge fireplace in the State Dining Room
Notice the long and wide dining room table with more than thirty chairs
Above you on the wall is a painting of Abraham Lincoln
Continue your tour, visiting other rooms*
Your last stop is the White House family theater
See the President watching a movie and snacking
See yourself returning to the classroom
When I count to ten, open your eyes

VARIATIONS:

     Students could take imaginary visits to other famous and historical buildings located in the United States or in other parts of the world.

FOLLOW UP ACTIVITIES:

     Draw pictures of the various rooms visited while touring the White House. Create your own executive mansion where a president could live. Research facts about the White House.

ACADEMIC AREA: SOCIAL STUDIES   **GRADE LEVEL:** Primary/Intermediate

SUB-AREA: United States   **SUGGESTED TIME:** 15 mins.

IMAGERY DESCRIPTION:

Students are taken by helicopter for an exciting adventure through mid-western farm country. Many aspects of farming will be pointed out along the way. Students will see both small and large farms with many different types of livestock and produce. They will talk to farmers and learn what it's like to live on a farm.

IMAGERY EXERCISE:

Sit comfortably and relax

See yourself boarding a turbo-jet helicopter with other students

for a visit to some exciting farm country

Feel yourself taking off...lifting, lifting up...up

In a few minutes you will be over some beautiful farm land

Feel the helicopter slowing up as you come in for a close look at

your large farm

Notice the vegetation growing in the fields*

See the cows and horses grazing peacefully

Notice the different buildings on the farm...look closely

See a tractor plowing a new area of land

See the farmer waving as you fly by

You're off again to another area

See the clouds go by as you speed through the air

You are going to stop at the next farm

Now see yourself climbing onto a horse-drawn wagon

Take a nice visit through the farm

Stopping whenever you like...enjoy*

Smell the odor in the air...watch the animals grazing

See yourself talking to some children who live on the farm

Listen to what they're saying

See yourself saying goodbye

Now begin to return to the classroom

When I count to ten, open your eyes

VARIATIONS:

Students could spend several days on a farm doing many different things. Students could actually spend a day working on the farm. Certain types of farms could be designated for visiting.

FOLLOW UP ACTIVITIES:

Write a story about your travels. Construct a farm. Research some aspect of farming that excites you. Write to the National Farming Association for literature about the farming industry.

ACADEMIC AREA: SOCIAL STUDIES   GRADE LEVEL: Intermediate

SUB-AREA: United States   SUGGESTED TIME: 15 mins.

IMAGERY DESCRIPTION:

The activity will take students to different geographical locations throughout the United States. They will observe the construction of homes and buildings and the adjustments made by engineers in order to build safely in different land areas.

IMAGERY EXERCISE:

Sit comfortably and relax

You're boarding a private plane which is going to take you to many places

You're part of a construction engineering team inspecting various building sites

Feel the plane taking off up...up

See yourself arriving at your first site, a marshy, wet low-land area

See yourself walking on this marshy land

Listen to the other engineers discussing how they would have to build here*

See yourself arriving near a high mountainous area

See yourself inspecting a rocky, hilly area

Observe construction that is going on presently

Continue to see yourself visiting other different land surface areas

Notice the variations in construction*

Listen to the explosion as rock is being dynamited

See yourself holding your ears

Watch large poles being hammered into the earth

Observe other construction means being used for adapting to the different land surfaces

See yourself returning to the classroom

When I count to ten, open your eyes

VARIATIONS:

Students could participate in the construction of a certain type of building in one type of land surface area. They could become a piece of equipment or machinery. They could film different stages of construction.

FOLLOW UP ACTIVITIES:

Draw or diagram different land surface areas depicting the variations for building foundations. Construct an actual model of a building, built in a marshy area, highlighting the various engineering strategies for building the foundation. Interview a construction engineer.

ACADEMIC AREA: SOCIAL STUDIES   **GRADE LEVEL:** Intermediate

SUB-AREA: United States   **SUGGESTED TIME:**   20 mins.

IMAGERY DESCRIPTION:

Fishing is a big industry in some parts of the United States. Whole villages or towns are engaged in the catching and selling of fish. Students will have an opportunity to visit a small fishing village, talk with the people and watch their daily involvement in the fishing business.

IMAGERY EXERCISE:

> Sit comfortably and relax
> See yourself arriving at a small fishing village located along the Pacific Ocean
> Take a walk through town and notice all the fish markets*
> Smell the ocean air and the fish smell everywhere
> See yourself walking down to the boat dock where many boats are leaving for their daily catch
> Talk to some of the fishermen
> Listen to what they have to say*
> Feel the ocean breeze
> Listen to the sounds of the boats' engines
> See yourself boarding a commercial fishing boat
> Enjoy the trip and observe how the fish are being caught and brought on deck*
> See yourself coming into port with a boatload of large tuna fish
> Notice all the fishermen who have already begun to sell to market owners
> Notice the many different kinds of fish
> Notice how men, women and children are all involved in the selling of their catch
> Observe the sun slowly setting as this beautiful day comes to an end
> See yourself slowly returning to class
> When I count to ten, open your eyes

VARIATIONS:

Students could visit other villages or towns where the focus may be on a different industry, e.g., coal mining town, the timber lands of the northwest, a cotton-growing town of the south, etc.

FOLLOW UP ACTIVITIES:

Draw a large mural showing the different aspects of life in a fishing village. Send away for literature about a commercial fishing village. Illustrate the different techniques used in catching fish.

NO:**140**   TITLE: MAKING A TEPEE OF BUFFALO SKIN

ACADEMIC AREA: SOCIAL STUDIES   GRADE LEVEL: Primary/Intermed.

SUB-AREA: United States   SUGGESTED TIME: 10 mins.

IMAGERY DESCRIPTION:

Students will watch an actual, real-life tepee being constructed by a group of Navajo Indians. They will learn how the Indians used buffalo skin to make the tepee durable and warm for the winter months. They will observe the tools and material used in constructing the tepee.

IMAGERY EXERCISE:

Sit comfortably and relax
You are at a Navajo Indian Village in Western United States about the year 1800
See yourself watching several Indians spreading out
Watch others finish the wooden frame of a large tepee
See the wooden branches being tied and fastened together
Observe how the buffalo skin is being fastened to the frame*
Feel the heat of the blazing sun
Taste the dryness in the air
Smell the smoke coming from an open fire
Continue to watch the skin being wrapped around the tepee*
See yourself looking inside the tepee
Notice the small opening at the top
Feel the dried buffalo skin
Notice its texture
Feel its strength
Notice its different shades
Smell the skin
Observe the Indians decorating the tepee with colored paint and ornaments
Notice how clearly you can see the finished tepee
Take several photos of the completed tepee
See yourself slowly returning to the class
When I count to ten, open your eyes

VARIATIONS:

Have students observe the Indians using buffalo skins for other purposes. Have students observe the Indians' preparing the buffalo for cooking. See themselves actually building the tepee.

FOLLOW UP ACTIVITIES:

Make a colorful drawing of a real-life tepee. Construct a model. Prepare an oral report on how the Indians used various animal skin for building, for weapons, for games. Build an actual tepee in class.

NO:141   **TITLE:**   NATIONAL POLITICAL CONVENTION

ACADEMIC AREA: SOCIAL STUDIES   **GRADE LEVEL:** Intermediate

SUB-AREA: United States   **SUGGESTED TIME:**   10 mins.

IMAGERY DESCRIPTION:

Students will have an opportunity of participating at a National Political Convention. They will listen to major issues being debated as well as hear the voices of many, many people supporting their political beliefs. They will become aware of the role that media plays at a National Convention.

IMAGERY EXERCISE:

> Sit comfortably and relax
> See yourself walking into a huge Convention Hall
> Look at the gigantic signs and decorations
> Hear the yelling and screaming of thousands of political supporters
> See all the colors
> See yourself being escorted to where your state representatives are seated
> Listen to a speech being made by a famous senator in support of a new presidential candidate*
> Watch the convention chairperson taking a vote, state by state
> Listen to the representatives discussing how they will vote
> Hear the confusion
> Notice how everyone is dressed
> Notice all the cameras and TV personnel
> Listen to someone being interviewed
> Notice how this person is dressed
> Listen to the excitement of the conversation
> See yourself talking to a representative from another state
> Feel the excitement as people begin to clap
> Feel the vibrations in the floor
> See everyone starting to leave the huge hall
> See yourself leaving and returning to the classroom
> When I count to ten, open your eyes

VARIATIONS:

Students could attend other types of political meetings or rallies. Students could work as a TV commentator interviewing various politicians. Students could be a member of a political convention planning committee.

FOLLOW UP ACTIVITIES:

Write a newspaper story on important aspects of the convention. Have the class stage a political rally. Have the class design slogans, banners, and other political paraphernalia.

TITLE: PEOPLE AND NATURAL RESOURCES: A TRIP DOWN
THE MISSISSIPPI RIVER

ACADEMIC AREA: SOCIAL STUDIES   GRADE LEVEL: Primary/Intermed.

SUB-AREA: United States   SUGGESTED TIME: 15 mins.

IMAGERY DESCRIPTION:

Students will discover the variety of natural resources found in
different geographical locations. They will observe people
working at and developing these natural resources. They will
understand and appreciate the value of a large river and its relationship to the conservation of natural resources.

IMAGERY EXERCISE:

> **Sit comfortably and relax**
> **See yourself on a boat journeying down the Mississippi River**
> **Notice what a beautiful day it is**
> **Feel the warmth of the sun**
> **Feel a slight, gentle breeze blowing on your face**
> **Notice the trees and wild life all around you**
> **As your trip continues...notice people working and developing**
> **our natural resources***
> **See these resources being transported along the river**
> **Notice boats loaded with natural resources**
> **See yourself stopping at a coal mining town**
> **Notice the equipment**
> **See huge piles of coal**
> **Next see yourself talking to workers at a lumber mill**
> **Hear the noise of wood being cut by giant machines**
> **Take a deep breath...feel the freshness in the air**
> **Notice all the fishing boats**
> **See yourself stopping at a large city where people are trading**
> **and selling products made of natural resources**
> **See yourself talking with these trade merchants***
> **See your journey coming to an end**
> **See yourself coming back to class**
> **When I count to ten, open your eyes**

VARIATIONS:

Students could visit any number of places where natural resources
are being developed. They could spend their entire time visiting
a lumber mill, coal yard, fishing village, etc. They·could work
in one of these natural resource producing facilities.

FOLLOW UP ACTIVITIES:

Write a story about your trip down the Mississippi. Research
how the development of natural resources along the Mississippi
has changed during the last 100 years. Make a chart indicating
the location of different natural resources along the Mississippi.
Create a short story or poem.

NO:143   TITLE: THE MAKING OF THE CONSTITUTION--1787

ACADEMIC AREA: SOCIAL STUDIES   **GRADE LEVEL:** Intermediate
SUB-AREA: United States   **SUGGESTED TIME:**   20 mins.

IMAGERY DESCRIPTION:

Students will participate in the long, tedious task of developing
the constitution of the United States. They will be a delegate
responsible for developing a new plan of government for the
United States. After many months of debating and arguing, the
delegates were ready to agree and sign this famous document.

IMAGERY EXERCISE:

Sit comfortably and relax
You are a delegate who has just arrived at Independence Hall,
Philadelphia, Pennsylvania, 1787
Your job over the next few months is to develop and adopt a new
constitution of government for the United States of America
You're sitting in a hall with many delegates
See the chairperson of this convention, General George
Washington, on a platform in front
Feel the dampness as you sit on wooden benches
Listen to other delegates argue and shout
See yourself standing up and recommending three things for the
new constitution*
Hear the applause from the other delegates as you make some
favorable suggestions
Return to the Hall after several weeks of re-writing parts of the
new constitution
Notice how weary and tired the delegates are
It's September 17, 1787; after months of work, the delegates are
signing approval for the new constitution of the United States
See the relief and joy on their faces
You're shaking hands, congratulating delegates
You're leaving the Convention Hall, feeling proud
See yourself returning to the classroom
When I count to ten, open your eyes

VARIATIONS:

Students could have seen themselves as a newspaper reporter
writing headlines each day. Students could have acted as pro-
testors demonstrating for a certain cause they wished to have
included in the new document.

FOLLOW UP ACTIVITIES:

Write a newspaper story highlighting this famous event. Write
a script which could be a play dramatizing the process that the
delegates had to go through. Draw a mural of the Convention
Hall where the constitution was signed on September 17, 1787.

NO:**144**   TITLE: THE MAKING OF SUGAR

ACADEMIC AREA: SOCIAL STUDIES   GRADE LEVEL: Intermediate
SUB-AREA: United States   SUGGESTED TIME: 10 mins.

IMAGERY DESCRIPTION:

Students will learn the process of making sugar. They will follow a process that begins with the harvesting of cane stalks and
concludes in the packaging of pure sugar. Each step will be
vividly experienced as if the students were actually there.

IMAGERY EXERCISE:

Sit comfortably and relax
You're on a sugar cane field in Louisiana
Feel the warmth and moistness of the climate
Notice the rich soil
See a big power-driver machine cutting cane stalks
Listen to the slashing of the stalks*
Watch trucks carrying the cane stalks to the processing plants
See yourself walking into a large factory
Watch the leaves being cut from the cane stalks and burned
Smell the odor in the air
Observe the cane being crushed in great machines*
Hear the noise
Notice the crushed cane moving along large conveyor belts as it
flows into huge tanks with heating juices
Listen to the cane after it has mixed with the juice traveling inside
a long circular tube on the way to a purifying tank
See the large tanks cooking the liquid sugar
Finally, observe the liquid sugar being spun at tremendous speed
Listen to the loud noise
Watch workmen loading huge bags of raw sugar in preparation
for shipping
See yourself leaving the factory and returning to class
When I count to ten, open your eyes

VARIATIONS:

Students could experience any number of products being harvested
and processed. Students could focus in on one particular aspect
of the processing and actually see themselves physically involved.
They could become one of the machines.

FOLLOW UP ACTIVITIES:

Have a student locate and bring in a sugarcane stalk. Describe
the various steps used in processing pure sugar. Make colorful
charts illustrating each of the required steps in processing
sugar. Write to a sugar manufacturer and obtain information and
material that describes the process. Create a bulletin board.

ACADEMIC AREA: SOCIAL STUDIES   GRADE LEVEL: Primary/Intermed.

SUB-AREA: United States   SUGGESTED TIME: 30 mins.

IMAGERY DESCRIPTION:

Students will experience what it was like to travel across country in a covered wagon. They will learn about the difficulties and hardships that faced the pioneers. They will see roads being made, rivers being crossed and pathways being cut. An adventurous trip filled with excitement and realism.

IMAGERY EXERCISE:

> **Sit comfortably and relax**
> **You're leaving on a wagon train in 1843**
> **See all the other people loading the wagons**
> **Notice what people are bringing**
> **Listen to the excitement in people's voices**
> **Listen to the wagon-train master describing the trip and giving the rules***
> **See many wagons beginning to move**
> **Feel the hot sun and the dryness of the climate**
> **Listen to the noise as the wagons roll**
> **See yourself sitting on the wagon**
> **Feel the bumps and rocking**
> **Smell the horses as they begin to sweat**
> **See yourself traveling for three days***
> **You're sitting around a campfire singing songs**
> **Smell the odor of rabbits being roasted**
> **Hear the hand clapping and foot stomping**
> **See yourself sleeping at night...hear the distant screams of coyotes**
> **See yourself continuing and moving on, day after day***
> **See the wagon train coming down the mountain and into a California town**
> **Hear the cheers as the wagon train reaches its destination**
> **See yourself returning to the classroom**
> **When I count to ten, open your eyes**

VARIATIONS:

Students could experience other types of early travel, e.g., horseback, train, etc. Students could experience the wagon train from the Indian's perspective. They could be a cook, a scout or wagon-train master.

FOLLOW UP ACTIVITIES:

Write a diary of the trip. Draw some of the beautiful sites viewed during the trip. Build a model of an authentic wagon coach. Research an actual account of a wagon train during the mid-1800's.

7. Imagery in Art

ACADEMIC AREA: ART   GRADE LEVEL: Intermediate
SUB-AREA :   SUGGESTED TIME: 10 mins.

IMAGERY DESCRIPTION:

Students will use a recording by an artist of their choice to
design an appropriate cover to an album that features that song.
Students may use headphones to listen before the Imagery Exercise and later while they work to reinforce ideas.

IMAGERY EXERCISE:

Sit comfortably and relax
Hear your favorite group performing their best recording
**Observe each member, noting clothing...hairstyle...facial expres-
sions...and movements***
Scan the surroundings where the performance is taking place
Listen to the message of the song*
See the singer in a different setting*
Scan the scene for other people...and background details
Put yourself into the song
Feel the rhythm and flow of the tune
Become the music
See your newly created album cover
Look closely at the design*
See everyone looking at it with pleasure
See yourself returning to the classroom
When I count to ten, open your eyes

VARIATIONS:

One recording may be chosen for the entire group to use.

FOLLOW UP ACTIVITIES:

Design an album cover depicting one or a combination of images
you saw during the Exercise.

ACADEMIC AREA: ART   **GRADE LEVEL:** Intermediate

SUB-AREA: **SUGGESTED TIME:**   10 mins.

IMAGERY DESCRIPTION:

Students will create a cartoon character using themselves as the model.

IMAGERY EXERCISE:

Sit comfortably and relax
Look closely at yourself
Put yourself in an unusual place
Scan the setting of this place*
Hear yourself talking in a funny voice
Say some funny things that make you laugh
Watch as you do something impossible
Put an animal's body with your face
Feel your fur...change it to feathers
Listen as you make animal noises
Climb out of that body
Give yourself a different one*
Focus on your face
Look at each feature
Emphasize each part of it, one-by-one
Make your eye color deeper...different
Make your mouth strange
Change your nose
Look at the cartoon you, you have created*
See yourself returning to the classroom
When I count to ten, open your eyes

VARIATIONS:

Other directions could be given which include different animals, places, colors, activities, detail, etc.

FOLLOW UP ACTIVITIES:

Draw a comic strip featuring the cartoon you. Create a script for the cartoon you.

NO:**148**   TITLE: CLOWN FACE

ACADEMIC AREA: ART   GRADE LEVEL: Primary/Intermed.

SUB-AREA: SUGGESTED TIME: 10 mins.

IMAGERY DESCRIPTION:

Students will watch their own faces being made up as clowns, then recreate that face.

IMAGERY EXERCISE:

> **Sit comfortably and relax**
> **See your own face**
> **Notice your hair...forehead...eyes...nose...mouth...chin**
> **Watch makeup being taken out of a bag**
> **Notice the different colors**
> **Smell them as the containers are opened**
> **Observe your face being transformed to one of a clown***
> **Feel your mouth as it's painted**
> **Examine what was done to your eyes...and nose**
> **Move like a clown in a circus***
> **Hear laughter...and applause**
> **Bow**
> **Look into the mirror**
> **Study your face one last time***
> **Now see your makeup disappearing**
> **See yourself returning to the classroom**
> **When I count to ten, open your eyes**

VARIATIONS:

Other face types could be created, e.g., monster, cartoon characters, TV stars, etc.

FOLLOW UP ACTIVITIES:

Draw or make a model of the face you imaged. Write a description of what your face looked like.

NO:**149**   TITLE: CLAY

ACADEMIC AREA: ART   GRADE LEVEL: Primary/Intermed.
SUB-AREA: SUGGESTED TIME: 5 mins.

IMAGERY DESCRIPTION:

Students will take a ride in an imaginary vehicle and recreate
it with clay.

IMAGERY EXERCISE:

Sit comfortably and relax
See yourself leaving school to go home
Notice an unusual vehicle waiting to take you
See its color and shape
Move closer to examine it
Count the windows...look inside
Observe the controls
Find a way to get in
Get comfortable and make it start
Listen to the engine
Test the controls
Find out what each one makes it do
Take an exciting ride
See yourself approaching home
Park...get out
Inspect the vehicle one last time from the top...bottom...and
sides*
Watch as the vehicle shrinks slowly, becoming a lump of clay
See yourself returning to the classroom
When I count to ten, open your eyes

VARIATIONS:

Vehicle may be built with other materials such as boxes, food
containers, wood shapes, etc.

FOLLOW UP ACTIVITIES:

Write a description of your vehicle. Make your imaged vehicle
out of clay.

170

ACADEMIC AREA: ART   GRADE LEVEL: Primary/Intermed.

SUB-AREA: SUGGESTED TIME: 15 mins.

IMAGERY DESCRIPTION:

After a marionette has been made, students will see themselves creating a scene or stage for it to perform on. You can use a simple cardboard box with a large rectangle cut from the top, to start with.

IMAGERY EXERCISE:

Sit comfortably and relax
Listen to the curtains rising, showing a beautifully decorated stage for your puppet*
Watch your puppet moving.,..performing for a large audience
Listen to the applause
Scan the scene for details
Notice the different colors and shapes painted on the left wall…the back wall…and the wall on the right*
Look at the floor
See the footlights along the outer edge
See other important details
Examine the ceiling
See the opening for the marionette's strings
See yourself controlling the puppet from above
Notice the placement of props on the set
Scan the scene one more time
See something you didn't notice before*
See yourself returning to the classroom
When I count to ten, open your eyes

VARIATIONS:

Have the stage be a movie or TV set including cameras and technical equipment.

FOLLOW UP ACTIVITIES:

Build the scenery and stage.

ACADEMIC AREA: ART   **GRADE LEVEL:** Primary/Intermediate
SUB-AREA: **SUGGESTED TIME:**   10 mins.

IMAGERY DESCRIPTION:

Students will actually become finger paint and experience themselves being used to create a picture.

IMAGERY EXERCISE:

> **Sit comfortably and relax**
> **Feel yourself inside a jar of finger paint**
> **Listen as the lid is unscrewed**
> **Feel a hand scooping you out and plopping you onto the wet, slippery paper**
> **See your color against the white background**
> **Smell your odor**
> **Feel yourself gliding back and forth...making swirls...first little...then bigger***
> **Become thick and thin as you are poked and smoothed by giant fingers**
> **Hear the splatter of another color against you**
> **See yourself as mixing and blending with it***
> **Watch as a picture begins to form***
> **Hear the water washing the messy hands while you admire yourself---a completed picture**
> **See yourself returning to the classroom**
> **When I count to ten, open your eyes**

VARIATIONS:

Water color, acrylic or oil paint may be used for older students.

FOLLOW UP ACTIVITIES:

Finger paint.

NO:**152**   TITLE: GEOMETRIC DESIGN

ACADEMIC AREA: ART   GRADE LEVEL: Intermediate
SUB-AREA: SUGGESTED TIME: 10 mins.

IMAGERY DESCRIPTION:

Students will use the computer to experiment with geometric designs (circles and lines).

IMAGERY EXERCISE:

Sit comfortably and relax
See yourself before a large screen
Feel the control buttons as you settle into the comfortable chair
Program the special computer for "Geometric Design"
Put a line on the screen...give it color
Add more like it...move them as you wish*
Change their brightness and colors...have them disappear and come back
Make them 3-dimensional
Give them sound
Listen while they move...fast...and slowly
Clear the screen
Push "circles"
Watch them appear
Change their sizes...give them depth*
Have them move
Give them sound
Put a spotlight on them...watch their shadows
Make them blink...overlap...split apart...and fit together differently
Add lines...have them do something with the circles
Create designs
See yourself returning to the classroom
When I count to ten, open your eyes

VARIATIONS:

Students could create the designs in the sky, on a movie screen, on large paper, using different objects, etc.

FOLLOW UP ACTIVITIES:

Using only a ruler, create designs in one color, then many. Using only a compass, create designs in one color, then many. Combine compass and ruler to create designs. Research the use of designs.

ACADEMIC AREA: ART   **GRADE LEVEL:**   Primary/Intermed.

SUB-AREA: **SUGGESTED TIME:**   5 mins.

IMAGERY DESCRIPTION:

Students will experience finger painting from different and unusual aspects.

IMAGERY EXERCISE:

> **Sit comfortably and relax**
> **See yourself ready to begin finger painting**
> **Feel the wet paper and soft paint with your fingers**
> **Give it color**
> **Swirl it around...poke it...spread it**
> **Give it a flavor...taste it**
> **Make shapes with it**
> **Change the color**
> **Give it a fragrance...smell it**
> **Climb into it**
> **Skate on it**
> **Slide on it...roll in it...play***
> **Make footprints in it**
> **Give it sound...listen to it...move with it***
> **Pile it up...add another color**
> **Drink some...splash in it...blow bubbles with it**
> **Do something with it that you know will be fun**
> **See a teacher enjoying it too**
> **See yourself returning to the classroom**
> **When I count to ten, open your eyes**

VARIATIONS:

Instrumental music may be played during the Exercise.

FOLLOW UP ACTIVITIES:

Write about the imagery experience. Set it to music. Draw a picture showing the imagery experience.

NO: **154**   TITLE: GLOBS TO GOBLINS

ACADEMIC AREA: ART   GRADE LEVEL: Primary/Intermed.

SUB-AREA: SUGGESTED TIME: 10 mins.

IMAGERY DESCRIPTION:

Students will become clay and experience being shaped into
many things.

IMAGERY EXERCISE:

>   Sit comfortably and relax
>   See yourself as a compact glob of clay
>   Notice your color and texture
>   Notice how you smell
>   Scan your surroundings
>   Feel a warm hand begin to soften you
>   Become a ball...a snake...and a new shape
>   Feel yourself being rolled...poked...pounded to flatness
>   Become something funny*
>   Become something strange
>   Feel stretched...and squashed
>   Become a flower*
>   Smell your fragrance...feel your texture
>   Change into an animal...move and make a noise
>   Become something big and scary
>   Feel your power*
>   Note how you move and sound
>   Listen to yourself
>   Feel your skin texture
>   Examine your feet...make a footprint
>   Watch as your face gets stranger
>   Change your color and shape
>   See yourself returning to the classroom
>   When I count to ten, open your eyes

VARIATIONS:

The clay could be changed into many different things. Other
senses could be included.

FOLLOW UP ACTIVITIES:

Experiment with clay, building some of the figures seen during
the Exercise. Create a slide show with tape, taking photos
of a clay figure, manipulated to show continuous action and
movement. Write about Planet Clay.

ACADEMIC AREA: ART   **GRADE LEVEL:** Intermediate

SUB-AREA: **SUGGESTED TIME:**   5 mins.

IMAGERY DESCRIPTION:

Students will make greeting cards with messages after becoming one.

IMAGERY EXERCISE:

Sit comfortably and relax
Put yourself inside a flat, dark envelope
Feel the weight of other mail on top of you
Hear yourself hitting the inside of a mailbox and the door shutting
Smell the mailbox odors
Feel the relief at being pulled out
Watch the face of the one receiving you
Study the eyes...mouth...and other features
Scan your surroundings
Feel the fingers opening you
Hear a voice reading your message aloud
Look at your picture...on the front and inside...noting every detail
Smell your paper smell
Shout your message one more time
Close yourself
See yourself returning to the classroom
When I count to ten, open your eyes

VARIATIONS:

Students could be different types of cards or letters. They could be signs, posters, etc. They could be 3-D, have sound, photographs, etc.

FOLLOW UP ACTIVITIES:

Create an actual postcard. Make copies and send to friends.

NO:**156**   TITLE: INSIDE THE WIRE

ACADEMIC AREA: ART   GRADE LEVEL: Intermediate

SUB-AREA: SUGGESTED TIME: 15 mins.

IMAGERY DESCRIPTION:

Students will capture themselves in wire doing something they do well or would like to be able to do well.

IMAGERY EXERCISE:

Sit comfortably and relax
See yourself in front of a large movie screen with a control box
Start the movie
Watch yourself doing something you enjoy doing
Listen to what they say about your special skill
Feel the pride swelling inside of you as you perform to the best of your ability*
You are truly wonderful doing this
Freeze the action and examine your concentration
Note it in your face...neck...shoulders*
Zoom in for a close-up of each part
Observe how each body part is positioned...feet...ankles...calves...knees...and so on
Back up the film, frame-by-frame...study it...slowly run it forward
Feel the muscle tension and flow of movement
Stop the action again
Watch as your stilled pose slowly becomes a wire sculpture*
Watch your wire body move
Give it color...sound...lighting*
Now see yourself returning to the classroom
When I count to ten, open your eyes

VARIATIONS:

Other sculpting mediums could be substituted.

FOLLOW UP ACTIVITIES:

Create a wire sculpture or mobile of yourself in action. Make a movie or slide presentation of the Imagery Exercise. Write about becoming made of wire and how you solved the problem.

NO: **157** TITLE: LETTERING

ACADEMIC AREA: ART GRADE LEVEL: Intermediate

SUB-AREA: SUGGESTED TIME: 10 mins.

IMAGERY DESCRIPTION:

Students will use the computer to experiment with lettering.

IMAGERY EXERCISE:

>**Sit comfortably and relax**
>**See yourself before a large screen**
>**Feel the control buttons as you settle into the comfortable chair**
>**Program the special computer for lettering**
>**Put your name on the screen**
>**Give it color...change its size**
>**Make it look shiny and new**
>**Watch it grow old**
>**Feel it moving to music***
>**Make it melt...and freeze**
>**Have it become an animal**
>**Watch the animal tracks spelling something***
>**Make a loud word, give it sound**
>**Listen to it**
>**Make a rough word...give it a colorful design**
>**Feel it**
>**Make a word that can stretch...and grow**
>**Write an emotion**
>**Give it color and sound**
>**Make it smell good...enjoy the fragrance**
>**Watch it change...and rot**
>**Continue to make words with different lettering***
>**See yourself returning to the classroom**
>**When I count to ten, open your eyes**

VARIATIONS:

Students could select different lettering to be used in creating signs, posters, etc. They could become letters and feel themselves being used in graphic designing.

FOLLOW UP ACTIVITIES:

Make words whose letters show their meaning (e.g., "hot" in flames). Write animal names depicting some trait of the lettering ("rabbit" in fur, or tracks). Use objects to form letters of a word ("brush" written with brushes overlapping).

NO:**158**   TITLE: MONSTER BUILDING

ACADEMIC AREA: ART   GRADE LEVEL: Primary/Intermed.
SUB-AREA: SUGGESTED TIME: 10 mins.

IMAGERY DESCRIPTION:

Students will watch rocks come together to form living "monsters", then attempt to build them. Begin by giving each student several rocks to "play with."

IMAGERY EXERCISE:

Sit comfortably and relax
See rocks on a table in front of you
Feel their shapes
See their colors
Examine their dents, bumps and textures
See them fitting together to make a body*
Watch them move
First slowly...then faster
See it from every angle and direction
Give color to the head...body...arms...and legs
Focus on the face
Observe its expressions
Listen to it speak*
Ask its name
Watch it do something unusual and interesting*
See your monster going away
See yourself returning to the classroom
When I count to ten, open your eyes

VARIATIONS:

Use other materials such as wood scraps, styrofoam, wire, leaves, etc., or one larger piece of driftwood.

FOLLOW UP ACTIVITIES:

Recreate the "monster" from the Exercise, using rocks of various shapes and sizes, clay, paint, etc.

NO: **159**   TITLE: MOSAIC

ACADEMIC AREA: ART   GRADE LEVEL: Intermediate
SUB-AREA: SUGGESTED TIME: 5 mins.

IMAGERY DESCRIPTION:

Students will create a mosaic design or picture by first focusing on one tile and slowly moving away to see the entire piece.

IMAGERY EXERCISE:

> Sit comfortably and relax
> See yourself standing on a large, flat, tile square
> Feel its smoothness
> See its color
> Examine the grout around the edges
> Slowly rise above the tile
> Look down at the shapes that surround the square
> Observe how they fit together
> Continue to rise, seeing more tiles of many shapes
> Watch as a pattern of colors and shapes begins to form
> See the individual tiles blend together
> Move farther away still
> Feel yourself drifting high above as you scan the picture below
> Try to focus on your starting square
> See it again as part of the larger scene
> See yourself returning to the classroom
> When I count to ten, open your eyes

VARIATIONS:

Students could be taking pictures of mosaic designs or they could see themselves constructing such designs.

FOLLOW UP ACTIVITIES:

Make a mosaic using cut paper, bits of colored material, plastic or tiles.

NO:**160**   **TITLE:**   PATTERNS

ACADEMIC AREA: ART   **GRADE LEVEL:** Primary/Intermed.

SUB-AREA: **SUGGESTED TIME:** 5 mins.

IMAGERY DESCRIPTION:

Students will experiment with different shapes, colors and textures to create patterns.

IMAGERY EXERCISE:

> **Sit comfortably and relax**
> **See yourself in front of a large computer**
> **Program a familiar object to appear on the wide video screen**
> **See the object**
> **Notice its color...and shape**
> **Change its color**
> **Fill the space with more of these objects***
> **Move them around...take some away...let them overlap**
> **Enlarge some**
> **Add an object with a different shape**
> **Make lots of these**
> **See the objects mix...and change***
> **Clear the screen**
> **Smell a fruit flavor...put it on the screen**
> **Split it...make more and more of them**
> **Make them flash...give them sound**
> **Stretch them...stack them**
> **Clear the screen**
> **Hear an animal**
> **Put it on the screen**
> **Change its color**
> **Make a lot of them***
> **See yourself returning to the classroom**
> **When I count to ten, open your eyes**

VARIATIONS:

Use different senses. Use different objects, things or events.

FOLLOW UP ACTIVITIES:

Have the students recreate designs for printmaking. Have students use seeds, cereal, etc., to create patterns. Use finger paints to create patterns. Trace shapes of leaves or simple objects to create patterns.

ACADEMIC AREA: ART   GRADE LEVEL: Intermediate

SUB-AREA: SUGGESTED TIME: 10 mins.

IMAGERY DESCRIPTION:

Students will use a slogan as the starting point for creating a poster. This could be a contest slogan (e.g., Prevent Forest Fires) or a quote they or the teacher chose to use.

IMAGERY EXERCISE:

> **Sit comfortably and relax**
> **See yourself sitting on a large white cloud**
> **Feel yourself getting comfortable**
> **Hear words being spoken by a soft voice**
> **Listen as it repeats the phrase***
> **Write the words in the sky**
> **Ride the cloud to a scene that depicts what the words are saying***
> **Make it silly**
> **Make it serious**
> **Scan the view**
> **See the words with the view**
> **Give the scene action and music**
> **Feel the mood of the words**
> **Observe any characters in the scene**
> **Watch them...listen to them...talk to them**
> **See the scene change when the words are not listened to**
> **Return to the words and the first scene**
> **Put a frame around it**
> **Write them again**
> **Settle back on your cloud**
> **Admire your work***
> **See yourself returning to the classroom**
> **When I count to ten, open your eyes**

VARIATIONS:

Reverse the process, giving a picture as the stimulus and have students create the words they feel are appropriate.

FOLLOW UP ACTIVITIES:

Design an ad slogan with pictures. Design a poster with words of wisdom. Create the scene to be photographed and blown up for a poster. Paint a mural for a school spirit slogan.

NO:**162**   TITLE: PHOTOGRAPHY

ACADEMIC AREA: ART   GRADE LEVEL: Intermediate
SUB-AREA: SUGGESTED TIME: 10 mins.

IMAGERY DESCRIPTION:

Using a slide, photo, magazine or newspaper picture, students will "back up" in time and create the events that preceded the ones in the picture. Students should examine the photo before the Exercise begins.

IMAGERY EXERCISE:

Sit comfortably and relax
See the photo projected onto a large screen with the words "The End" written across it
Scan the scene for details...people's faces...actions...and background*
You are the projectionist
Feel yourself flipping a switch to reverse the film
Watch as characters move in reverse, slowly*
Continue the process until you reach a new scene
Run the scene forward to the end without sound*
Focus on the actors
Reverse it once more
This time quickly
Add sound (music and voices) and again watch the ending of the movie*
See the final scene again with "The End" written across it
See yourself returning to the classroom
When I count to ten, open your eyes

VARIATIONS:

Have students repeat the Exercise, this time moving forward.

FOLLOW UP ACTIVITIES:

Draw the scene that preceded the photo used. Recreate the scene that preceded the photo and capture it on film. Make a short movie, using the photo as the final scene.

ACADEMIC AREA: ART

GRADE LEVEL: Primary/Intermed.

SUB-AREA:

SUGGESTED TIME: 15 mins.

IMAGERY DESCRIPTION:

Students will see themselves building marionettes from step one to completion. It is suggested that if the project takes several sessions, children be encouraged to refocus on the steps to be done for each session before beginning the actual work.

IMAGERY EXERCISE:

Sit comfortably and relax
You're at a large work table
Scan your supplies...wooden shapes...string...paint...cloth...and other items you'll need
Feel the sandpaper as you smooth each piece of wood
Place the wood shapes to form a
body...head...arms...legs...feet...hands
Feel yourself attaching the strings to the control rods for each body part
Focus on the blank face
Put in details...eyes...nose...mouth...ears..hair*
Smell the paint as you select a color for the
feet...legs...hands...arms
Watch as you create a costume for this character, noting colors...textures...and designs*
Listen to the click of the feet on the floor as you control the finished puppet
Make it walk...sit...lie down
Have it do something interesting*
See yourself returning to the classroom
When I count to ten, open your eyes

VARIATIONS:

Activity may be altered to the specific type of puppet to be made (e.g., paper bag, sock, finger, etc.).

FOLLOW UP ACTIVITIES:

Build the marionette.

NO:**164**   TITLE: PUPPETRY: NO STRINGS ATTACHED

ACADEMIC AREA: ART   GRADE LEVEL: Primary/Intermed.

SUB-AREA: SUGGESTED TIME: 10 mins.

IMAGERY DESCRIPTION:

Students will experience being a puppet--how they are constructed and controlled.

IMAGERY EXERCISE:

Sit comfortably and relax
See yourself lying on a large work table
Scan the materials around you...paints...glue...brushes...and
other things
You look different
You're all apart
Hear the door open as the puppet builder comes in
Feel your face being painted
Smell the glue as your hair is attached
Listen to the puppet builder whistling a tune wh   tting you
together
Watch a wonderful costume being made for you
Note its color...texture...and special trimmings*
See the puppet builder's smile as finishing touches are added
Feel yourself being lifted
Watch your mouth move
Say something to the puppet-maker
Feel the puppeteer moving your head...legs...arms
See yourself doing something all puppets can do*
See yourself returning to the classroom
When I count to ten, open your eyes

VARIATIONS:

Students could see themselves being constructed into a specific
type of puppet, e.g., one of the muppets.

FOLLOW UP ACTIVITIES:

Act out being a puppet while dressed in a special costume. Build
a puppet that resembles you as you appeared in the Imagery Exercise. Use a friend as the model for making a puppet, or "decorate" them as a puppet. Research the many types of puppets.

NO: **165**   TITLE: SELF-COLLAGE

ACADEMIC AREA: ART   GRADE LEVEL: Primary/Intermed.

SUB-AREA: SUGGESTED TIME: 10 mins.

IMAGERY DESCRIPTION:

Students will look at all aspects of their lives to gain ideas
for a collage about themselves.

IMAGERY EXERCISE:

Sit comfortably and relax
See yourself in front of a large canvas
Examine the magical brush in your hand
Use it to guide ideas as they flow from you to the canvas
Paint three words that tell about you
Create the scene of your favorite place*
Hear music you enjoy
Paint it*
Show yourself in action...doing what you do best
See yourself doing something you want to learn to do
Add it to the masterpiece*
Use color and shapes to show your moods
Paint a plane writing a message for the world to see
See yourself returning to the classroom
When I count to ten, open your eyes

VARIATIONS:

A video game could be used for creating the self-collage.
Specific instructions could be given classifying things to
include.

FOLLOW UP ACTIVITIES:

Cut pictures and words that describe you and arrange them to
make a collage. Add actual photos, ticket stubs, etc. Give
the entire collage a significant shape (e.g., capital letter,
car, etc.) that relates to your uniqueness.

NO:**166**   TITLE: SELF-TIME LINE

ACADEMIC AREA: ART   GRADE LEVEL: Intermediate

SUB-AREA :   SUGGESTED TIME: 15 mins.

IMAGERY DESCRIPTION:

Students will watch their life from infancy to senior citizen in order to create a time line about themselves.

IMAGERY EXERCISE:

Sit comfortably and relax
See yourself in front of a large screen
Watch as your name appears on the screen
You are today's feature
Hear yourself crying as a newborn baby
Watch your parents as they care for you
See yourself growing...learning to sit...crawl...walk...and talk*
Watch as you play with your favorite toy
See your first classroom...and teacher
Scan the room...find your best friend*
Watch yourself thinking...and learning
Observe yourself as you look today
See yourself doing something you love to do*
Feel your arms and legs growing longer
Listen to your voice changing
See yourself in high school
Talk with your friends
Drive your first car...go somewhere special*
Become something you've wanted to be*
See yourself growing old
See other things in this older life
See yourself coming back to happy you
See yourself returning to the classroom
When I count to ten, open your eyes

VARIATIONS:

Primary may cut pictures and paste rather than draw onto time line.

FOLLOW UP ACTIVITIES:

Using paper from adding machine rolls, design a time line of your life, drawing scenes for each important event. Write an autobiography and design a cover that's you. Make a movie.
Focus only on events of the Past, Present, or Future, writing down ideas for each before going on.

NO:**167**   TITLE: TEXTURES

ACADEMIC AREA: ART   GRADE LEVEL: Primary/Intermed.

SUB-AREA: SUGGESTED TIME: 15 mins.

IMAGERY DESCRIPTION:

Students will explore various objects to understand textures
more fully.

IMAGERY EXERCISE:

> **Sit comfortably and relax**
> **See yourself on a beach**
> **Feel the sand under your feet**
> **Lie on your belly**
> **Examine the sand closely**
> **Look at each grain***
> **Pick up a shell...touch the ridges**
> **Note its color and size**
> **Catch a feather in the air**
> **Touch it to your cheek**
> **See its pattern**
> **Move the sand with your toe**
> **Write something**
> **Make it lumpy...and smooth***
> **Drag a giant piece of seaweed from the water**
> **Feel its weight...slide your fingers over it**
> **Smell it**
> **See green squares on a turtle's back**
> **Feel them**
> **Listen to your hands rubbing over them**
> **Pick up a fish skeleton...note its color**
> **Play a tune on the ribs***
> **See yourself returning to the classroom**
> **When I count to ten, open your eyes**

VARIATIONS:

Other objects could be substituted. Different senses could
be included.

FOLLOW UP ACTIVITIES:

Make collages with different textured objects. Take a familiar
object and give it a new texture, making it from something else
(e.g., rough feathers cut from sandpaper). Use objects with different textures to make prints and designs or "rub" over them
for varied effects.

188

NO:**168**   TITLE: TEXTURE TRANSFORMATION

ACADEMIC AREA: ART   GRADE LEVEL: Primary/Intermed.

SUB-AREA: SUGGESTED TIME: 5 mins.

IMAGERY DESCRIPTION:

Students will watch themselves replacing their facial parts with objects of different textures and colors.

IMAGERY EXERCISE:

> Sit comfortably and relax
> See yourself before a magical mirror
> Study the features of your face
> Focus on your hair
> Feel it...smell it
> Watch it become a food of the same color
> Feel it...smell it
> Move to your eyes
> Make them larger...and smaller
> Close them...watch them become flowers as they begin to bloom
> Feel them...smell them
> Make them change size...and color
> Examine your skin
> Feel it
> Cover it with fur...feathers...scales
> Change it to something that feels nice
> Give it color
> Feel your teeth
> Make them soft...change their color
> Replace them with something rough
> Change other parts of you
> See yourself returning to the classroom
> When I count to ten, open your eyes

VARIATIONS:

Use other objects for creature texture transformation. Suggest what objects to be used and the senses involved.

FOLLOW UP ACTIVITIES:

Use a paper plate and glue on objects of different textures to form a face (e.g., grains, materials, nature objects). Use only color and shading to create the appearance of unusual textures in a face.

189

ACADEMIC AREA: ART   GRADE LEVEL: Intermediate

SUB-AREA: SUGGESTED TIME: 10 mins.

IMAGERY DESCRIPTION:

Students will enter a painting to gain new insight into the subject. Students should be familiar with the painting before the Imagery Exercise.

MATERIALS NEEDED: Copy of <u>Arrangement in Grey and Black</u>, Whistler, J. M.

IMAGERY EXERCISE:

> **Sit comfortably and relax**
> **See yourself in a large art museum**
> **Feel the smooth marble pillars as you pass them**
> **Hear the echo of footsteps on the stone floors...and the whispers of other visitors**
> **Stop in front of "Whistler's Mother"**
> **Examine the different shades of gray and black**
> **Study the painting behind her**
> **Notice how she's dressed and where she is**
> **Scan the room for details and odors**
> **Look into her eyes**
> **Feel her mood**
> **Give color to the drapes, change the design**
> **Speak to her**
> **Watch her lips as you hear her answer**
> **Tell her about something that's happened in history since she was painted***
> **Watch her reaction to the news**
> **Change the chair to a rocking chair**
> **Listen to it rock**
> **Ask her advice about something***
> **See yourself returning to the classroom**
> **When I count to ten, open your eyes**

VARIATIONS:

Use any painting to be studied. Word the Exercise to emphasize key aspects of the painting.

FOLLOW UP ACTIVITIES:

Write and act out an interview with Whistler's mother. Draw what you think Whistler's father or Whistler looks like. Research other works of the same time period and compare them to this.

NO: **170**　　　　TITLE:　　WIRE HEROES

ACADEMIC AREA:　　ART　　　　　　GRADE LEVEL:　Intermediate

SUB-AREA:　　　　　　　　　　　　SUGGESTED TIME:　　10 mins.

IMAGERY DESCRIPTION:

Students will transform a favorite hero to wire sculpture.

IMAGERY EXERCISE:

Sit comfortably and relax
See yourself in a large crowd of people
Feel them pushing past you to find their seats
See yourself sitting in the best seat with the best view
Hear the applause for your favorite performer
As the action begins, examine the clothing...and surroundings*
Enjoy the perfect performance as it appears before you*
You are in control
Whenever you wish, you may freeze the action
Test your power
Stop it at an interesting pose*
Get out of your seat
Go up to the frozen performer and begin wrapping wire around the entire body*
Begin at the feet
Describe each part as you wrap
Listen to yourself talking
See the balance and symmetry of the pose
Watch the end of the performance in wire*
See yourself returning to the classroom
When I count to ten, open your eyes

VARIATIONS:

You may wish to confine the theme only to one area (e.g., athletics). Other sculpting mediums may be substituted.

FOLLOW UP ACTIVITIES:

Create or draw your wire sculpture, giving it a special name.

8. Imagery in Music

NO:**171**   TITLE: A VISIT TO THE ORIENT

ACADEMIC AREA: MUSIC   GRADE LEVEL: Primary/Intermed.

SUB-AREA: SUGGESTED TIME: 15 mins.

IMAGERY DESCRIPTION:

Students will visit Japan and sightsee while listening to appropriate music.

MATERIALS NEEDED: Recording of Japanese music.

IMAGERY EXERCISE:

Sit comfortably and relax
See yourself sitting in a large plane
Look out the window as you approach a group of islands sur-
rounded by clear blue water
(BEGIN TAPE, PLAY SOFTLY)
Scan the view...seeing cities, harbors...and mountains*
See a fishing boat
Notice how the people are dressed
Feel the plane landing smoothly
Listen to Japanese being spoken*
Study the strange figures on the signs
Ask someone how to get to the Kabuki Theater
Watch dancers with painted faces perform in bright costumes*
Smell the rice and fish as you pass a restaurant
See customers sitting on straw mats using chopsticks
See the dragon-like figures painted on the sides of buildings
Feel the silk kimono as a woman passes
Continue to visit other exciting places*
See yourself returning to the classroom
When I count to ten, open your eyes

VARIATIONS:

Use any culture(Italy, Ancient Egypt) exposing students to that style of music.

FOLLOW UP ACTIVITIES:

Write haiku poetry for some of the images experienced. Learn origami (Japanese art of paper folding). Draw a map of your tour. Make a travel log for others who may wish to visit Japan. Research Japanese music.

NO:**172**   TITLE: DISAPPEARING ORCHESTRA

ACADEMIC AREA: MUSIC   GRADE LEVEL: Primary/Intermed.

SUB-AREA: SUGGESTED TIME: 10 mins.

IMAGERY DESCRIPTION:

Students will watch an orchestra as it changes from people to food, colors, animals, etc. You may want to shift each scene with the natural musical transitions of the piece.

MATERIALS NEEDED: Orchestra music.

IMAGERY EXERCISE:

Sit comfortably and relax
See yourself in a large concert hall
Scan the stage, noting each musician and instrument
Hear the conductor tap his baton
(BEGIN TAPE)
Watch the people of the orchestra play their instruments*
See them fade until all that's left are the instruments -- playing by themselves
Smell sweetness as flowers appear where the instruments were*
Give them colors
Listen as they play...hear their sounds
Watch them grow
See them change to different fruits*
Taste them
Change their colors
Put them underwater
Listen to them move
Have them become animals...move them
Listen to them communicate with each other
Make them something strange
Feel the music drawing to an end
(TAPE ENDS)
See yourself returning to the classroom
When I count to ten, open your eyes

VARIATIONS:

Substitute key words (animal, flower, fruit, underwater) with other desired phrases (e.g., insects, vegetables, etc.). Eliminate key words and allow students to create their own changes.

FOLLOW UP ACTIVITIES:

Write a poem about the changes. Draw an orchestra in sections, choosing appropriate substitutes for each instrument (e.g., all types and sizes of animals).

NO:**173** TITLE: FANTASY ORCHESTRA

ACADEMIC AREA: MUSIC GRADE LEVEL: Primary/Intermed.

SUB-AREA: SUGGESTED TIME: 10 mins.

IMAGERY DESCRIPTION:

Students will become a conductor of a large orchestra. They will lead the orchestra in playing different types of music.

IMAGERY EXERCISE:

> Sit comfortably and relax
> You're a conductor of a large orchestra
> See yourself walking out on the stage
> Hear the applause*
> Pick up your baton and raise it
> Begin with your first selection of music*
> See all the musicians
> Hear the beautiful music
> Hear different sections of the orchestra playing
> Have the orchestra change their dress
> Begin a new piece of music*
> Have someone play a solo
> Take the orchestra somewhere*
> Lead the orchestra in another song
> See the orchestra playing inside a 747 plane*
> See the orchestra returning
> See yourself returning to the classroom
> When I count to ten, open your eyes

VARIATIONS:

Certain selections of music could be suggested to the students.

FOLLOW UP ACTIVITIES:

Draw a picture of your fantasy orchestra. Write a new piece of music for your orchestra. Research the role of the conductor.

NO:**174**   TITLE: FUTURISTIC MUSIC

ACADEMIC AREA: MUSIC   GRADE LEVEL: Primary/Intermed.

SUB-AREA: SUGGESTED TIME: 10 mins.

IMAGERY DESCRIPTION:

Students will create music of the future. They will incorporate advanced technology in communications and electronics.

IMAGERY EXERCISE:

> Sit comfortably and relax
> You're in a music studio, year 2000
> Look around...notice all the modern equipment
> See a large special-effects control unit
> Try some of these special effects
> Try your automatic voicing unit
> See yourself sitting in front of all the control switches now ready to create music
> Begin exploring and combining*
> Hear this new music blasting*
> Feel the vibrations
> See the active dials on your control panel for volume, pitch, tone, balance*
> See your new music being recorded*
> Give it a special name
> See yourself driving home and hearing it on your own car radio
> See yourself returning to the classroom
> When I count to ten, open your eyes

VARIATIONS:

Create a certain type of music, e.g., instrumental, vocal, etc. Develop music for space travel or undersea exploration. Create music for the different planets.

FOLLOW UP ACTIVITIES:

Describe the special effects imaged in the Exercise. Predict what music will be like in the year 2000. Develop a time line showing the different styles of music (past to present).

ACADEMIC AREA: MUSIC   GRADE LEVEL: Intermediate

SUB-AREA: SUGGESTED TIME: 15 mins.

IMAGERY DESCRIPTION:

Students will see themselves emerging from an instrument as the music is being played.

MATERIALS NEEDED: Recording of guitar music.

IMAGERY EXERCISE:

>Sit comfortably and relax
>See yourself inside a guitar
>Smell the wood...and metal
>You are music about to be played
>Listen to your silence
>Examine yourself
>Look out through the opening
>*(BEGIN TAPE)*
>Feel yourself emerging into the air*
>Give yourself color...texture
>Ride the air waves
>Travel wherever you wish*
>Feel yourself going high...and low
>Become shoes that move to the beat
>Feel yourself dancing
>Look at the prints you're leaving behind*
>See a rhythm pattern being created with colors...and shapes
>*(TAPE NEARS END)*
>Feel yourself fading to silence
>Come to rest somewhere pleasant
>See yourself returning to the classroom
>When I count to ten, open your eyes

VARIATIONS:

Substitute the word "guitar" with any other instrument desired.

FOLLOW UP ACTIVITIES:

Draw the rhythm pattern that was seen. Compare it to a musical score. Write about an adventure while riding the sound waves.

ACADEMIC AREA: MUSIC   GRADE LEVEL: Primary/Intermed.

SUB-AREA: SUGGESTED TIME: 10 mins.

IMAGERY DESCRIPTION:

Students will listen to an instrument as it is being played as if they were the instrument. A recording for this Exercise could be Carlo Maria von Weber's Concerto for Clarinet and Orchestra, No. 1 in F Minor (1811), Columbia Records, Harcourt Brace Jovanovich, Music in Today's Classroom.

IMAGERY EXERCISE:

Sit comfortably and relax
See yourself as a clarinet
Feel your damp reed being adjusted in the mouthpiece
Notice how long and smooth and dark you are
Count your keys
Examine your tallness
Feel hands gently lifting you, fingers testing all of your keys*
(BEGIN RECORDING, ALLOW TO PLAY TO END WHILE READING PHRASES BELOW)
Listen to your sound as warm breath passes through you
Watch the music notes in front of you
Feel your sounds rise and fall as the notes do on the lines of the staff*
Smell the sweaty stickiness of the fingers as they play you
Observe other clarinets moving in harmony with you*
Feel yourself coming to the end of the piece
(TAPE ENDS)
Drop back onto the lap of your owner
Hear the applause
See yourself returning to the classroom
When I count to ten, open your eyes

VARIATIONS:

Become another instrument being studied and use appropriate recording. Actually play clarinet for students during Exercise.

FOLLOW UP ACTIVITIES:

Find other musical records featuring this instrument. Compare the music styles and time periods. Interview a clarinet player. Write a story and be the instrument of a famous performer.

NO:**177**   TITLE: I'M A VIOLINIST!

ACADEMIC AREA: MUSIC   GRADE LEVEL: Intermediate
SUB-AREA: SUGGESTED TIME: 15 mins.

IMAGERY DESCRIPTION:

After studying the violin, students will be musicians in the string section of the orchestra during a performance.

MATERIALS NEEDED: Recording of orchestra music featuring strings.

IMAGERY EXERCISE:

Sit comfortably and relax
You're sitting on stage in the string section of the orchestra
Note your formal dress
Pluck each string with your finger
Listen to the tone...see each one vibrate
Adjust the pegs to change the tone
Tighten the bow...loosen up your wrist...first slowly and lightly...then with more pressure
Scan the rest of the orchestra, noting where each group is positioned...strings...woodwinds...brass...percussion*
Raise your violin at the conductor's signal
Feel the tightness under your chin
(BEGIN TAPE, PLAY TO END, READING THE FOLLOWING PHRASES WHEN APPROPRIATE)
See the notes on your music sheet
Hear the vibration of your instrument*
Hear the blending of instruments*
Feel the mood of the music
Observe all of the bows moving with yours*
(TAPE ENDS)
See yourself returning to the classroom
When I count to ten, open your eyes

VARIATIONS:

Be part of a rock, jazz, etc., band. Do not play a tape, rather have students create music mentally or hear a melody they have been practicing as members of the school orchestra or band.

FOLLOW UP ACTIVITIES:

Draw a diagram of orchestra positions. Keep a current events notebook of large orchestras throughout the country. Compare and contrast a school orchestra to a symphony orchestra.

NO:178   **TITLE:**   LIVE AT THE CONCERT HALL

ACADEMIC AREA: MUSIC   **GRADE LEVEL:** Intermediate

SUB-AREA: **SUGGESTED TIME:**   10 mins.

IMAGERY DESCRIPTION:

Students will listen to a vocal music selection as if experiencing a live performance. Emphasis will be on the message of the lyrics. A recording of a live performance can be used.

MATERIALS NEEDED: Vocal recording.

IMAGERY EXERCISE:

Sit comfortably and relax
You're entering a large concert hall
Locate your seat
Feel the audience focus attention on the closed curtain and dim lights
Study the curtain as it slowly rises, noting lighting...technical equipment...instruments and musicians*
Observe how they are dressed
See the leader signal to begin
Feel the excitement as they start to play*
(BEGIN TAPE, SOFTLY)
Listen to the message of the song
Observe each member's face
Feel the mood of their expressions*
See people enjoying themselves
Watch the performers bow as the song is lost in the roar of applause
Listen to what others are saying about the performance as the curtain descends
See yourself returning to the classroom
When I count to ten, open your eyes

VARIATIONS:

Adapt the Exercise so that students take the role of the performers rather than the audience. Use Exercise with different styles (rock, jazz, opera) as means for comparison and contrast.

FOLLOW UP ACTIVITIES:

Perform a mime of a favorite recording for the class. Present a puppet play or short movie of the performance accompanied by the recording. Write new lyrics for the tune to change the mood of the message.

NO: 179   **TITLE:** LIVE AT THE SYMPHONY

ACADEMIC AREA: MUSIC   **GRADE LEVEL:** Primary/Intermed.

SUB-AREA: **SUGGESTED TIME:** 15 mins.

IMAGERY DESCRIPTION:

Students will listen to an instrumental selection as if experiencing a live performance. Emphasis will be upon interactions of musicians and the conductor.

MATERIALS NEEDED: Recording of orchestra performance.

IMAGERY EXERCISE:

Sit comfortably and relax

See yourself entering a large concert hall

Feel the audience focus attention on the closed curtain ahead as the lights dim

Study the stage as the curtain slowly rises, noting lighting...instruments...music stands...and musicians*

Hear the discord of sounds as the performers tune their instruments

See the conductor enter...hear the silence as she taps and raises her baton

Feel the excitement as they begin to play

(BEGIN TAPE, PLAY TO THE END)

Notice the concentration of the musicians*

Feel the rhythm

Study each group of instruments as they move together in time with each other...(the strings...the brass, etc.)*

Watch the conductor's movements*

Feel the mood of the music

(TAPE ENDS)

Watch the conductor turn and bow

Feel the room shake with applause

See yourself returning to the classroom

When I count to ten, open your eyes

VARIATIONS:

Students are the musicians. Students become the conductor. Use Exercise with recordings of the same piece by different groups as a means of comparing styles.

FOLLOW UP ACTIVITIES:

List the instruments that you heard. Take roles as conductor and musicians and mime the performance with imaginary instruments. Interview a conductor or professional musician.

NO:**180**   TITLE: MAGIC CARPET RIDE

ACADEMIC AREA: MUSIC   GRADE LEVEL: Primary/Intermed.
SUB-AREA: SUGGESTED TIME: 15 mins.

IMAGERY DESCRIPTION:

Students will ride a magic carpet listening to the sounds and rhythms of things viewed.

IMAGERY EXERCISE:

> **Sit comfortably and relax**
> **See yourself on a large, soft carpet**
> **Feel its plush contours**
> **Trace its colorful patterns**
> **Test the controls...position your headphones**
> **You will be hearing and recording many sounds today**
> **Rise into the air***
> **Hear the calling of geese***
> **See the V-formation shifting as they move**
> **Hear the vigorous beating of wings as they continue their honking**
> **Fly to the ocean and feel the crashing of water against rock cliffs***
> **Record some fish sounds**
> **Rise again, fly to a rain forest**
> **Listen to the tapping of raindrops***
> **Hear a strange, colorful bird calling***
> **Hear the mud under the belly of an alligator as it slides into the water**
> **Dodge a mosquito as it buzzes at you**
> **Hear a wild animal calling to its mate***
> **Set your controls for home**
> **Hear the whistling of the wind as you fly**
> **See yourself returning to the classroom**
> **When I count to ten, open your eyes**

VARIATIONS:

Students can ride through a city and hear cars honking, signs blinking, etc.

FOLLOW UP ACTIVITIES:

Make a tape of household sounds for a study in contrasting rhythms. Make a scrapbook of things that make sound. Develop a unique system of classification for them (i.e., loud/soft, nature/man-made, real/unreal, etc.).

ACADEMIC AREA: MUSIC   **GRADE LEVEL:** Intermediate

SUB-AREA: **SUGGESTED TIME:**   15 mins.

IMAGERY DESCRIPTION:

   Students will prepare to listen to a recording from a Broadway musical by imaging the characters, setting and situations, before listening.

MATERIALS NEEDED: *Man of La Mancha* recording.

IMAGERY EXERCISE:

> **Sit comfortably and relax**
> **See a brave knight on a beautiful horse**
> **Hear the powerful animal stamping and snorting**
> **Examine the colorful armour worn by both**
> **Notice a squire with the Knight, as they travel on the road toward a castle***
> **Observe their weapons**
> **Scan the countryside**
> **Hear the strange noises made by an unknown enemy in the distance**
> **Watch the picture fade away**
> **Bring it back into focus**
> **The picture has changed**
> **See an old man on a tired mule**
> **Hear the hooves as they plod along***
> **Notice the servant following as they ride toward an Inn**
> **Smell the country air**
> **Hear the windmills turning steadily on a hill in the distance***
> **Listen as the old man, Don Quixote, speaks to Sancho, his servant**
> *(BEGIN TAPE, PLAY TO END)*
> **See yourself returning to the classroom**
> **When I count to ten, open your eyes**

VARIATIONS:

   Describe the scene as it would be viewed from your seat in the theater, ending with the curtain falling.

FOLLOW UP ACTIVITIES:

   Draw the character in the scene. Listen to and interpret other songs from the same show. Predict your own ending and write it. Listen to the other songs of the show out of sequence and attempt to put the story together.

NO:**182**   TITLE: MARCHING

ACADEMIC AREA: MUSIC   GRADE LEVEL: Primary/Intermed.

SUB-AREA: SUGGESTED TIME: 10 mins.

IMAGERY DESCRIPTION:

Students will see different objects and animals marching to the music heard.

MATERIALS NEEDED: Marching music.

IMAGERY EXERCISE:

Sit comfortably and relax
You are waiting for the parade to pass
Listen to it in the distance*
(BEGIN TAPE, SOFTLY AT FIRST, INCREASE VOLUME SLIGHTLY)
See the band uniforms
Notice the shiny buttons, tall hats...and bright colors
Watch feet stepping together...see the color of the shoes
Watch them change to bugs
Hear them march
Change their color
See them stepping together as they pass
Fall in behind them...in time with the music
See them become ants
Follow them into the earth
Smell the dirt...feel its texture
Travel the tunnels back to the surface
March through the grass
Watch it move with you
See it change to marching pencils*
See colorful tips bobbing as they go
See other things marching*
See yourself returning to the classroom
When I count to ten, open your eyes

VARIATIONS:

Different objects and animals can be substituted or added.

FOLLOW UP ACTIVITIES:

Draw one of the scenes viewed. Use objects and create a visual performance to marching music for the class. Draw an animated cartoon sequence from the experience.

NO:**183**   TITLE: MUSICAL MOVIE

ACADEMIC AREA: MUSIC   GRADE LEVEL: Primary/Intermed.

SUB-AREA: SUGGESTED TIME: 15 mins.

IMAGERY DESCRIPTION:

   Students will listen to a vocal music selection, creating a
   movie to view as it plays.

MATERIALS NEEDED: Vocal recording.

IMAGERY EXERCISE:

   Sit comfortably and relax
   See yourself in a movie theater
   Feel yourself in a comfortable seat
   Smell the popcorn and soda
   Taste it
   Enjoy it
   Watch the lights dim slowly
   Hear people become quiet
   (BEGIN TAPE)
   Watch as the movie begins
   Notice each character in the story*
   See how they are dressed
   Notice where they are
   Observe what they are doing
   Continue creating your own movie*
   Now see the words "The End" appear on the screen
   See yourself returning to the classroom
   When I count to ten, open your eyes

VARIATIONS:

   Substitute the word "movie" with play, ballet, opera, Broadway
   show, etc., to create different interpretations.

FOLLOW UP ACTIVITIES:

   Create a slide show or movie to accompany the recording. Write
   the story viewed during the Exercise.

204

NO:**184**   TITLE: ONE OF A KIND INSTRUMENT

ACADEMIC AREA: MUSIC   GRADE LEVEL: Primary/Intermed.

SUB-AREA: SUGGESTED TIME: 10 mins.

IMAGERY DESCRIPTION:

Students will create an instrument that they think could create the sounds they hear.

MATERIALS NEEDED: Recording of an instrument <u>not</u> familiar to students.

IMAGERY EXERCISE:

Sit comfortably and relax
See yourself in a place you've never been before
Scan the room for details...colors...unusual objects
(BEGIN TAPE, SOFTLY)
Focus on the object making the music
Feel its surface
Examine its construction
Pick it up and feel its weight
Play it*
Experiment with all its parts*
(INCREASE VOLUME)
Feel the moods you are creating
Give them colors...patterns...designs*
Tell a friend about this unusual musical instrument
Listen to what you say*
See it again from a different angle
Put it in a safe place
See yourself returning to the classroom
When I count to ten, open your eyes

VARIATIONS:

Add words to suggest specific parts (strings, keys) or how it's played (blow into it, strum it, slide it. etc.).

FOLLOW UP ACTIVITIES:

Design and build the instrument visualized. Attempt to recreate the type of sounds heard and tape them. Compare the real instrument with the one imagined, using diagrams.

NO:**185**   TITLE: UP AND DOWN AT THE ZOO

ACADEMIC AREA: MUSIC   GRADE LEVEL: Primary
SUB-AREA: SUGGESTED TIME: 10 mins.

IMAGERY DESCRIPTION:

   Students will visit the zoo to become familiar with high and
   low pitches in relation to the staff.

IMAGERY EXERCISE:

           Sit comfortably and relax
           You're entering a large zoo
           Notice cages with different animals*
           Notice that the bars go back and forth instead of up and down
           Count the bars of one cage
           There are 5
           Climb up the side of the bird cage...stopping at the top
           See birds of many colors and sizes
           Listen to their high voices
           Sing high with them*
           Listen to the music change
           Go to the elephant cage
           Smell the peanuts
           Listen to the low, loud footsteps he makes when he walks
           See him raise his trunk and make high, loud calls
           Hear another one answering
           Look at the monkeys climbing up and down on the bars
           Hear their voices get higher when they go up to the top and lower
           when they come down
           Have them sing a song
           Make them move up and down with the notes*
           See yourself returning to the classroom
           When I count to ten, open your eyes

VARIATIONS:

   Other animals, birds, insects, etc,, could be used to emphasize
   high and low sounds.

FOLLOW UP ACTIVITIES:

   Draw animals with high-pitch sounds and low-pitch sounds.

ACADEMIC AREA: MUSIC   GRADE LEVEL: Primary/Intermed.

SUB-AREA: SUGGESTED TIME: 15 mins.

IMAGERY DESCRIPTION:

Students will view the ocean as a scuba diver while listening to the recording.

MATERIALS NEEDED: Recording of water sounds (Oliveros, Sound Patterns).

IMAGERY EXERCISE:

Sit comfortably and relax

See yourself on the edge of a boat

Feel it rocking with the waves

Check your air tank...air hoses...mask...and other scuba equipment

Smell the salty air

Taste it on your lips

Fall back gently into the blue, clear ocean water and swim to the bottom*

(BEGIN TAPE)

Feel the movements

Hear the air bubbles rising from you

Watch them reaching the top

Examine the strange plant life...their shapes...colors...and movements in the water*

Hear fish passing around you

Notice their unusual designs and colors

Observe an animal you've never seen before

Watch it...follow it...communicate with it

Make friends with it

Enjoy your sea hunt*

You're now coming back up...up

See yourself returning to the classroom

When I count to ten, open your eyes

VARIATIONS:

Students travel through the digestive system in little boats. Students travel through underground caves in little boats. Watch the movement of bacteria under a microscope.

FOLLOW UP ACTIVITIES:

Write a poem contrasting the sea bottom to land, comparing sea creatures to land creatures, etc.   Make an animated cartoon about a sea creature. Create an "Air Tape" or "Soil Tape", etc., experimenting with sounds.

NO:**187**   TITLE: STORY IN A SONG

ACADEMIC AREA: MUSIC   GRADE LEVEL: Primary/Intermed.

SUB-AREA: SUGGESTED TIME: 5 mins.

IMAGERY DESCRIPTION:

   Students will listen to a vocal music selection and create appropriate surroundings and situations to fit the message. Bal-
   lads can be used effectively with this Exercise.

MATERIALS NEEDED: Vocal recording.

IMAGERY EXERCISE:

   Sit comfortably and relax
   Listen to yourself as you sing this song
   (BEGIN RECORDING SOFTLY)
   Note how you are dressed...and where you are*
   Scan your surroundings for details
   See who is with you
   Feel your mood
   Show your mood
   Watch as people and surroundings become hazy and fade away
   See colors reflecting your mood
   Feel the microphone in your hands
   Feel the success as your song nears the end*
   See yourself returning to the classroom
   When I count to ten, open your eyes

VARIATIONS:

   Replace the second line with:
            "Listen as this song is being sung to you
            (BEGIN RECORDING)
            See the one singing to you..."

FOLLOW UP ACTIVITIES:

   Write your version of the story of this song using first person.
   Write a new verse or response to the song heard. Create a
   melody for it. Act out the story of the song.

ACADEMIC AREA: MUSIC   **GRADE LEVEL:** Primary/Intermed.

SUB-AREA: **SUGGESTED TIME:**

IMAGERY DESCRIPTION:

Students will listen to The Nutcracker Suite as they visualize the story being told with the music. Teacher should become familiar with the piece so as to know when to suggest each scene.

MATERIALS NEEDED: Recording of The Nutcracker Suite, Tchaikovsky.

IMAGERY EXERCISE:

> **Sit comfortably and relax**
> **See yourself in a large crowded theater**
> **Hear the orchestra in the pit tuning their instruments**
> **Watch the lights get dim**
> *(BEGIN RECORDING, PLAY TO END)*
> **Observe a Christmas party scene**
> **See Clara, a young beautiful ballerina***
> **Notice her hair...face...costume**
> **See the nutcracker doll in Bavarian dress that Clara gets as a present***
> **Watch as Clara leaves to go to bed**
> **Feel the excitement as the nutcracker doll changes into a handsome prince**
> **Watch him move...like a prince***
> **Listen as he invites Clara to go with him**
> **Feel the coolness in the Land of Snow**
> **Scan the surroundings...ice...frost**
> **Smell the Kingdom of Sweets...taste your favorite candy**
> **Hear the Sugar Plum Fairy greeting them***
> **Feel the floor vibrating as they dance**
> **See two funny Chinamen dancing about quickly**
> **Observe them doing the Dance of Tea***
> **See yourself returning to the classroom**
> **When I count to ten, open your eyes**

VARIATIONS:

Teacher may wish to break lessons down even more for the first experience hearing the music, then play the entire ballet at another time without narration.

FOLLOW UP ACTIVITIES:

Design and construct one of the scenes. Build puppets and reinact the ballet to music. Role play the story to music. Write a script for the story. Write a new scene for another fantasy land to be visited.

ACADEMIC AREA: MUSIC   **GRADE LEVEL:** Primary/Intermed.

SUB-AREA: **SUGGESTED TIME:** 10 mins.

IMAGERY DESCRIPTION:

Same as The Nutcracker Suite: Part I

MATERIALS NEEDED: Recording of The Nutcracker Suite, Tchaikovsky

IMAGERY EXERCISE:

> **Sit comfortably and relax**
> *(BEGIN RECORDING AT THE TEA DANCE)*
> **See yourself sitting in a darkened theater**
> **Feel your comfortable soft seat**
> **Notice the dancers on the stage dressed as delicate beautiful fairies***
> **Listen as they play long reed pipes**
> **Feel the smoothness of the pipes***
> **Watch them glitter**
> **Notice their shapes**
> **Watch them dance lightly into a lovely garden***
> **Smell the sweet fragrance of flowers**
> **Examine each color and shape**
> **See them waltz to the music***
> **Feel their leaves...and petals**
> **Waltz with them on the stage**
> **See yourself returning to the classroom**
> **When I count to ten, open your eyes**

VARIATIONS:

See Part I

FOLLOW UP ACTIVITIES:

See Part I

NO:**190**   TITLE: THE ROARING 20'S

ACADEMIC AREA: MUSIC   GRADE LEVEL: Intermediate
SUB-AREA: SUGGESTED TIME: 15 mins.

IMAGERY DESCRIPTION:

Students will experience the 1920's time period seeing events, dress style, transportation modes, etc., while associating them with the music of the time.

MATERIALS NEEDED: Instrumental recording of Charleston.

IMAGERY EXERCISE:

Sit comfortably and relax
(BEGIN RECORDING, PLAY SOFTLY)
You're back in time...in the 1920's
You are on a busy city street*
Hear the chugging of a Model T
Notice its spoked tires*
Stop in front of a movie theater and read the sign to see what's showing
Hear the ringing of a bell as you enter a drugstore
Taste your favorite ice cream soda
Hear the voice of President Hoover on the large wooden radio
Listen as he urges factories not to lay off their workers
Watch as a dance competition begins
Notice the ruffled dresses...colorful beads...feathered headbands worn by the women*
See the vested suits and colorful shoes of the men
Choose a favorite couple and see numbers on their backs
Watch them dance the Charleston, kicking high...stepping fast*
See yourself returning to the classroom
When I count to ten, open your eyes

VARIATIONS:

Use another time period with identifiable music (e.g., Waltz, Minuet, etc.).

FOLLOW UP ACTIVITIES:

Select a type of music from the past and research aspects of that time period (i.e., economy, government, fashion, etc.). Write a skit based on the 1920's era. Learn the Charleston. Have a dance contest.

ACADEMIC AREA: MUSIC   **GRADE LEVEL:** Primary/Intermed.

SUB-AREA: **SUGGESTED TIME:** 10 mins.

IMAGERY DESCRIPTION:

Students will hear their names expressed with many different sounds in many different ways.

IMAGERY EXERCISE:

> **Sit comfortably and relax**
> **See yourself in a listening booth**
> **Notice a controlo panel in front of you**
> **Press "Name"**
> **Hear your name being whispered very softly...over and over***
> **Feel the rhythm...give it color***
> **Increase the volume slowly**
> **Use drums to beat the pattern**
> **See your name in musical notes**
> **Hear a voice singing it**
> **Hear a choir singing it**
> **Feel the vibrations as giant church bells play your name**
> **Hear a bird chirping your name**
> **See his color and softness**
> **Watch your name become that color**
> **Clap your name**
> **Tap your name**
> **Whistle your name**
> **Hear a frog croaking your name***
> **Listen as your name slides...skips**
> **Hear an orchestra playing your name***
> **Hear one instrument play it softly**
> **See yourself returning to the classroom**
> **When I count to ten, open your eyes**

VARIATIONS:

Select other animals, instruments or things to sing student's name.

FOLLOW UP ACTIVITIES:

Write a limerick or poem about your name. Create a design including your name, for a book cover, ad, or poster. Create a design for your name and find music that duplicates the same mood.

9. Imagery in Guided Fantasy

See yourself sitting on a shiny new bicycle
Look at a special switch which allows the bicycle to fly
Before you fly, just ride down the street and get used to your
new bike
Notice how easy it is to pedal
See the shiny spoked wheels and beautiful colors
Now it's time to test this magical bike
Push the special switch forward
Feel the bicycle beginning to lift off the ground
Feel yourself lifting up...up into the air
Feel the wind blowing against your face
Feel the excitement of going up and over the houses and streets
Look below. See all the people waving to you
Look at the amazement on their faces
See yourself just pedaling effortlessly through the sky
Turn and go through a soft white cloud
Feel the silence as you float gently through the cloud
Go visit a special place now...
You are back flying again
Notice some people looking out of a plane window
Wave at them
See the beautiful trees and flowers as you fly peacefully above
It's time to return home
See yourself coming lower and lower toward the ground
See your house and street
See yourself landing right in front of your house
Listen to everyone greeting you with smiles
See yourself returning to the classroom
When I count to ten open your eyes

You are high off the ground
You are hanging from a branch of a large oak tree
Notice how your stem is attached to the thick branch
Look at your beautiful colors
Notice your shape...size
Feel your thin and silk-like texture
Look around and see thousands of other leaves, all a little different
from you
Feel yourself beginning to sway, as a strong breeze starts to blow
from the north
Listen, as the huge branches begin to bend and twist
Hear the leaves flapping
Notice one leaf floating...floating...slowly to the ground
See it lying there...peacefully
It's now getting dark...feel the dampness and moisture settling
upon you
Hear the small creatures of the night
Feel yourself becoming tired and sleepy
You are motionless...ready to enjoy the stillness of night
See yourself returning to the classroom
When I count to ten, open your eyes

See yourself walking toward the entrance of a magical candy land
Walk through the gate and see a large mountain made of thick dripping chocolate and mounds of ice cream
See trees made of chewy gumdrops of all colors
See the streets lined with silver-wrapped candy kisses
See children riding on a giant milky way
Feel multi-colored chocolate sprinkles falling on you
See a huge marshmallow rock
Feel its softness
Listen to roasted walnuts floating in a sea of hot melting chocolate
See yourself sliding down the sides of giant lollipops
See yourself climbing into an enormous peanut butter cup
See yourself breaking off a piece of chocolate and dipping it into the smooth peanut butter
Smell all the candy
Now see yourself hanging and swinging on a long red piece of licorice
Feel its stickiness
See yourself getting ready to leap into a large Hershey bar
See yourself walking on the squares of the Hershey bar
Notice the footprints as you sink into the chocolate
Look around and notice all the different candy
You are leaving...take a bag filled with your favorite candy
See yourself returning to the classroom
When I count to ten, open your eyes

See yourself as a small rabbit
Feel your soft fur
Notice your little paws
Touch your long soft ears
See your little pink nose
See a lovely garden in the middle of a park
See yourself hopping along
Feel the bounce and spring in your legs
Feel how nice it is to hop over rocks and branches
In front of you is a gorgeous rose bush
See yourself putting your little pink nose up close for a terrific
sweet smell
Look over to the side
See some fresh wild strawberries
Go over and taste them
Feel the delicious strawberry juice in your mouth
See another rabbit coming toward you
See both of you running and playing
Listen to the birds in the trees above
See yourself coming to a playground area
Look at the children playing
See one of the children start to chase you
See yourself running and hopping through the flower bushes and
away from everyone
See yourself looking for a soft grassy area where you can take a
quiet nap
Feel the softness of the grass as you start to close your tired eyes
Enjoy this calm and comfortable feeling
See yourself returning to the classroom
When I count to ten, open your eyes

You are lying down in a canoe
Your head is on a soft fluffy pillow
You are calm and comfortable
See yourself in the middle of a beautiful gentle lake
Look at the calmness of the water
See it as still as glass
Feel the sun shining down on you
Feel its warmth on your arms...legs...whole body
Listen to the sounds coming from the nearby woods
Hear the birds singing
Listen to the chatter of crickets
Feel a soft cool breeze blowing gently on your face
Feel a very slight swaying as your canoe drifts and drifts
Smell the cleanness in the air
Look up and see a magnificent blue sky with small ruffle-like
white clouds moving slowly by
Let your hand float in the cool water
Feel the wet and tingling sensation
Notice how peaceful everything is
Enjoy this comfortable and relaxing place
Notice some beautiful little fish swimming freely in the water
Notice how clean and clear the water is
Look around and see all the beauty of this magnificent place
See yourself leaving and returning to the classroom
When I count to ten open your eyes

See yourself diving into warm, clear, crystal, ocean water
Feel the water pressure as you slowly descend toward the bottom
Notice all the different species of fish
See yourself reaching the bottom
See different shaped rocks imbedded in the sand
Notice the seaweed and magnificent underwater plant life
See a huge clam slowly opening its gigantic mouth
Feel yourself pushing through the water as you walk on the bottom
of the sea
See an enormous stingray above you
Notice its huge wings flapping and long tail waving as it moves
swiftly through the water
Hear the silence of the sea
See hundreds of striped, multi-colored fish
See their glass-like eyes and sharp white teeth
Watch them move and turn in many directions
Notice a giant sea turtle
Get on its back
Feel the hardness of its huge shell
Watch its flipper-feet dig and push through the sand
Feel the smooth silk-like sea plants brushing you
Watch the plants swing and move with the ocean current
Enjoy the peacefulness and calmness
Look ahead and see the remains of an old wooden ship
Notice how rusted and decrepit the ship's anchor is
Feel it...feel how brittle it is
Watch the pieces just flake off and float away
Feel yourself starting to rise...moving up...up
See yourself leaving this beautiful place
See yourself coming back to the classroom
When I count to ten, open your eyes

Feel the cold as you sit in a chair lift moving slowly up a ski slope
Feel the wind blowing
Feel the chair swaying and rocking
Feel your feet dangling as your skis hang tightly fastened to your boots
Feel the coldness in your hands
Feel your eyes tearing and your nose running
See yourself getting off the chair lift
Feel the slickness of the white snow as you move toward the starting point
Look down and see a cabin at the finishing point, far below
Smell the freshness in the air
See yourself ready to begin the long and daring trip down the slope
You're off…feel the speed as you race over the packed white snow
Feel yourself turning to the right and gliding back to the center
Feel the pressure on your legs
Feel your leg muscles flexing and straining
Feel the wind blasting against your face
See the whirling snow almost blinding you in the face
Feel the excitement of roaring down the slope
Feel your breathing getting heavier
See yourself digging and pushing into the snow with your poles as you break to the left
You're almost to the bottom
See the finishing point becoming closer and closer
Feel the satisfaction and success as you approach the finishing point
See your friends greeting you with congratulations
See yourself returning to the classroom
When I count to ten, open your eyes

See yourself climbing on the back of a giant eagle
Feel the beautiful feathers as you sit firmly on the eagle's back
You are...off...lifting up...up...up into the sky
Feel yourself gaining speed as the eagle flaps its giant wings
Notice how far the eagle's wings extend
Feel the wind soaring against your face
Feel yourself floating through a large white cloud
Feel the sensation of gliding without noise
Feel the eagle turning
Look down and notice how clear everything is
See yourself heading toward a huge mountain
Feel the eagle slowing and gliding toward the mountain
See yourself landing on a gigantic rock
As you sit on the eagle's back feel the eagle breathing more heavily
See yourself taking off again
Feel the coolness in the air
See yourself flying over beautiful valleys and streams
Notice all the colors
Feel the calmness as you float effortlessly through the sky
See yourself returning to the classroom
When I count to ten, open your eyes

You are in the middle of a forest

You are searching for the Lost Cave

Suddenly, you see a small opening between two giant rocks

You are now entering the cave

Feel the coolness

Smell the damp air

Notice spider webs...everywhere

As you shine your flash light...notice the different kinds and colors of rocks

Feel the side walls of the cave

Feel the dirt and dust

Listen to water dripping

See old wooden beams lying on the ground

Listen to your voice echo, as you talk to other members of your group

Hear a strange noise in the distance

Find out what it is

Find something unusual

Notice its detail

Now find another way out of the cave

See light ahead of you

See yourself returning to the classroom

When I count to ten, open your eyes

You are entering a large amusement park
In your pocket are hundreds of tickets to all the rides
Hear the sounds of the amusement park
Listen to the thunder of the roller coaster
See yourself getting on a thrilling ride
Feel it beginning to start
Feel the movement...the shaking...and terrific speed
Listen to the screams as people enjoy the ride
See yourself holding a piece of foam rubber getting ready to come
down a steep water slide
You're off...feel the splashing as you wind and curve down the
slide
Feel the sharp turns as you speed down
Notice how fast you are going
See yourself finishing the run by landing in a giant pool
You are now eating popcorn...hear it crumble in your mouth
Feel your hands getting sticky
You are now getting into a midget car
Hear the racing of the engine
Feel the rubber steering wheel
Feel your body shift as you speed around your first turn
Feel the wind in your face and hair in your eyes
See yourself braking and finishing the ride
Next...see yourself in a bumper car
Hear the electricity exploding on the ceiling
Feel the crashing, jolting and bumping
See your friends laughing as you bump them from behind
See yourself visiting other favorite rides...enjoy yourself
It's now time to leave the park
As you walk toward the gate sipping on your cold drink, turn
around and take one more look at this exciting place
See yourself returning to the classroom
When I count to ten, open your eyes

See a big rocket ship waiting for blast off

Feel the heavy space suit you are wearing

Look through your glass space helmet and see hundreds of buttons and control switches

Hear the control tower telling you to prepare for blast off

Listen to the countdown

10...9...8...7...6...5...4...3...2...1...BLAST OFF!

Hear the explosion...feel the vibrations as the huge ship begins to lift off the ground

Up...up...up

Feel the excitement as your rocket ship moves swiftly through the sky

Look out the window and notice how small things are becoming

See your altitude screen reading 5000...10,000...20,000

Feel the rocket ship climbing higher and higher...further and further into space

See it becoming darker and darker

Begin to see the shape and curve of the earth's surface

See yourself penetrating high-level clouds

Feel the roar of the engines becoming quieter as you move into the silence of outer space

Through your window you can see the craters of the moon's surface

See the stars and planets ahead

Notice meteorites flaring in the distance

See yourself coming closer to a huge planet

Look closely at its surface

Feel yourself getting out of your seat and floating weightlessly in the space cabin

See yourself looking out through a small porthole into space

Notice how quiet and still everything is

Feel the motionless, floating sensation of outer space

See your space ship turning around and heading back to earth

Down...down...down...see the planet earth getting closer

See yourself gliding down the runway heading for a safe landing

See yourself returning to the classroom

When I count to ten, open your eyes

BIBLIOGRAPHY

Ahsen, A. "Eidetics: An overview." *Journal of Mental Imagery,* 1, 1977, 5-38.

Ahsen, A. *Psycheye: Self-analytic Consciousness.* New York: Brandon House, 1977.

Bagley, M. & Barrett, M. "A study of the relationship between learning style and imaging ability." Unpublished research paper, College of New Rochelle, New York. 1982.

Benson, H. *The Relaxation Response.* New York: Avon Books, 1975.

Gallwey, W. *The Inner Game of Tennis.* New York: Bantam Books, 1975.

Haber, R. N. & Haber, R. B. "Eidetic Imagery 1: Frequency, Perceptual and Motor Skills," 19, 1964, 131-138.

Hebb, D. *Textbook of Psychology.* Philadelphia: W. B. Saunders Co., 1972.

Jacobson, E. *Progressive Relaxation.* Chicago: University of Chicago Press, 1938.

Jaensch, E. *Eidetic Imagery.* Trans. by Oscar Oeser. New York: Harcourt, Brace & Co., 1930.

Khatena, J. *Educational Psychology of the Gifted.* New York: John Wiley & Sons, 1982.

Parnes, S. et. al. *Guide to Creative Action.* New York: Scribners, 1977.

Powers, M. and Starrett, R. *A Practical Guide to Better Concentration.* Hollywood, California: Wilshire Book Co., 1962.

Richardson, A. *Mental Imagery.* New York: Springer, 1969.

Rogers, C. *On Becoming A Person: A Therapist's View of Psychotherapy.* Boston, Mass: Houghton Mifflin, 1967.

Rugg, H. *Imagination.* New York: Harper & Row, 1963.

Samuels, M. & Samuels, N. *Seeing with the Mind's Eye.* New York: Random House, 1975.

Tutko, T. & Tosi, U. *Sports Psyching.* Los Angeles: J. P. Tarcher, Inc., 1976.

Arnheim, R. *Visual Thinking.* Berkeley: University of California Press, 1969.

Bagley, M. & Lynch, V. *Units: A Resource Guide of Differentiated Learning Experiences for Elementary Gifted Students.* New York, NY: Trillium Press, 1984.

Croley, J. & Bagley, M. *Suppose the Wolf Were an Octopus?* New York, NY: Trillium Press, 1984.

Durio, H. "Mental Imagery and Creativity." *Journal of Creative Behavior,* 9, 4, 1975, 233-244.

Ewards, B. *Drawing on the Right Side of the Brain.* Los Angeles, J. P. Tarcher, Inc., 1979.

Gordon, W. *Synectics.* New York: Harper & Row, 1961.

Gough, H. "Incubation, Imagery and Creativity." *Journal of Mental Imagery,* 2, 2, 1978, 23-32.

Harrison, A. & Musial, D. *Other Ways, Other Means: Altered Awareness Activities for Receptive Learning.* Calif: Goodyear Publishing Co., Inc., 1978.

Holland, M. & Strickland, A. *Making Movies in Your Mind.* Columbus, Ohio: School Book Fairs, Inc., 1980.

Holt, R. "Imagery: The Return of the Ostracized." *American Psychologist,* 19, 1964, 254-264.

Horowitz, M. *Image Formation and Cognition.* New York: Appleton-Century-Crofts, 1970.

Kenny, A. *A Creative Writing Companion.* New York, NY: Trillium Press, 1984.

Khatena, J. "Creative Imagination Imagery and Analogy." *Gifted Child Quarterly,* 19, 2, 1975, 149-160.

Khatena, J. "Creative Imagination Imagery: Where Is It Going?" *Journal of Creative Behavior,* 10, 3, 1976, 189-192.

Khatena, J. "Imagination Imagery by Children and the Production of Analogy." *Gifted Child Quarterly,* 17, 2, 1973, 98-102,

Khatena, J. "Nurture of Imagery in the Visual and Performing Arts." *Gifted Child Quarterly,* 23, 4, 1979, 735-747.

Koestler, A. *The Act of Creation.* New York: MacMillan, 1964.

Kravette, S. *Complete Relaxation.* Rockport, Mass: Para Research, 1979.

Krueger, T. *Visual Imagery in Problem Solving and Scientific Creativity.* Derby, Conn: Seal Press, 1976.

Maltz, M. *Psycho-Cybernetics.* New York: Pocket Books, 1960.

McKim, R. *Experience in Visual Thinking.* Belmont, Ca: Wadsworth, 1972.

McKellar, P. *Imagination and Thinking.* New York: Basic Books, 1957.

Murphy, J. *The Power of Your Subconscious Mind.* Englewood Cliffs, New Jersey: Prentice Hall, Inc., 1963.

Paivio, A. *Imagery and Verbal Processes.* New York: Holt, Rinehart & Winston, 1971.

Paivio, A. "On the Functional Significance of Imagery." *Psychological Bulletin,* 73, 1970, 385-392.

Olson, M. "Right or Left Hemisphere Processing in the Gifted." *Gifted Child Quarterly,* 21, 1, 1977, 116-121.

Ornstein, R. *The Psychology of Consciousness.* San Francisco: W. H. Freeman, 1972.

Sheehan, P. ed. *The Function and Nature of Imagery.* New York: Academic Press, 1972.

Singer, J. *Daydreaming.* New York: Random House, 1966.

Singer, J. *Imagery and Daydream Methods in Psychotherapy and Behavior Modification.* New York: Academic Press, 1974.

Torrance, E. "Can We Teach Children to Think Creatively?" *Journal of Creative Behavior,* 6, 2, 1972, 114-143.

Torrance, E. *Education of the Creative Potential.* Minneapolis: University of Minnesota Press, 1963.

Vezza, T. & Bagley, M. *The Investigation of Real Problems.* New York, NY: Trillium Press, 1984.

Wittrock, M. *The Human Brain.* New Jersey: Prentice-Hall, Inc., 1977.

INFORMATION AND RESOURCES

American Imagery Conference
c/o Brandon House
P.O. Box 240
Bronx, New York 10471

Department of Education
Psychology
University of Georgia
Athens, Georgia 30602

Department of Education
Psychology
California State University
Los Angeles, Ca. 90058

Gifted & Creative Education
c/o Graduate School
College of New Rochelle
New Rochelle, N.Y. 10801

Journal of Mental Imagery
Brandon House
P.O. Box 240
Bronx, N.Y. 10471

Department of Creative Studies
State University College at Buffalo
1300 Elmwood Ave
Chase Hall
Buffalo, N.YU. 14222

Department of Psychology
University of Illinois at Chicago
Circle
Chicago, Il.

Dept. of Educational Psychology
Mississippi State University
Mississippi 39762

Center for Integrative Learning
767 Gladys Ave.
Long Beach, Ca 90804

Superlearning Inc.
450 Seventh Ave., Suite 500
New York, N.Y. 10123

IMAGE (Institute for Maximizing
Affective Growth in Education)
P.O. Box 612
Portland, Pa 18351